BLUE LIES

THE WAR ON JUSTICE AND THE CONSPIRACY TO WEAKEN AMERICA'S COPS

SGT. JEFF WOLF (RET.)

———— FOREWORD BY ————
LT. COL. DAVE GROSSMAN

Library of Congress Control Number: 2021924216

ISBN: 978-1-0881-3910-3

Published by:

Resurgence Publishing, LLC

P.O. Box 514

Goshen, OH 45122

Cover Design: Aaftab Sheikh

Printed in the United States of America

Dedication

Dedicated to the men and women of law enforcement, especially those who have given their lives to protect their fellow man.

Praise for Blue Lies

"This book is a must-read for those with an open mind about the current attack by the liberal left on our police agencies. The author combines statistical analysis, evidence-based facts regarding high-profile cases, and a career of personal experience to refute efforts to paint our officers in an unfavorable light. These statistics obtained from well-recognized academia have shown the lack of data to support any systemic racism but raw data is often dismissed or not even read by our media and the public. Jeff weaves these facts into an analysis of use of force events that are regularly tainted by the media in their initial reporting. He continues with a review of the conclusion of numerous investigations to refute these inflammatory statements. If you are open to discussion and interested in a personal perspective from a career officer, this is a great read."

–Scott Barker
Supervisory Special Agent (Ret.),
Federal Bureau of Investigation

"Truth may sometimes be hard to hear and difficult to explore but it must be told, truth follows the proof. Join me in walking with Jeff Wolf as we journey to hear the other side of the story! In the pages that follow, Jeff—a retired police officer—takes us on the inside. We get to review several of today's headline-grabbing matters through the mindset and eyes of a law enforcement officer. Through these pages we get the rest of the story. Through these pages, we explore what the evidence shows, the truth will follow the proof."

–Hon. Valerie Roller
Administrative Judge

"Jeff Wolf has captured the real issues facing American Law Enforcement Officers and presented them in a way that the reader can not only understand but can "feel." His personal stories concerning his own career enhance the readers' experience and allow a glimpse into the heart and soul of a true Blue Warrior"

–Lt. Randy Sutton, (Ret.)
Las Vegas Metro Police,
Founder of The Wounded Blue,
Author of "True Blue: to Protect and Serve", "A Cops Life" and
"The Power of Legacy"

"Academics can write a book about police work. However, from where have they collected their information? Jeff Wolf has written "Blue Lies," a book about the false narrative used by the media in order to fuel anti-police sentiments. He obviously did thorough research, and he definitely knows what he is writing about. Jeff Wolf has vast real-life experiences stemming from his many years as a police officer! What Americans don't understand is, it's not just a job. It's our life. We dedicate it to our communities. I have attended way too many police funerals paying last respect to officers who sacrificed their lives while protecting their citizens. As a police officer of 38 years, I concur author Jeff Wolf has written about the truth of current policing in America! "Blue Lies" is a must read for officers and those that we serve!"

–Chief Dave Hayes
Sagamore Hills, OH Police
Acting Lieutenant, (Ret.),
Prince George's County, MD Police

"Blue Lies is a must-read book for anyone and everyone who wants to understand the reasons for the increasing lawlessness across America. Jeff Wolf has taken a complex issue, an issue which has been demonized by the media, politicians, and the judiciary, and he has lifted the fog of mistruths about those who serve in law enforcement in a way that everyone can understand. Sadly, if Americans do not listen to the sage advice which fills the pages of Blue Lies, it may be too late to turn back the calendar on the destruction of America."

Jeff Wolf spent his law enforcement career on the streets of his community as a true, very first responder. In his roles as a patrolman and patrol supervisor, he has experienced all of the issues and scenarios that law enforcement faces. In his book, he has skillfully taken those experiences, good, bad, ugly, and sometimes humorous, and added pertinent academics and research. Most importantly, he has anchored his book to the most important aspect of policing that a community requires–protecting that community as a sheepdog–to truly protect and serve.

Acknowledgments

First and foremost, I want to acknowledge my wife, Christal, for enduring my long days and nights of research and writing, and for encouraging me through the challenges of the process.

Completing this project without my friend, Lt. Col. Dave Grossman would've been difficult. Thank you, Sir, for expressing your faith in me and for agreeing to be the "Godfather" of my "baby."

Special thanks to Dr. Tony Pinizzotto and Lt. Ed Davis (Ret), formerly of the FBI Behavioral Sciences Unit and FBI Academy, respectively, for sharing their invaluable research and consulting with me on the "Deadly Force Encounters" chapter.

Special thanks to the Honorable Valerie Roller for consulting with me on the subject of race relations, and spending many hours scrutinizing the manuscript to advise on matters of culture and context.

Special thanks to the military service members and law enforcement officers (active and retired) for sharing their deadly force encounter stories and experiences.

Contents

Preface

This book was born out of frustration. When I wore the badge, I didn't pay much attention to media scrutiny. Rather, I did what a vast majority of police officers do on a daily basis: I behaved professionally, ethically, and morally and remained above reproach.

It wasn't until I walked away from law enforcement that I began to digest all the noise made by the mainstream media about cops. It made me angry. Not because activists and their media allies call for police accountability—even cops want dirty cops to be held accountable and ultimately rooted out—but because they are unjustly attacking my family. When my family is under fire, I don't have the ability to keep my mouth shut; I have to say something.

The media has locked arms with liberal activists and politicians to "misrepresent" our good, noble, and brave police officers. Where I come from, misrepresenting the facts is just an old-fashioned lie. But why? Why do those with a voice and a platform spread blatant lies about the police? I don't believe they hate the police as human beings, but they hate what the police represent: law and order, personal responsibility, righteousness, and justice.

I know there are bad cops, but they represent only a minute fraction of the hundreds of thousands of men and women who wear the badge and do their duty with integrity and love for their fellow man. Not everything you see on television or the internet is true. Even when it's called "news."

The narrative of widespread police racism and corruption is manufactured to further a political agenda. The opposite is actually the truth. But, the men and women of law enforcement hesitate to stand up for themselves for fear of retaliation from police leadership, local politicians, and the media mob. That's why I wrote this book. I decided to come out of the shadows and stand up for police officers.

The general public has somewhat of a naive view of what the police actually do and underestimates the impact of the job on the people who bear its burden. Therefore, the public is vulnerable to the biased, anti-police message that makes its way into the media coverage of most high-profile police encounters. To put it bluntly: the media often take advantage of their ability to shape the opinions of the public, allowing misrepresentations–or "lies"–whether explicit or implicit, to hang in the social atmosphere. Consequently, the general public is so often exposed to the lies, they accept them as truth.

I'm not a famous influencer, I don't have a massive social media following or a household name. I'm just a beat cop from the suburbs of Cincinnati who is frustrated with the blue lies hanging over the police. There is a thin blue line that stands between fact and fiction, and it's about time we change the narrative.

–Jeff Wolf

Foreword

Jeff Wolf's book, *Blue Lies,* is one of the *most important books of our time.*

The breakdown of law and order, and the systematic erosion of the fabric of our civilization, is the single most important issue facing us today. And the most horrific part of this issue is that most people don't even know what is happening!

The annual increase in homicides is a key factor in assessing the degree of violence in our society. But, one critical factor concerning homicide rates, one that desperately needs to be taken into consideration, is the fact that the murder rate under-represents the level of violence because medical technology is saving even more lives.

In 2002, Anthony Harris and a team of scholars from the University of Massachusetts and Harvard published their landmark research in the journal *Homicide Studies.* They concluded that advances in medical technology, between 1960 and 1999, *cut the murder rate to a third, or a quarter, of what it would otherwise be.* And the leaps and bounds of life-saving technology in the decades since then, have saved the lives of even more victims of violence. Thus "preventing" many more murders.

Everyone understands the concept of "inflation-adjusted dollars." When we finally start reporting "medically adjusted murders" then we will begin to appreciate just how desperately, tragically *bad* the situation has become. For every murder we report, *there are ever-increasing numbers of our citizens* physically maimed and scarred, and emotionally crippled and traumatized by violence.

Thus, you must multiply homicides in the 1960s by a factor of about 3.5 to compare with the 1990s. And a similar dynamic is in play between the 1990s and the 2020s.

Many medical experts believe that tourniquets alone may have cut the murder rate in half in just the last decade. We must understand that, if a cop slaps on a tourniquet and saves a crime victim's life, he has prevented a murder! Two decades ago, no one carried a tourniquet. Today, as a result of life-saving lessons learned in two decades of war, virtually every cop, and every EMS, and firefighter, and many civilians all carry tourniquets, and they are saving many lives, every day. And that is just one aspect of the astounding medical technology being applied every day, to save lives, but also to hold down the murder rate and conceal just how violent and destructive our nation has become.

(There is a temptation to use the "aggravated assault" data instead of murder data, but it is too easy to "fudge the figures" on aggravated assault. Every cop will tell you that we can make the aggravated assault rate say whatever you want it to say, by shifting that "magic line" between aggravated assault and simple assault. Very much like "grade inflation" in our schools. Murder is good data, dead is dead, and it is hard to "fudge" those numbers. But to use murder rates over any period of time, we must allow for medical technology, just like allowing for inflation when comparing minimum wages across time.)

Thus, the entire field of criminology and criminal justice has been systematically misrepresenting the magnitude of the problem of violent crime in America! It is like the entire field of economics not taking inflation into account. The reason for this is the same as the reasons for not reporting homicide rates in the media today. They do not like where that information takes us!

The annual increase in homicides in 2020 was over 30%, and the worst we have ever seen previously is a 12% annual increase in the 1960s. But that comparison between 2020 and the 60s completely breaks down! You must multiply homicides today by a factor of seven (and that is a *very* conservative estimate) to compare with the 60s! What happened in 2020 is at least *20 times worse than anything we have ever seen before, and 2021 is even worse.*

There is one other important dynamic that we must consider. A monstrous mass murder, by a single individual, can create more psychosocial trauma than countless deaths by disease. In its section on PTSD, the *DSM* (the "bible" of psychology and psychiatry) tells us that, whenever the cause of trauma is "human in nature" (such as assault, torture, or rape) the degree of trauma is "more severe and long-lasting." Millions die from disease every day, and it has little impact on our behavior, but one serial killer or serial rapist can paralyze a city.

Thus, the overall societal harm of violent crime can be far greater than the harm caused by disease or any other factor. It is like a body suffering horrendous trauma, but the pain receptors are turned off! The trauma is still there, and the breakdown of the "body" is still happening. Where this will take us is an entirely different subject, but you can bet anything you want that it is not good.

This brings us back to the book you hold in your hand. Amazingly well written, informative, and empowering, *this* is *the* book for every citizen to understand how and *why* this explosion of violence is playing out in our cities and our streets today.

A virus of violence, a cancer of crime, is exploding in our streets and our lives. The "lies" about our men and women in "blue" are exposed in this book. The "war on justice" is very, very real, and we desperately need to understand the "conspiracy to weaken our cops" that is aiding and abetting the destruction of our nation.

It is absolutely vital that we understand the "Blue Lies" that Jeff Wolf has so powerfully outlined in this book! Read this book! Then buy copies and send them to all your friends! This is one way that you can help fight back! Our lives depend on it! The survival of our nation and our way of life depend on it!

–Lt. Col. Dave Grossman (U.S. Army, Ret.),
Author of *On Killing, On Combat,* and *On Spiritual Combat.*

LT. COL. DAVE GROSSMAN, U.S. Army (Ret.)
Director, Killology Research Group
www.killology.com

Lt. Col. Dave Grossman is an award-winning author and nationally recognized as a powerful, dynamic speaker. He has authored over a dozen books, including his "perennial bestseller" *On Killing* and a *New York Times* best-selling book co-authored with Glenn Beck. His books are "required" or "recommended" reading in all four branches of the U.S. Armed Forces, and in federal and local law enforcement academies nationwide.

He is a U.S. Army Ranger, a paratrooper, a prior service sergeant, and a former West Point Psychology Professor. He has five patents to his name, has earned a Black Belt in Hojutsu (the martial art of the firearm), and has been inducted into the USA Martial Arts Hall of Fame.

His research was cited by the President of the United States in a national address; he has testified before the U.S. Senate, the U.S. Congress, and numerous state legislatures, and has been invited to the White House on two occasions to brief the President and the Vice President in his areas of expertise.

Since his retirement from the U.S. Army in 1998, he has been on the road over 200 days a year, for over 24 years, as one of our nation's leading trainers for military, law enforcement, mental health providers, and school safety organizations. He has been inducted as a "Life Diplomate" by the American Board for Certification in Homeland Security, and a "Life Member" of the American College of Forensic Examiners Institute.

Chapter 1
Black and Blue

"The wicked flee when no man pursueth; but the righteous are bold as a lion." —Proverbs 28:1

Imagine an America without law and order, a mobocracy where the government submits to the demands of domestic terrorists, where criminals are glorified and police are vilified, where your child's killer walks free because an activist prosecutor failed to appear in court, where drug traffickers are given free rein of our highways, where you are charged with a crime for defending your home against riotous thugs, where cop killers sit in seats of government, where entire police forces quit, and others no longer come when you call. Imagine an America where good is evil and evil is good, and the fascism our forefathers died to defeat is championed. Sadly, this is our America. An America that would make our founding fathers lament the day they set foot on its soil.

It is extraordinary how the voices of our past continue to speak to our present circumstances as if they could see into the future. Such were the words of the 40th President of the United States.

"But liberty, without law, without legal safeguards is not and cannot be liberty in the long run. It becomes, instead, license, revolution, and anarchy. It leads, without qualification, to mob rule and from there to the rule of the many by the few. And these in turn establish or disestablish law as they see fit, or ignore the law and rule by fiat or edict. What free men must achieve in order to remain free is a delicate balance wherein some liberty is sacrificed in order that the remainder can be preserved." —Ronald Reagan

President Reagan cautioned us to embrace law and order as the safeguards of our liberty. He admonished us to steward the freedom of America without allowing it to give way to mob-ocratic rule. He warned against the establishment and disestablishment of laws based on the will of the few. He encouraged us to embrace sacrifice so that liberty could be preserved.

Nevertheless, our democracy has been abdicated by its leaders to the whims of the mob as a politically powerful force. Law and order are being displaced by the infancy of anarchy, born to domestic terrorism masquerading as social activism. This mobocracy has created a fractionalization in our nation, the worst casualties of which are the men and women who are charged with maintaining law and order—the men and women of law enforcement. Maintaining law and order has been likened to oppression. Personal responsibility has been replaced with society's collective guilt. The peace pirates have declared war on the peacemakers.

No matter where you live, you are exposed to the war on American law enforcement. In Charlotte, North Carolina a headline reads, *"Councilman Wants to Disarm Police so Cops Must Use Words Instead of Force."*[1] An Ithaca, New York headline reads: *"Mayor Proposes Ending City's Police Force, Replacing It With New Civilian-Led Agency."*[2] In St. Louis, Missouri a headline reads, *"St. Louis Mayor Votes to Defund Police, Cut 100 Sworn Positions From Force."*[3] A New York City headline reads, *"Cop Killer Given Seat on Governor-Mandated Police Reform Panel."*[4] An Indianapolis headline reports: *"NFL Honors Gunman Killed While Trying to Murder Cops."*[5]

These are just a few of the ridiculous headlines feeding the anti-police sentiment that has been dominating the media. What's perplexing is that some people don't think these headlines are all that ridiculous. Those are the people who believe the narrative they are fed without considering that it may be misrepresented—or even blatantly false. For those who will unsuspectingly swallow the pill they are given, the narrative is carefully crafted to control their thinking and create fear. "Fear of what," you ask? Fear of personal responsibility, fear of others, fear of being labeled, fear of being canceled, and—the topic of our discussion—fear of the police.

Those that mix the message—like a carefully followed secret recipe—want Joe and Jane Public to believe that their actions and reactions are not their fault; they are the result of cultural constraints and societal sins, therefore, making them exempt from personal responsibility. In other words, neither Michael Brown, Alton Sterling nor anyone else killed in police encounters is at fault for their actions that led to being shot by police, and society as a whole must bear the collective guilt. Once this narrative is widely received and becomes the unofficial doctrine of a society, any push against it will be viewed as an attack on that society, and anyone who pushes back will be considered an enemy who must be feared and canceled. Subsequently, the police, the first line representatives of law and order, are the enemy who must be feared, delegitimized, resisted, and even preyed upon and attacked. Those attacks are coming more frequently and ferociously than ever before in history—sadly illustrated by a 40% increase in police officers feloniously killed in the line of duty in the first half of 2021.

At the center of this manufactured narrative is the issue of racism in American Law Enforcement. Discounting that one-in-three police officers in the United States is a member of a minority community, we are being compelled to believe that law enforcement is corrupted with "systemic" racism. Rejecting The Washington Post's statistic that twice as many whites than African Americans are killed in confrontations with police each year, we are dutifully corrected that African Americans are killed in disproportionate numbers to whites[6], as per population ratios.

A 2019 study published by the Proceedings of the National Academy of Sciences (PNAS) claimed there is "no evidence for anti-Black or anti-Hispanic disparity in police use of force... and, if anything, [there are] anti-White disparities[7]... " The authors of the study, Psychologists Joseph Cesario of Michigan State and David Johnson of the University of Maryland, later retracted their article, after receiving pressure from the MSU press office, who apologized for the "harm it caused."[8] Basically, a study painting cops in a positive light was retracted because of liberal academic peer pressure and fear of professional cancel culture.

Mainstream media—who has unashamedly aligned themselves with the anti-police mob—won't allow the truth to be published if it doesn't agree with the narrative. Why are we so determined to prove American police officers are racist? Why do we resist the faintest notion that police in our great nation are not murderous sociopaths, bent on exterminating African Americans? Cops are fathers and mothers, sons and daughters, sisters and brothers. They are patriotic people, just like Joe and Jane Public, who want to live the American dream and raise their families in the peace and safety of the greatest nation in the world. Every day they risk their lives to preserve that dream, standing against the evil we would rather pretend doesn't exist.

I get frustrated when I see asinine headlines such as these. They represent a society that is slowly weakening a thin blue line they cannot afford to erase. I think about the impact these would-be-policies would have on the safety of police officers, the price to be paid by law-abiding citizens, and the people who will ultimately be victimized by these irresponsible measures.

In this book I'm going to take you behind the scenes, giving you an inside view—from a beat cop's perspective—on some incendiary issues including traffic stops, deadly force encounters, and some of the high-profile shootings that were extorted by the Black Lives Matter organization to shove their agenda down our throats, and aggressively leverage an offensive against law enforcement. I'm going to expose the real domestic terrorist agenda and examine the What, Who, Why, and How of today's fulminating war on police, and its deadly consequences. I'm going to show you why the narrative of systemic racism in law enforcement is false, and explain how the defund, disarm, and disband the police movement is making America weaker while emboldening the lawless.

Our investigation together will be threaded with moderate statistics, but this will not primarily be a numbers book. There are books out there that contain thorough research into crime rates and demographics—making a solid case in favor of the police by the numbers—such as Heather MacDonald's *"The War On Cops."* This book, however, is an endeavor to take you on a literary "ride-a-long" with a cop who can't remain silent, as social and political bullies wage war against our men and women in blue. Cops are making heavy sacrifices in a society that no longer understands the meaning of the word, *sacrifice*. Buckle your seat belt. It's going to be a bumpy, but interesting ride.

Statement Against Racism

As the author, I believe it is important to give you a personal perspective on racism before going any further. I don't understand racism. Racism doesn't register with me. I grew up on a dead-end street, with eight houses, in the middle of the cornfields of north-central Ohio. The families that lived in our closely-knit neighborhood were lifers. Across the street from our house lived two of my childhood buddies. I didn't know them as the "Black kids" that lived across the street; I knew them as Robbie and Steven. We played together, got into mischief together, rode the bus to school together, and remained friends through high school until life took us in opposite directions.

No one taught me to dislike Robbie and Steven because of the color of their skin. Their family is one of the most loving families I've ever known. They still live across the street from my Mom. At Christmas time, they come over to deliver cookies and exchange gifts. When my Dad passed away, they brought over food for the family. Through the years, we've celebrated together in life's blessings and mourned together in life's tragedies. They aren't the "Black family" across the street. They are family. This is why I don't understand racism.

I spent two decades in law enforcement. I believe it is one of the noblest professions one can join. I worked hard to obtain the honor of serving and wore the badge with integrity and professionalism. Being a police officer was not always easy, or enjoyable for that matter. I saw some of the most gruesome, heartbreaking things wearing that uniform; things that will never leave me. But, I also had the privilege of making a difference in the lives of people. Like the 80-year-old lady who was phone-scammed out of over $8,000 cash by someone posing as her grandson. I was able to recover every dime of her money. It was a good feeling. One Christmas, I was assigned the task of distributing donated gift cards to families in need. I still remember the faces and reactions of the recipients. I felt like Santa Claus. I loved serving just as much as I loved protecting.

On the other hand, police work is sometimes violent. Every day, police officers leave their families at home and put their lives on the line to do a job that is difficult, selfless, thankless, dangerous, and under more scrutiny than ever before in the history of our nation. Statistics say that every fifty-three (53) hours a cop is killed in the line of duty. Every instance is felt by the entire law enforcement community. It's a brotherhood/sisterhood that is unlike any other I've ever been a part of.

In my career I've arrested hundreds of people, some of them more than once. Some of them were African American. In those encounters, I didn't view them any differently than my friends, Robbie and Steven. They were just people like anyone else. Many times, an offender would make a statement like, "You're only arresting me because I'm Black." My response was normally something like, "No, I'm arresting you because you were drunk driving," or "because you hit your girlfriend," or "because you broke a fellow nursing student's nose in class (true story)." As a police officer, I never dealt with anyone a certain way because of the color of their skin. I just enforced the law as fairly and professionally as I knew how. This is why I don't understand racism.

Nevertheless, it would be terribly naive to deny the existence of racism in America. It is our black eye, our scarlet letter, our collective criminal record, the smudge on our armor. It makes me cringe to know that the country I love once condoned slavery, and, as recently as 60 years ago, segregated universities, schools, businesses, buses, restrooms, and drinking fountains. Instead of trying to erase our history, or insist that our children pay for the sins of their fathers, we Americans should hold our heads high, knowing that we have grown as a nation. We aren't perfect, but since the Civil Rights movement of the 1960s, we have worked to right our wrongs and learn from a troubled history and, though we have a long way to go, we will continue to do so.

It would also be terribly naive to deny the existence of racism in law enforcement. Senior Lead Officer Deon Joseph, a twenty-five-year veteran of the LAPD said it best. "The vast majority of officers are decent human beings, but there is a negative exception that we all need to work hard to try to root out. And I think we're trying to do that."[9] I agree. Racism is the exception, not the rule. I don't believe the force-fed false narrative of *systemic* racism in law enforcement. In two decades of service, I never once acted, or witnessed another officer act, in a manner that could even remotely be considered—or misunderstood—as racist. Let me ask you a question. If police racism is so systemic, shouldn't I have seen it for myself at least once in twenty years?

What I *have* witnessed is the determination of dedicated men and women who rise above the noise to make a difference. I've witnessed their bravery in the face of danger, and I've witnessed their courage under fire.

Chapter 2
Courage Under Fire

"Evil is powerless if the good are unafraid."
—President Ronald Reagan

January 21, 2005, would become the bloodiest day in the history of Brimfield Township, an Ohio community situated in Portage County on the southern tip of Lake Erie's snow belt. A winter storm was moving in with more than a foot of accumulation expected. By nightfall, the silent beauty of a fresh blanket of pure, sparkling, heavy snow would stand in dark contrast to the brutal violence that was looming. Before the night was over, this small community would be rocked by the tragedy of a triple murder.[1]

Renee Bauer was a 42-year-old home health aide. She and her seven-year-old son, Dakota lived with her boyfriend of two years, James Trimble. Trimble, an Air Force veteran, had recently moved back to Brimfield after living in Texas. He and Renee were now living in his childhood home on Sandylake Drive, still owned by his mother. Friends of the couple described their relationship as a happy one, initially. Over time, though, the warning signs of domestic violence began to surface.

Trimble spent a lot of time in his basement where he kept his collection of firearms. He had multiple handguns and long guns, countless magazines and rounds of ammunition, camouflage gear, and other military-style items. Trimble's neighbor often heard him firing his guns in the woods behind his home. The problem with this was that he was a convicted felon, on probation, and couldn't legally own or possess firearms. But Trimble was no stranger to criminal activity.

According to friends, Trimble and Bauer both drank a lot, which seemed to be what precipitated the fighting. To make matters worse, Trimble had a methamphetamine addiction which, allegedly, was being supplied by Renee's ex-husband. She had apparently confronted her ex and told him to stop giving Trimble meth because it was causing him to act "weird."

Renee had also confided in three separate people that Trimble had been beating her and had threatened to kill Dakota if she went to the police or left him. She told all three that if anything ever happened to her, it would be Trimble who did it. According to one of Renee's co-workers, she claimed Trimble had once put her in handcuffs and pointed a gun at her head. Nevertheless, Renee believed that if she stayed and kept the peace no harm would come to them.

According to Trimble's ex-wife, he had beaten her many times, had pointed guns at her, and had locked her in a room for several days at a time. She cited a specific incident, in 2001, when Trimble pointed a gun at her and told her he was going to kill her, burn the house down, and kill himself. He eventually let her go, fired shots in the air, and fled into the woods with a rifle. When police arrived, they talked Trimble out, arrested him, and charged him with aggravated assault and having weapons under disability (a person convicted of a violent felony in possession of a firearm). That was the last time she ever saw him. Unfortunately, it would not be the last time he became violent.

James Trimble's history of mental instability, domestic violence, use of firearms, and abuse of illegal drugs was a recipe for disaster which would culminate on January 21st. According to friends, Renee had mustered the courage to leave and this was the night.

Renee had been working that evening and had clocked out at 5:37 PM. It is not known if she went straight home or stopped somewhere along the way. At approximately 7:18 PM, Trimble received a phone call from his mother, Elizabeth Trimble Bresley. She said Trimble was at home and waiting for a pizza he had ordered and she thought everything sounded normal. At approximately 7:45 PM, the pizza delivery driver pulled up to the Sandylake home. The driver said Trimble was in the driveway tinkering around with his truck. He told the driver to take the pizza up to the front door, where "the boy" would give him the money. When he left, Trimble said, "Be safe tonight." The driver said he never saw Renee Bauer, but didn't observe anything out of the ordinary either, just a family having pizza for dinner during a snowstorm on Saturday night.

At 8:10 PM Trimble's mother called him again. Since her first call, Renee had returned home and she and Dakota had tried to leave the residence. An altercation occurred and things went bad very quickly. Elizabeth Trimble Bresley could never have expected the words that came out of her son's mouth when he answered the phone. He said, "I just shot Renee and Dakota," and hung up the phone. Within minutes, James' brother, Art Trimble in Florida, received a call from their mother. She was hysterical and repeated what James had told her. Art immediately called his brother to find out what happened. James confirmed to his brother that he had shot and killed both Renee and Dakota Bauer. As Art Trimble was hanging up to call the police, James Trimble was gathering his weapons to flee into the woods.

Two 911 calls came into Brimfield Township Police at approximately 9:00 PM. One was from a resident on Ranfield Road, which ran adjacent to Sandylake Drive, on the other side of the woods. The resident reported working in his garage when he heard someone outside. He walked out of the garage and was confronted by a man in camouflage clothing, armed with a rifle. The gunman, who was later identified as James Trimble, told him to put his hands up, that he had just killed three people, and he was going to kill him as well. The resident pleaded for his life until suddenly his mother walked outside to see what was going on. They somehow talked Trimble into just walking away, reasoning with him that they couldn't see his face and therefore couldn't identify him. Miraculously, Trimble did just that, fleeing back into the woods.

The second 911 call, also coming in at approximately 9:00 PM, was from Art Trimble. He reported what his brother had told him on the phone and requested police respond to the house on Sandylake Drive to check their welfare.

Brimfield Township Police, covering an area of about 20 square miles and 10,000 residents, had two police officers on duty that night. Two cops. Additionally, in 2005, patrol rifles were not standard issue to police officers. If an agency had any, they were assigned to supervisors or S.W.A.T. officers. The average road cop carried a semi-automatic pistol, about 45 rounds of ammunition, and a 12-gauge shotgun. In short, Brimfield officers were outgunned on this bloody night.

These two 911 calls were both considered high-priority calls. One was a "check the welfare" at a residence where two people were possibly shot and killed. The other was a "man with a gun" call. Both calls were in close proximity and, by any agency's standards, would require the response of more than one officer. What is typical in such a dilemma is the use of what is called, "mutual aid." Most police agencies have mutual aid agreements with surrounding agencies. It basically says, when an agency needs help they can make a mutual aid request, which gives cops from nearby jurisdictions the authority to respond across jurisdictional lines. Smaller police agencies regularly rely on this fail-safe. That's what Brimfield officers did.

Officer Knarr responded to Ranfield Road with the assistance of two nearby Kent City Police officers. After speaking with the caller, he quickly moved to establish a perimeter to try to contain and ultimately locate Trimble. He requested more officers from Talmadge and Kent State University Police. In the meantime,

Knarr communicated briefly with his shift partner, Officer Peterman, who had responded to the Sandylake Drive call.

When Officer Peterman arrived on Sandylake Drive, she checked the perimeter of the home, trying to get a look inside. She looked in through a back window and saw what she believed was a body laying on the floor. When deputies from the Portage County Sheriff's Office arrived, they made entry into the house and found Renee and Dakota Bauer dead in the master bedroom. The investigation would later reveal that James Trimble had opened up with an AR-15 rifle on Renee, as she used her body to shield her small son. She was shot thirteen times; six of those rounds passed through Renee and hit Dakota. He was found underneath his mother's body, clutching his teddy bear. They were wearing jackets, their bags were packed and sitting by the front door. Renee's plan to escape the violence had ended in their deaths, just as she had predicted.

Back on Ranfield Road, Officer Knarr and his backup suddenly began taking fire from the woods. The officers took cover and were pinned down for some time, as Trimble fired several bursts of 5-10 rounds each. Officer Knarr contacted the Chief of Police to update him on the situation. At 9:37 PM the Chief requested the response of the Metro S.W.A.T. team from the Akron area. For more than two hours Trimble roamed the woods between Sandylake and Ranfield Rd, firing hundreds of rounds at a growing number of responding officers.

The situation quickly changed as an additional 911 call came in at 11:18 PM. This call was from a 22-year-old Kent State University student named, Sarah Positano from a separate residence on Ranfield Road. Sarah was an assistant gymnastics coach from Ontario, Canada, who was expected to graduate at the end of the semester. She had been the only one of three roommates home that night when James Trimble randomly entered her residence and held her hostage. Positano told dispatchers Trimble wanted police to leave the area and would shoot her if they tried to enter the residence. She could be heard asking Trimble not to put the gun to her head.[2]

The two-story duplex sat about 100 yards off the road and was surrounded by enough open land for Trimble to have a line of sight all the way around the residence. Metro S.W.A.T. established a perimeter and attempted to get as close to the house as safely possible using an armored vehicle. Unfortunately, it had become stuck in the rapidly accumulating snow, leaving officers with insufficient cover beyond their vehicle to make an escape, as Trimble continued to take shots at them.

When someone shoots at cops, more cops come running. So, by this time more than 100 police officers from surrounding agencies had amassed on or near the scene. Neighbors, awakened by a combination of red and blue lights reflecting off the snowy surface of everything, sirens, and gunfire, were told by police officers to go to the back of their homes or even shelter in their basements. The atmosphere was filled with fear and uncertainty. No one, however, could have been experiencing more fear and terror than Positano.

There were long periods of silence pierced by the occasional crack of rifle fire coming from inside the house, each one reminding officers that vigilance would mean the difference in surviving this standoff. Faint police radio chatter, multiplied by scores of portable radios, sounded like stereo surround sound in the cold open atmosphere. The scene was surreal.

About three miles to the East was the Brimfield Township police station which was serving as the command post. Citizens and the media had already gathered outside. Word that something was going on had spread through the tight-knit community when police had closed the road to the residence where the murders had occurred. As of yet, no official statement had been released and people wanted answers.

I was summoned to the command post by Chief Deputy Dave Doak of the Portage County Sheriff's Office. Dave was a mild-mannered, laid-back, cop's cop. He was old school; he smoked a pipe and still carried a "wheel" gun (what old-timers call revolvers). I never saw him rattled and I don't recall ever hearing him raise his voice. Dave retired as a lieutenant from the Kent City

Police Department after a twenty-seven-year career, then served twelve years as Chief Deputy of the Sheriff's Office, and went on to serve three terms (12 years) as the Sheriff. Dave is partly responsible for my law enforcement career. I was then serving as the department chaplain and would be needed to assist in making a death notification to Renee and Dakota's family.

Among the people congregated outside were Renee Bauer's sister and brother-in-law. As they were being escorted into the building to meet with us, they were approached by a reporter. In true form to American media, the reporter blurted out something to the effect of, "You know Renee and Dakota are dead, don't you?" What kind of heartless human being does that just to get a reaction, therefore robbing the family of their dignity? Why, a member of the media, of course.

It was becoming obvious that information was beginning to get out. Something this big couldn't be concealed for very long, and the night was far from over. All efforts were being focused on saving a hostage and capturing a killer. Unfortunately, only one of those objectives would be accomplished.

Back on Ranfield Road, negotiators were preparing to make contact with James Trimble. When they got him on the phone, he identified himself as, "Camo Jim." He claimed that if police would give him two hours, he would release the hostage. He also said he didn't want to hurt any innocent people and had already let two people go. Meanwhile, Positano was on the phone with a different negotiator. She told him she was scared and didn't want to die, and asked to speak to her mother.[3]

What happened next is unclear and later became a source of contention in court. At approximately 12:04 AM, a faint, single gunshot was heard on the phone, followed by Positano screaming, "I've been shot!" She was heard gasping for air before the line went dead. They were not able to reestablish communication with Trimble or Positano. For more than two hours following the call, Trimble fired at officers from inside the duplex. Early in the morning hours, Metro S.W.A.T. entered the house to find James Trimble hiding in a closet and Sarah Positano dead of a single gunshot wound to the neck.[4]

James Trimble's drug-induced, bloody reign of terror on this quiet Northeast Ohio community had finally come to an end, leaving three people dead including a seven-year-old little boy. This unspeakable, senseless tragedy was not only felt by their families but by a college campus, mourning the loss of one of their own. The investigation and trial that followed overshadowed news coverage for several months. On November 21, 2005, James Trimble was convicted of all three murders and sentenced to death by lethal injection. Despite numerous appeals, as recently as 2015, his death sentence has been upheld. As of the date of this writing, he sits on death row at the Chillicothe Correctional Institution.[5]

On that infamous January night back in 2005, officers remained in the line of fire for several hours while enduring the chilling temperatures and precipitation of a winter storm. When duty called, the men and women of the thin blue line came running from multiple counties. In the face of impossible odds, police officers put themselves in harm's way to stop the murderous rage of an evil monster. It is nothing short of a miracle that none of them were hit in the process. The bravery, dedication, and character of every officer on that scene was brighter still the following day when they all put on the uniform, kissed their families goodbye, and went back to work to do it all over again.

These are the people who chose a profession that could not guarantee their survival. These are folks who spend a career having to see things that the general public could never stomach, having to keep their emotions in check, having to endure the hatred of society that tasks them with protecting but then criticizes the manner in which they have to do so. Every man and woman who wears the badge is faced with the reality that today, doing their job may make them a hero, but tomorrow, doing their job may make them the criminal. Taking action in the face of danger today may be rewarded with a medal or the thanks of a victim saved, but tomorrow taking action may cost them their reputation, career, freedom, or ultimately their lives. Yet, these blue warriors keep suiting up for the task, for if they didn't the nation would crumble under the evil and violence of anarchy.

That must be why Jesus said, "Blessed are the peacemakers, For they shall be called sons of God." (Matthew 5:9 NKJV)

Chapter 3
The Making of a Sheepdog

"There is no elegant way to protect sheep from hungry wolves." —
Unknown

Do you remember the days when the public respected and even admired police officers? They once stood as pillars of the community, examples of leadership, symbols of bravery, and all that society was supposed to be. America loved our men and women in uniform and depended on them to come running if and when we needed them. Those were the days when I decided I wanted to be one of them.

The biggest influence in my decision to become a police officer was my Uncle, my favorite cop whom I looked up to as a child. He looked larger than life when I saw him in uniform; it made an impression upon me that would shape my career. I was always proud to see him on the local news, like when he worked the riots during the AK Steel Strike, or when he was standing next to one of the many 18-wheelers that have been stuck under the Park Avenue East underpass. I knew I wanted to be like him, but I could never have prepared myself for the price that would have to be paid.

Things are much different now. War has been declared on police by liberal politicians, activist organizations, and anti-police prosecutors who have criminalized cops and victimized criminals. Celebrities and professional athletes have also jumped on the bandwagon, fueling the already divisive and toxic rhetoric that has many Americans convinced police are nothing more than racist murderers bent on terrorizing the public.

As much was said by a woman who was stopped by a Los Angeles County Sheriff's Deputy in April of 2021. In a widely circulated police bodycam video, the woman went on a rant akin to a toddler's temper tantrum, repeatedly calling the Hispanic deputy a murderer and racist Mexican. The deputy, who maintained a calm and professional demeanor, was praised by L.A. County Sheriff Alex Villanueva who said the woman filed a complaint immediately following the traffic stop.[1] Imagine that.

This type of hostile response to police officers isn't all that rare. Quite the contrary, it has become the norm in a national environment that is becoming increasingly contemptuous of law enforcement. Officers have grown to expect it; good officers know how to maintain courtesy and professionalism in the face of such contempt from a society that has the luxury of not knowing what we know—that the sheep ultimately survive because the sheepdog stands his watch.

Sheepdogs Live to Protect

It takes a special person to be a good police officer. Being a person of moral character is a prerequisite, but it's not enough. Being a person of integrity and trustworthiness is critical, but it's not enough. Having keen physical and mental health is necessary, but even that is not enough. Good cops have to be sheepdogs.

Perhaps you're familiar with the "Wolves, Sheep, and Sheepdog" speech from the movie, *American Sniper*. It originated from Lt. Col. Dave Grossman's book, *On Combat*. Col. Grossman, a

U.S. Army Ranger, paratrooper, and former West Point Psychology Professor, is the Director of the Killology Research Group. He trains law enforcement officers around the world. I had the privilege of attending one of his seminars on the Bulletproof Mind. He writes:

> *"If you have no capacity for violence then you are a healthy productive citizen: a sheep. If you have a capacity for violence and no empathy for your fellow citizens, then you have defined an aggressive sociopath—a wolf. But what if you have a capacity for violence and a deep love for your fellow citizens? Then you are a sheepdog, a warrior, someone who is walking the hero's path. Someone who can walk into the heart of darkness, into the universal human phobia, and walk out unscathed."[2]*

To understand Col. Grossman's metaphor, you have to accept an unsavory but undeniable fact. Wolves, like James Trimble, live among the sheep. According to FBI statistics, more than 1.2 million people were victimized by violent crime in 2019. That may seem like only a fraction of the population unless you are one of those victims. A society infested with wolves needs sheepdogs.

Take the beautiful Gran Sasso National Park in Italy, for instance. It is home to a large and thriving population of wolves. It also boasts rolling hills where shepherds keep their vast flocks of sheep. It is said that the predators and prey can successfully coexist because the wolf instinctively knows to leave the sheep alone due to the presence of the sheepdog. But what if you remove the sheepdog from the equation? What would keep the wolf from devouring the flock? What would become of the innocent sheep?

This is a microcosm of the role of law enforcement in society. The sheepdog has become a popular euphemism for the American police officer. Sheepdogs must be trusted to live among but not hurt the sheep. They must be instinctively attentive to the threat that the sheep don't see. They must be protective by bearing their teeth of aggression to deter evil predators. And if deterrence fails, sheepdogs must be willing to fight to the death if necessary to protect the sheep. There has never been a more fitting and accurate analogy to describe the brave and selfless men and women of law enforcement.

Col. Grossman goes on to say,

> *"To be a sheepdog you must make a conscious and moral decision every day to dedicate, equip and prepare yourself to thrive in that toxic, corrosive moment when the wolf comes knocking at the door."*[3]

Becoming a sheepdog requires a unique mindset. One that acknowledges the presence of the wolf and its savage nature. One that is prepared to do what is necessary when the wolf is relentless against the deterrent presence of the protector. The wolf is a trained predator; it lives by violence. Violence is something that never enters the sheep's imagination. But because it exists, the sheep need the sheepdog. Cops are ordinary people who are asked to do extraordinary things. Things for which most people are not mentally prepared.

Law Enforcement expert and trainer Ken Murray notes the sharp contrast.

> *"Many criminals grow up with a greater exposure to violence... The contrast and implications to police officers who typically have a much different upbringing—close to family, invested in a career, impacted by public expectations, and legal constraints—should be obvious."*[4]

The conservative, Christian environment in which I was raised served as a social and mental barrier from the fallen world around me. That barrier was unexpectedly shattered the first time I looked at society through the windshield of a patrol car. For the first time, outside of the nightly news, I witnessed first-hand the depravity of humanity. I was awakened to the presence and danger of the wolf, and the silent, often unnoticed deterrence of the sheepdog. I was enlightened to the strength of the thin blue line, taken for granted by the average citizen protected by it, that holds back the evil that the average citizen doesn't want to see.

Why Do Cops Become Cops?

So, why would someone choose law enforcement as a career? It certainly isn't for the money. In fact, most cops work second jobs or have a side gig on their days off. It definitely isn't for fame. Unwanted negative press is usually what makes a cop famous— or infamous. It isn't for awards or recognition; law enforcement is largely a thankless profession. It is positively not because they want a job that offers flexibility for family life. The words *divorce* and *police* are almost synonymous. Even if a cop is fortunate enough to stay happily married, they will inevitably miss birthdays, ball games, anniversaries, church, and important holidays like Thanksgiving and Christmas. People choose law enforcement because it's a calling; an internal instinct. Sheepdogs are born, not taught.

Cops don't become cops because it's easy. Law enforcement was once a very competitive profession. The hiring process lasts on average about 4-6 months. It includes written tests, physical agility tests, oral panel interviews, extensive background investigations, medical evaluations, psychological exams, drugs tests, and often a polygraph or voice stress analysis. Once an applicant passes all of those criteria, they may get a conditional offer of employment. Then again, they may not, depending on openings and how they stand in the applicant pool.

If you are fortunate enough to earn a position, the next step is police academy. Each state has its own criteria for training police officers, commonly known as P.O.S.T., or peace officer standards and training. In Ohio, police academy is over 700 hours, approximately six months, during which cadets will undergo classroom training in topics such as traffic and criminal law, search and seizure, and ethics and professionalism. They will also undergo training in physical fitness, police tactics, investigation, driving, self-defense, and everything else that falls under the job description of a police officer. They will be tested mentally, emotionally, and physically. The process is grueling, stressful, and difficult. Many don't make it through. Department of Justice national statistics report that only 86% of cadets complete police academy each year.[5]

After you have risen to the top of the selection process and have successfully completed the academy, you are still not finished. When you report for duty on your first day as a police officer, you are assigned a field training officer, affectionately referred to as an F.T.O., who supervises your on-the-job training. Field training lasts about six months. You will be constantly evaluated, scrutinized, tested, and corrected. You are on probation and can be dismissed without cause. If you make it through this rigorous 16-18 month induction into the blue family, then and only then are you "cut loose," the universal term for graduating to solo patrol.

So, when you encounter a man or woman wearing a badge, rest assured they have earned that badge by dedication, commitment, and perseverance. And, it only begins once they are sworn in. Their training never ends. Their job is never done. Their lives are never the same. They are now part of a fraternity of brothers and sisters that requires them to live their lives differently than everyone else. For instance, a cop will never be able to sit with their back to the door. They will have to take the "power seat" in every room they enter— the seat from which all people and entrances are visible. Why do they do this? Because of days like the one in June of 2014, when two Las Vegas Metro Police officers were eating lunch in a CiCi's Pizza restaurant. Two gunmen entered and opened fire, killing both of them.[6]

A cop will never be able to eat at a restaurant in uniform without watching their food being prepared. Though it is often mentioned tongue-in-cheek, cops are generally cautious about what and where they eat on duty, and for good reason. In 2019, management at a Bakersfield, California McDonald's restaurant caught an employee tampering with a Bakersfield Police officer's food. The employee was arrested and charged with a felony.[7]

A cop will rarely be able to go out in public with his family without running into someone they've dealt with on the job, or even had in handcuffs at one time or another. Even if they *do* manage to avoid that, they will invariably be recognized as a cop by someone who wants them to "pass the word" about some random violation of law. When a cop witnesses a serious crime while off-duty, they no longer have the luxury of not getting involved. They have a moral and ethical duty to act. Cops never really clock out. They take it home and everywhere they go. A sheepdog is *always* a sheepdog.

Cops accept a certain amount of risk when they enter their careers. Beyond the risk to their physical safety is the risk to their mental and emotional wellbeing. Many cops survive relatively unscathed, but many are those whose career has rewarded them with varying degrees of Post Traumatic Stress Disorder. Constant exposure to crime, violence, and death, and dealing with the people who maliciously victimize the innocent, is a burden most people outside the law enforcement circle don't understand. It takes a toll on officers, their marriages, families, and health. Additionally, rotating work schedules, long hours, and mandatory court appearances cause sleep problems and the ancillary issues that follow. Cops don't become cops because it's easy, but because it's their calling, and it's worth it.

The Days You Remember

Even when you're doing what you love, you don't always love what you're doing. Believe it or not, police officers do have unremarkable days. They are not all filled will heart-pounding, adrenaline-pumping action. Sometimes a shift consists of humdrum activities like phone calls and follow-ups on open cases, lock-outs, vacation house checks, checking business doors, online training courses, washing your cruiser, directed patrols, and other "check the box" activities that have to be done. But the days you remember are the ones when your monotony is suddenly interrupted by what I call a "shift-ender," a call that has all the characteristics of a reality police show, and will consume the rest of your day. Those are the days cops live for.

I recall one such day that landed me a local news interview. Cops typically don't like getting anywhere near a television camera, but on this occasion, there was a happy ending to tell. I was in a mobile home park taking a simple theft report. As I was speaking with the victim inside her residence, a neighbor came bursting through her front door yelling something to the effect of, "Somebody's house is on fire!" I guess they saw my cruiser parked in front of the residence and decided finding me was quicker than calling 911. It was a life-saving move.

I left my clipboard, as I recall, and ran outside, following the guy who alerted me. I quickly located the burning home one street over–which was now fully engulfed in flames with smoke pouring out of the windows–and alerted my dispatch to the fire. I noticed there were no cars in the driveway and asked a group of neighbors–who had come outside–if anyone was home. Nobody knew. I don't remember formulating a plan in my head, or considering the consequences of my actions, I just ran up to the front door and began banging and screaming, "Is there anybody in there?"

When I banged on the door, it came open! The home was so filled with smoke I couldn't see anything, so I got down on my hands and knees to try to look under the smoke for anyone inside. There was about six inches of visibility between the floor and the smoke. I could see shoes on the floor about 8-10 feet inside the living room. I could hear a man calling out and quickly realized his feet were in those shoes. I yelled for him to follow the sound of my voice and come toward me. I reached out and got a hold of his arm and began pulling him toward the doorway. Once we were outside, I helped the elderly man get across the street and sat him down on the sidewalk. He had sustained burns on his face, arms and hands. About that time I heard the fire department's sirens coming down the street. I truly believe if I had not been at the right place at the right time, that gentleman would have perished in the fire.

My superiors and colleagues honored me with the medal of valor. I received congratulatory letters from my Senator and Congressman. I was interviewed by a local radio personality. When I interviewed on scene with the local news, I heard this statement come out of my mouth in response to one of the reporter's questions, "Once I knew there was someone inside the home, I wasn't going to retreat until I got him out." In an obviously dangerous situation, my own safety was the least of my worries. I was determined that, Katy bar the door, I was not going to let someone lose their life. My actions that day were not necessarily a conscious decision as much as they were instinctual. I don't share that to sound brave, but to say that I believe any police officer in my shoes would—and often have—done the same.

Another highlight of my career was a meeting that took place in my office in 2017. Though it sounds rather routine, it was quite exciting—for me, anyway. I used to love to watch Manhunters, a show about the U.S. Marshalls Fugitive Task Force. As you can probably imagine, the afternoon they walked into my office I was star-struck. Yeah, I know it wasn't the same team that was featured on the show, but it was still pretty cool.

We were working a homicide that was only a few hours old; we had identified the suspect—who had stabbed his girlfriend and unborn child to death—and were pulling in every resource we had at our disposal. We sent cops to every known residence, hang out, hideout, and hole this monster was known to frequent. We decided to call the U.S. Marshalls field office on the off chance they might be able to help us out. Within an hour of making the call, I looked out my office window—which faced the parking lot—and saw several blacked-out SUVs rolling in like a convoy. It was just like the movies when the feds show up.

About a dozen guys, all "tacked out"—a common law enforcement phrase to describe officers dressed in tactical gear—were directed into my office, and made a semi-circle around my desk. They looked 8 feet tall and like they meant business. The group leader asked, "What can we do for you, Sarge?" I couldn't believe I was briefing the U.S. Marshalls Fugitive Task Force, just like they did on TV. I couldn't wait to tell my wife. (I'm easily amused.)

We had saturated the local news, radio stations, social media, and even the highway digital signs with information about our suspect and his vehicle, and it paid off. The same day, his vehicle was spotted by a motorist in an adjacent state who recognized it and was able to alert local law enforcement, directing them to his location. Following a short pursuit, the vehicle stopped, and the murderer was apprehended without incident. He had been captured within approximately twelve hours of the original call and was ultimately convicted and sentenced to life without parole.

The Days You Don't Remember

Then there are days that you don't remember, but someone else does because it changed their life. A police officer never knows how he or she has impacted someone's life until that person tells them. Several months after I retired, the PD forwarded to me a very kind letter from just such a person.

"I was a wild young man when I lived there. I struggled with a lot of issues with my upbringing and the environment I chose to be in. Long story short, I was a no-good thug. The reason I am writing this is because one of your officers really impacted me back then, Sergeant Wolf. He responded to an overdose where my mother had died. That wasn't our only encounter. He had also stopped me from taking my life and brought me to a mental health center. He never talked down to me. He never disrespected me. He treated me like a human and with compassion. I never got the chance to thank him. That is the point of this letter. I know right now a lot of people have hate for police but not me. I could never imagine doing what you guys do. I have a ton of respect for you guys and I just wanted to share it with you. Thanks so much to Sergeant Wolf, he is one hell of an officer and one hell of a person. Because of him and people like him, I turned my life around. I'm a father, a husband, and a tax-paying citizen. I try the best I can to be a good example for my son and others and I do all I can for my community. So thank you guys for all that you do. I appreciate you all."

I don't remember this person, but he remembered me. I don't recall the incident—it was one of many—but on a day that may have been inconsequential for me, a day that may not have been one of my best, I was able to make an impact on someone that changed their life. There is an untold number of stories out there, similar to this one, that tell the real story of American law enforcement officers. They care, they help, they love, and they change lives without even realizing it. This is the real reason why cops become cops.

The Days You Don't Want to Remember

Every cop has days they don't want to remember. Near the top of my list is the morning I was dispatched to a non-breather—a one-month-old infant. I raced to the residence to find a hysterical mother over the body of her child who was obviously deceased. Through sobs, she told me she had fallen asleep with the baby in bed next to her. During the night, she had rolled over on top of the baby in her sleep. The baby subsequently suffocated. That call pushed a personal button for me; my first daughter was born with a major heart defect and only lived to be ten weeks old. When I looked at that lifeless infant laying there, all I could see was my daughter. I was glad to eventually turn that scene over to a detective and get out of there, but it tormented me for several days.

I wish I could forget the violence and gore I witnessed, such as the man who walked away from a bar intoxicated one night and was hit by a vehicle. The force of the impact tore three of his limbs away from his body. I wish I could forget the smell of death and the faces of the deceased. I wish I could forget the sexual assaults that victimized children. There are so many things about law enforcement that took a mental and emotional toll on me. As tough as cops try to portray themselves—especially in front of other cops—the toll of the job is universal.

The Days You Tell Stories About

Then, there are the days you tell stories about because they were so ridiculous. One summer night I stopped a vehicle and arrested the driver for DUI and an outstanding warrant. I don't recall why, but I had to take him to the hospital to get medically cleared for the jail. While he was waiting to be seen in the E.R., I was getting my paperwork finished up. A DUI arrest generates several forms: a uniform traffic citation, misdemeanor summons for companion charges, vehicle tow sheet, BMV license suspension form, toxicology paperwork for a urine test, or Intoxylizer paperwork for a breath test, etc. I had it all finished by the time the medical staff finished up with my arrestee and put everything in my metal storage clipboard. I escorted him to my car and we headed toward the jail.

Once we arrived at the jail, I pulled into the sally port and took my guy inside to be booked. When the intake officer asked for my medical clearance paperwork from the hospital, I realized I didn't have it. I went back out to my car and realized I didn't have my clipboard, and I panicked. As I began to mentally retrace my steps, I figured I had left my clipboard laying at the hospital. So, I went back inside the jail and informed the booking officer I had to run back over to the hospital to get my clipboard and would return shortly.

I pulled up to the E.R., went inside, and asked one of the nurses if anyone had seen my clipboard. Crickets. I checked the exam room we had occupied. Nothing. Then it hit me. When I put my guest in the back seat of my cruiser, I set my clipboard on the roof so I could get him buckled in. As you've probably already guessed, I left my clipboard on the roof of my car and drove away. When I realized what I had done, I panicked again. My clipboard—which not only contained my arrest paperwork, but other important documents—could be anywhere between the hospital and the jail. The only thing I could do was drive the route and spotlight the side of the road until I found it.

I didn't have to go far. I pulled out onto the four-lane split highway in front of the hospital and spotted my metal box clipboard, empty and mangled up, in the middle of the road, about a hundred yards from the intersection. I hit my brights and shined my spotlight on the roadway ahead and found my paperwork. It was scattered for a quarter of a mile down the road like a ticker-tape parade. I was half relieved I found my paperwork and half sick to my stomach. So, I pulled off to the side of the road, lit up the blue lights, got out of the car, and started walking down the highway picking it up one piece of paper at a time. I was praying no other cops would come by and see me cleaning up my mess, but I wouldn't be that lucky. An officer whose jurisdiction I was going through stopped and asked me what was going on—he later told me he thought someone had run from me and I was looking for him. When I told him what happened, he laughed and said, "I'll help you look." And then there were two.

The more paper I picked up, the less hopeful I became. I was finding a lot of blank forms, but not my arrest paperwork. Another officer from a nearby jurisdiction was on his way home from work when he saw two police cruisers lit up on the side of the highway. He stopped to see what happened. My Good Samaritan told him what I did. He also laughed and said, "I'll help you guys out." And then there were three. We were about a half-mile from the Highway Patrol post; I guess it was inevitable that a trooper would eventually come by. She stopped and asked who we were looking for. One of my helpers told her what—not who—we were looking for, and she just drove off. I guess she figured we had enough help. After spending considerable time on the side of the road picking up what was now trash, I thanked my brothers in blue who so graciously lent a hand and headed back toward the jail. I never did find my paperwork. I had to redo all of it. Everyone had a good laugh at my expense, including the dispatchers who had already heard the story from another cop.

Then, there was the day I tried to stop a funeral escort. I was sitting at a fire station watching the world go by—also called stationary patrol—when a white, unmarked sedan, with a siren and green and orange lights on top, busted through the inter-section of two busy state routes. I'm pretty sure I said out loud, "What in the world is this guy doing?" I knew he wasn't a volunteer firefighter, they use red lights. I dropped the car in drive and attempted to catch up to investigate. We went a couple of miles, and the civilian running code stopped in the middle of the next intersection. I stopped behind him, wondering out loud, "Why is he stopping in the middle of the intersection?" It was then that I noticed the vehicles going by had blue funeral flags on them. I had just passed about two dozen cars in a funeral procession and was attempting to initiate a traffic stop on their escort! I don't believe I've ever felt like such an idiot. I decided to join the procession and make it look like I planned the whole thing. When the cars passed, the escort car fell in behind them, and I followed him all the way to the cemetery. When they pulled in, I turned around, shut the blue lights off, and went the other way. I hoped they thought I was providing a police escort to their funeral. To my knowledge, they were none the wiser. At least, no one ever called the police department to report one of their officers interfering with a funeral escort. I don't know what I was thinking.

I Would Do It All Over Again

Despite the daily mental and emotional roller coaster of the law enforcement profession, most cops absolutely love the job. I say, *most*, because I'm sure there are a few out there who don't necessarily *love* it, however, I've never personally met one. Most former or retired cops will say, *"Once a cop, always a cop,"* meaning, you can leave the job but the job will never leave you. It gets in your blood and becomes a part of you, almost like you were made to do this. It is your calling. The rewards far outweigh the risks. I interviewed a retiree recently who—when speaking of his 33-year career—said, *"I'd do it all over again."*

Mass Exodus

My generation joined up when law enforcement was a coveted and competitive career; a position of honor that only the most capable and diligent of recruits were fortunate enough to earn. Historically, there have always been more applicants than positions. When they couldn't land a job, young recruits would take auxiliary and reserve positions, enthusiastically working for free just to get their foot in the door, as they worked their way up to a full-time career. Across the country, many sheriff's deputies first paid their dues working in the county jail as they patiently waited for their turn to hit the streets. When every cop's turn came, they set out on a career to serve with honor and professionalism. They have run toward danger when others have run away. They have faced off with evil when others have looked away. And they have defended the helpless when others have walked away.

Unfortunately, that sentiment is changing. Thousands of men and women in law enforcement are reevaluating their commitment to the profession. Not because they don't love the job, but because they see the writing on the wall, as it were, that the balance of risk and reward is tipping too far in the wrong direction. The political shock waves that have shaken the police community are felt in the squad car, in the station house, and around the dinner table of cops everywhere. They don't fear being wounded or killed. They don't fear criticism or scrutiny. They don't even fear the toll taken by the job—physically, mentally, and emotionally. They fear being sold out in the name of political expediency, and their fates being given over to the whims of a mobocratic society that will steal their freedom and come after the welfare of their families. To many, the risk has become greater than the reward.

Between the summers of 2020 and 2021, agencies across the nation reported police officers are leaving at unprecedented rates. The Los Angeles Police Department lost approximately 500 of its more than 10,000 sworn officers.[8] The New York Police Department lost more than 5,300 of its 36,000 sworn officers in 2020, either to resignation or retirement—that's 75% more than the previous year.[9] The Portland Police Bureau lost 115 of its 800 sworn officers.[10] The Atlanta Police Department lost 219 of its 1,822 sworn officers in 2020, which was already well below its authorized manpower of 2,046.[11] The Seattle Police Department lost more than 200, bringing them to an all-time record low of 10,800 "deployable officers."[12] The Louisville Metro Police Department lost almost 200 officers, which is equal to 20% of its sworn manpower.[13] The Asheville, North Carolina Police

Department lost 30% of its 238 sworn officers.[14] This trend perpetuates in agency after agency across the nation, with an 18% increase in resignations and a 45% increase in retirements.[15]

This mass exodus comes on the heels of a recruiting crisis that began brewing in 2013 when a consistent national uptick of full-time sworn officers began to decrease. By 2016, that number had plummeted by over 23,000 sworn officers.[16] The downward trend has continued, creating a national shortage of cops in 86% of the nation's police departments by 2020, according to the National Police Foundation.[17] A survey conducted in 2019 by the Police Executive Research Forum reports a decrease in applicants over a five-year period in 63% of law enforcement agencies.[18] Fast forward to 2021, and the situation has become so dire that some agencies have resorted to offering cash sign-on bonuses for new recruits and retention bonuses to keep existing officers.[19]

Although the recruit crisis predates the current national outcry, the mass exodus is a proximate result of the trickle-down effects of the "defund the police" movement. I'll save the in-depth exposition of those effects until later in our discussion. In the meantime, let's take a bird's eye view.

Disarm, Defund, Disband

At the heart of the crisis is a fallacious and obnoxious vocal minority who wants to disarm, defund, and even disband the police. They want to remove the thin blue line that has been drawn to keep the wolf at bay. Is this the misguided and deluded cause of naive and foolish sheep, or is it a calculated and socialistic movement seeking to cause mayhem and mobocracy?

According to the American Civil Liberties Union (ACLU), defunding the police actually makes us safer.[20] According to the American Public Health Association (APHA), a non-profit focussed on legislation and advocacy, police violence is a "serious public health issue."[21] Statements like this are made in contradiction to the real world. They are akin to claiming that defunding healthcare will make us healthier, or defunding fire departments will result in fewer fires. Or, as Rep. Alexandria Ocasio-Cortez claims, fewer prisons will mean fewer criminals.[22] It's absurd.

If that isn't injudicious enough, a CNN op-ed claimed that defunding police would "begin the process of ending the culture of punishment in the criminal justice system."[23] But, to remove the threat of punishment from the criminal justice system is to remove the deterrent effect the sheepdog has on the wolf. This is a calculated move to open the door for lawlessness and mob rule.

Crippling America's Cops

Law enforcement is already a difficult job by virtue of its demands. When the government begins to strip away the protections that police officers depend upon, it erodes confidence and destroys morale. The anti-police narrative has caused a systematic weakening of the thin blue line. The job is not what it used to be; it's much more difficult, risky, and dehumanizing now. Cops have lost a lot of public support, and worse yet, they've lost the support of their superiors, local politicians, and—in some cases—even prosecutors.

The ever-growing negative sentiment towards police officers has given most cops a bad taste in their mouth for the job. In the height of the 2020 Summer of protests, Calibre Press and Police1 polled 10,000 officers about their career satisfaction. Only half of them (50.8%) said they were satisfied in law enforcement, but not as much as in the past. Only 30% said they would remain on the job as long as possible. Almost half (44.5%) said they want to retire but are waiting for eligibility. More than 8% said they were either new to the profession, or not yet eligible for retirement, but were leaving the job regardless.

Despite my discouragement, my son and son-in-law are both seeking careers in law enforcement. I'm among the 80% that say they would not recommend their children go into the profession. When asked to select from a list of reasons why they felt that way, an overwhelming majority (88%) cited lack of departmental support and (83%) overall lack of respect for the profession.[24]

If I were to put in a sentence how a growing number of cops feel about the profession and why they are leaving in droves, it would be this: *It's just not worth the risk anymore.* Let me ask you a question. Do you blame them? Cops are tired of fighting for their own collective credibility, and their local government leaders who are buckling under the pressure of the anti-police mob, given a voice by the mainstream media. This is a national dilemma; it's bad for communities, it's bad for America, but it is exactly what the mob wants. The basis for the national narrative disparaging of police isn't even true. But the smoldering embers of the false narrative sparked a full-fledged war on police in Ferguson, Missouri—where the lies were born—and continues to leave destruction in its wake to this day.

Chapter 4
Ferguson, Missouri

"This dynamic is now widely accepted as the norm. Any officer-involved shooting—no matter how justified or illicit, whether we know everything about the circumstances or nothing at all—is simply assumed to be the occasion for mayhem." —Rich Lowry, New York Post[1]

Today there are more than 800,000 sworn law enforcement officers serving in the United States. In 2019, more than 56,000 of them were assaulted in the line of duty. Every 53 hours, one of those dedicated sheepdogs makes the ultimate sacrifice. In the words of a friend, colleague, and retired police officer, "I don't tell people I'm retired. I tell them I survived."

Officer Darren Wilson of the Ferguson, Missouri Police Department survived, but his deadly force encounter cost him everything *except* his life. Wilson became the most hated cop in America, and the most supported cop at the same time. In the aftermath of this and other high-profile deadly force encounters with minorities, by 2017 perhaps as many as 72% of law enforcement officers said they were hesitant to investigate suspicious activity or perform other protective measures out of fear they would become the next officer to face national scrutiny.[2] This is what many have called the Ferguson effect. Years later, it still impacts American law enforcement, with renewed momentum every time an African American is shot by police.

On August 9, 2014, Officer Darren Wilson shot and killed Michael Brown, an 18-year-old unarmed African American man. The incident quickly sparked widespread unrest in the St. Louis suburb and across the country. Rioting, looting, shooting, arson, blocking highways, and other illegal acts became the response of the rancorous public, ready to blame everyone *except* Michael Brown for the incident. As a result, the Black Lives Matter (BLM) organization—which began a year prior—rose to national prominence, propagating the narrative of systemic racism in law enforcement, and renewing the declaration of war on police in America.[3]

That I may dispel any notion that I am minimizing the death of Michael Brown, I will emphatically state that Brown's death was a tragic loss for his family and anyone who knew and loved him. I wholly concur with Lt. Col. Dave Grossman's quote in his book, *On Killing:*

> *"The [person] pulling the trigger never suffers as much as the person on the receiving end. It is the existence of the victim's pain and loss, echoing forever in the soul of the killer, that is at the heart of his pain." (Allen Cole and Christ Bunch)*[4]

Michael Brown's death was indeed a tragedy—but it was a tragedy of his own making.

The Original Call—Robbery

Missouri Revised Statutes § 570.025. Robbery in the second degree. A person commits the offense of robbery in the second degree if he or she forcibly steals property and in the course thereof causes physical injury to another person.[5]

The story begins on the morning of the 9th when Dorian Johnson and Michael Brown met up outside Johnson's apartment building on Canfield Drive to walk to a nearby convenience store to pick up cigars. While inside the store, Brown grabbed a box of cigars and began leaving the store, indicating no intention of paying for them. Surveillance video showed Michael Brown approaching the door and the store clerk coming around the counter to stop him. This is when Michael Brown, standing 6'4" and weighing approximately 300 pounds, pushed the store clerk into a display and left the store with Johnson. A customer called police to report the incident.

Later, during the robbery investigation, it was never disputed that Brown and Johnson were the two men seen on the store surveillance tape that morning. The nature of the incident, however, *was* disputed by the anti-police mob. In the days following the shooting several articles were published inferring that Michael Brown didn't rob anyone, he just harmlessly shoplifted a box of cigars from a convenience store. The Philadelphia Tribune published an article to that effect entitled "A Black Life Is Worth Less than a $50 Box of Cigars."[6] This type of incredulous media is designed to distract from the truth and infer that Brown was killed that day because he stole a box of cigars as if the degree of offense ultimately determined Officer Wilson's decision to use deadly force, i.e. Wilson shot him for shoplifting. That notion is ridiculous. Does any reasonable, prudent person really believe that? It's just an example of how the media irresponsibly twisted the facts and reported false information to pour gas on an already raging racial fire in Ferguson.

Another theory being peddled was that there was no robbery *or* shoplifting at all. In 2017, a documentary called, "Stranger Fruit" emerged claiming the altercation between Brown and the store clerk was the result of a misunderstanding about an earlier drug transaction.[7] Even if this information is true, it's irrelevant to the case. The information given to police at the time was that a robbery had occurred. Brown didn't simply shoplift cigars, he pushed the store clerk to the ground when the clerk tried to stop him at the door. The moment force was used, it became robbery in the second degree, a class B felony according to Missouri law.

The Stop

Probable cause is defined as facts and circumstances that would lead a reasonable officer to believe that a crime has been or is being committed.

Around noon, Officer Darren Wilson encountered Michael Brown and Dorian Johnson walking in the middle of the street. He had heard the radio traffic about the robbery but didn't make the connection. He stopped his patrol vehicle next to them to advise them to use the sidewalk. Instead of following Officer Wilson's instructions, Johnson quibbled that they were almost to their destination, and kept walking. Everything that took place after this was predicated by the initial contact Officer Wilson made with the two, which could be interpreted as a traffic stop. In other words, did Wilson have probable cause to stop them, especially since he later said he didn't initially connect them with the robbery? It may seem trivial in comparison to what ultimately occurred that day, but many Brown supporters based their case against Officer Wilson and the Ferguson Police Department on the false premise that Wilson had no legal reason to stop them in the first place. Let's start there.

Johnson and Brown were walking down the middle of Canfield Drive in Ferguson—a two-lane road with a double yellow line and paved sidewalks on both sides of the roadway. There is a City of Ferguson ordinance (in force in 2014) that prohibits walking on the roadway.

44-344. Manner of walking along roadway. Where sidewalks are provided, it shall be unlawful for any pedestrian to walk along and upon an adjacent roadway.[8]

Officer Wilson's probable cause to stop Brown and Johnson was as simple as that. His knowledge of the robbery was irrelevant. They were clearly in violation of a municipal ordinance and attracted Officer Wilson's attention. However, rather than taking enforcement action (writing them a citation), Wilson simply pulled up alongside them to advise them to get out of the roadway, intending to proceed down Canfield Road and go about his business.

Wilson did not stop, get out of his car, ask for identification, or check them for warrants—all things he would've done if he were writing them citations. Additionally, Officer Wilson clearly didn't view Johnson and/or Brown as a threat to his safety, otherwise, he never would have pulled up beside them. He would have made a U-turn, stopped his vehicle behind them, exited his vehicle, and approached them on foot, where he had options for cover if attacked. That is the tactical way to conduct a stop. But he wasn't doing that. He was just giving them a simple admonishment. No big deal. Just, "Hey, get out of the road, use the sidewalk." If they had complied, it would've ended there.

What happened next changed the trajectory of events. When someone's actions are intended to get a police officer's attention, that officer will pay attention. For instance, while investigating a drug complaint one night a man nearby began getting mouthy for the purpose of attracting my attention. I obliged, discovered he had a warrant, and arrested him. I explained that if he had not drawn attention to himself, I would've continued focussing on the task at hand, and likely wouldn't have even spoken to him. This is similar to what happened in this case.

According to Officer Wilson's statement to his supervisor, St. Louis County Police detectives, the FBI, and the grand jury, as he pulled away, Michael Brown said, "F—— what you have to say!" To be clear, there is absolutely nothing criminal about telling a police officer, "F—— what you have to say," but it will probably draw the officer's attention to your behavior. In this case, Wilson's attention was redirected to Brown, which is when he saw a Cigarillo pack in Brown's hand. That's when it clicked. He remembered the radio traffic about the robbery at a nearby convenience store; two African American men had stolen cigars. Wilson observed that Johnson's and Brown's clothing matched the description given, and he reasonably surmised they were possible robbery suspects.

The Assault on Officer Wilson

Officer Wilson stopped his vehicle and backed up to where they were, still walking in the roadway. He said, "Hey, come here for a minute," and attempted to get out of his patrol vehicle—a Chevy Tahoe. Michael Brown said, "What the f—— are you going to do about it?", and slammed the door shut, preventing Wilson from getting out. Wilson tried to open his door again, pushing Brown with it, and shouted, "Get the f—— back!" Officer Wilson gave Michael Brown the opportunity to reverse his behavior and de-escalate the situation. Instead, Brown slammed the door shut again, came through the open window, and began punching Wilson in the head and face.

What Officer Wilson had originally intended to be a brief warning for a misdemeanor traffic violation had escalated to assault on a police officer, a class B felony, in a matter of seconds. It was escalated by Michael Brown.

Missouri Revised Statutes § 565.082. Assault of a law enforcement officer in the second degree. 1. A person commits the crime of assault of a law enforcement officer in the second degree if such person (2) Knowingly causes or attempts to cause physical injury to a law enforcement officer by means other than a deadly weapon or dangerous instrument.[9]

As Wilson is using his hands to protect his head, he is contemplating how he's going to gain control of the situation, thinking through his force options. He can't use his pepper spray because it's on the left side of his duty belt, out of reach. Even if he could reach it, he doesn't believe it would be effective, and he could inadvertently incapacitate himself instead. He can't use his collapsible baton because there isn't sufficient room inside the vehicle to expand it and/or swing it. He considered using his flashlight as a weapon, but it was located in the passenger seat, and he didn't want to expose more of his body to Brown's assault just to reach over to grab it.

Brown had already rung his bell a couple of times, and Officer Wilson stated he feared that if a third punch connected it would render him unconscious, leaving him unable to defend himself. He stated his only other option was to pull his gun, so he did and shouted another command at Brown: "Get back or I'm going to shoot you!"

The Attempted Murder of Officer Wilson

Missouri Revised Statutes § 565.081. Assault of a law enforcement officer in the first degree. 1. A person commits the crime of assault of a law enforcement officer in the first degree if such person attempts to kill or knowingly causes or attempts to cause serious physical injury to a law enforcement officer.[10]

People need to realize that there is no such thing as an *unarmed* confrontation with police. Every single physical confrontation with a police officer involves at least one gun—the officer's gun. The moment Officer Wilson reasonably believed his life was in danger he was justified in using deadly force to protect himself.

Continuous punches to the head by someone Brown's size was not just a boxing match, it put Wilson's life in danger. Two things could've happened. Firstly, it could have rendered Wilson unconscious, which would've left him temporarily vulnerable to anything, up to and including Brown gaining control of Wilson's gun and using it on him. Secondly, the right punch in the right place could've killed Wilson. Before you roll your eyes, read about Thomas Driscoll, a retired 22-year veteran of the Connecticut State Police who was killed with a single punch in an unprovoked Las Vegas attack.[11] Officer Wilson testified that he had taken two solid punches and believed a third punch could be fatal. His display of deadly force was completely appropriate.

Officer Wilson didn't just draw his weapon and kill Michael Brown. He gave Brown a second chance to reverse his behavior and de-escalate the situation: "Get back or I'm going to shoot you!" Instead of complying, Brown's reaction was to say, "You're too much of a p—y to shoot me!" Brown then grabbed the top of Officer Wilson's gun, twisted it downward, and pressed the muzzle into the officer's hip. Wilson said as he began to scoot his body to the right while simultaneously pushing the muzzle away from his leg, he could feel Brown trying to get his fingers inside the trigger guard. Wilson said he believed he was about to be shot. Read this carefully. Brown tried to shoot the officer with his own gun! Michael Brown has now escalated the situation to assault on a law enforcement officer while attempting to kill or cause serious physical injury—a class A felony.

Missouri Revised Statutes § 563.046 (2014) Law enforcement officer's use of force in making an arrest. 1. A law enforcement officer need not retreat or desist from efforts to effect the arrest, or from efforts to prevent the escape from custody, of a person he or she reasonably believes to have committed an offense because of resistance or threatened resistance of the arrestee.[12]

During Officer Wilson's grand jury testimony, one of the jurors asked him if, during the altercation, he ever thought about putting his patrol vehicle in gear and getting out of there. He said he did not. I would expect that question from Joe Public; it's a completely logical train of thought. However, with the emergence of stand-your-ground laws around the country, citizens have no duty to retreat from any place where they are lawfully present if/when they are attacked. Police officers have *never* had the duty to retreat. On the contrary, they have a duty to *act*. Officer Wilson continued his attempt to apprehend Brown per Missouri law.

The Shooting

The shooting took place in two stages: inside Officer Wilson's patrol vehicle, and outside his vehicle. Click, click, fire, click, fire. That describes the first five times Officer Wilson pulled the trigger of his department-issued Sig Sauer P229 semi-automatic pistol, from inside his vehicle.

While Brown was pressing the muzzle into Wilson's hip, fortunately, Officer Wilson was able to leverage his body against the seat in order to force the muzzle of his weapon away from his body and back toward the door. If anyone had any doubts about whether or not Michael Brown had control of the weapon, it is proven by what happened next. Darren Wilson, with more than enough justification to use deadly force, pulls the trigger and nothing happens. He pulls the trigger a second time and nothing happens. There are specific and logical reasons for this. Wilson said Brown's hand was still on the slide of the weapon. Brown's grip could have prevented the hammer from operating, or it could have pushed the slide back just enough to put it out of battery, preventing the slide from cycling, therefore preventing the weapon from firing. This is *obvious* evidence that Brown had control of the weapon.

After Officer Wilson's gun misfired twice, he pulled the trigger a third time and it fired through the door panel, shattering the window rolled down inside it. Wilson said it startled Brown and he let go of the gun and stepped back, but only momentarily; he wasn't sure at this point if Brown had been hit. Rather than deterring Brown, though, the shot fired seemed to enrage him, and he lunged back at Wilson, punching him in the face again! When Wilson pulled the trigger the fourth time, it misfired again.

A firearms examiner for St. Louis County Police testified to the grand jury that this particular misfire could've been the result of what's called a "stovepipe." That's when a semi-automatic pistol fires a round, but the spent casing is not completely ejected from the weapon. It gets caught in the slide ejection port with the open end facing up so that it looks like a stovepipe sticking up out of the weapon. Officers are trained to correct a stovepipe malfunction by using their non-dominant hand to swipe the top of the weapon to knock the stuck casing loose, then pull the slide back to load another round into the chamber.

Officer Wilson instinctively cleared his weapon as he was trained. When he pulled the trigger the fifth time, the weapon fired a second round. This time, Brown ran. It is important to note that the investigation found that Brown was grazed by the first round fired. The autopsy showed a small grazing wound on one of his fingers; the spent round was later found inside the door panel. Officer Wilson testified that he saw a cloud of dust on the ground behind Brown when he started running and believed it was caused by the second fired round hitting the ground.

Wilson was able to get out of his vehicle for the first time since his original contact with Johnson and Brown. He called "shots fired" over the radio and ran after Brown, who had just committed two violent felonies against him. It's important that people wrap their minds around this and understand what's happening here. The irresponsible media convinced the public at large that Michael Brown was an innocent and unsuspecting victim, but the real victim here was Officer Wilson. He gave Brown multiple commands to "get back." He gave him multiple opportunities to stop his aggressive attack and comply with commands. Nevertheless, Brown continued to escalate his behavior, challenging Officer Wilson verbally, then physically, then with a deadly weapon. This is not the behavior of a victim— it's the behavior of a predator—a wolf.

As Officer Wilson pursued Michael Brown, he ran about two car lengths, referencing the cars that were stopped behind his patrol vehicle. When Brown reached the light pole that was situated on the opposite side of the road, Wilson said Brown suddenly stopped running and turned around to face him. Wilson also stopped running to maintain some reactionary distance between them. Once again, Wilson gave Brown an opportunity to de-escalate the situation, stop his aggressive behavior and comply with repeated commands to get down on the ground. Instead, Brown displayed his intention to attack Wilson a third time. According to Wilson's grand jury testimony, Brown took a step toward him and took a skipping step as if to begin running toward Wilson, all while simultaneously reaching into his waistband.

As Michael Brown charged Officer Wilson, Wilson began backpedaling and fired several rounds. He was unsure if he hit Brown because Brown continued to charge him, dropping his center of gravity and tucking his head in as if he was going to tackle Wilson. Wilson fired several more rounds which ultimately stopped Brown, who then fell dead.

From the time Officer Wilson stopped to talk to Johnson and Brown until the time Brown was killed was approximately two minutes. For 120 seconds Wilson fought for his life. He testified that he believed his life was in danger. I agree. Based upon the evidence, I believe if he had not shot Michael Brown, Brown would've overpowered him and seriously injured or killed him. Officer Wilson's use of force was justified, so said the grand jury and the U.S. Department of Justice. He survived. Unfortunately, his career didn't.

The Investigation

The leadership of the Ferguson Police Department called the St. Louis County Police to conduct the investigation into the shooting. This is standard procedure and best practice to eliminate any conflict of interest or appearance of impropriety. St. Louis County Detectives descended upon Canfield Drive to begin the tedious task of processing the crime scene—marking and collecting evidence, taking photographs, identifying and interviewing witnesses, etc. Due to an angry crowd—who were throwing objects at police, shouting threats, and attempting to encroach upon the crime scene—safety remained a concern. Investigators were even interrupted at least once by gunfire.

Before investigators could even finish processing the scene, Dorian Johnson—who disappeared after the shooting—was already on television, giving his account of what happened. The problem was, he lied through his teeth. While claiming to have witnessed the "cold-blooded" murder of his friend by a police officer, he wasn't as eager to tell investigators what happened as he was the reporters who were all too willing to give him airtime. In fact, it took detectives four days to find Johnson to get a statement. When they finally did interview him on August 13th, he had already retained an attorney.

The media was manufacturing the narrative before police could even make a statement—the narrative of systemic racism. They were lighting the fuse of a bomb that would explode before the weekend was over. What wasn't speculated by the news media was spread in the form of rumors on social media. As a result, racial unrest brewed to the point of combustion. The riots began the day after the shooting; stores were looted, buildings and vehicles were burned, and gunfire rang out. For eleven days, rioting and violence plagued Ferguson and other major American cities. Protesters marched with their hands up chanting, "Don't shoot," a plea they claimed Michael Brown made to Officer Wilson before he was shot. Civil rights activists, politicians, and even President Obama weighed in on the ordeal that gained national recognition for the Black Lives Matter organization. Michael Brown was transformed into a martyr, while the public was thirsty for blood. The media was quick to serve up Officer Darren Wilson's head on a silver platter.

Michael Brown's family released a statement on August 15th that echoed the false narrative.

> "Michael Brown's family is beyond outraged at the devious way the police chief has chosen to disseminate piece mil information in a manner intended to assassinate the character of their son, following such a brutal assassination of his person in broad daylight. There is nothing based on the facts that have been placed before us that can justify the execution-style murder of their child by this police officer as he held his hands up, which is the universal sign of surrender. The prolonged release of the officer's name and then the subsequent alleged information regarding a robbery is the reason why the family and the local community have such distrust for the local law enforcement agencies. It is no way transparent to release the still photographs alleged to be Michael Brown and refuse to release the photographs of the officer that executed him. The police strategy of attempting to blame the victim will not divert our attention, from being focused on the autopsy, ballistics report and the trajectory of the bullets that caused Michael's death and will demonstrate to the world this brutal execution of an unarmed teenager."[13]

Michael Brown was suspected of committing a robbery, then

an assault on a police officer, then the attempted murder of a police officer. He was not a victim, he was a wolf living among the sheep. When confronted by the sheepdog, he continued to escalate the confrontation until it ultimately led to his demise. Racism had nothing to do with it, but that didn't stop the likes of Al Sharpton from exploiting the incident on the basis of racism and ironically demanding "justice for Michael Brown."[14]

Granted, I understand how coming to this conclusion is completely dependent upon Officer Wilson's statement being accurate. No one is believed at their word, not even police officers. That's why independent investigations are conducted. As with almost any investigation, it is expected that there will be conflicting stories. There is a difference, however, between a conflicting story and a fabricated story. Fabricated stories usually have no basis in logic or reason. The story Dorian Johnson fabricated is that Officer Darren Wilson shot Michael Brown while Brown's hands were raised in surrender, and then stood over him and executed him in "cold blood," in broad daylight with the community watching. That is the kind of act that normal people don't have the capacity for—the act of a psychopathic killer that has no empathy for fellow human beings. Does anyone really believe that of Officer Darren Wilson? There is no evidence in Officer Wilson's background or behavior to support that.

The false narrative that brought down a city came from a fabricated story. People in the Canfield apartment complex were expected to stick to the story whether talking to the police or the media. They were threatened with harm if they deviated from that story. An unnamed witness told police there were threatening notes posted throughout the complex, warning residents about talking to the police and that gunshots rang out nightly to reinforce the threats. But even under threat of retaliation, multiple witnesses came forward to support Officer Wilson.

On August 9th, the day of the shooting, an anonymous eyewitness called in to St. Louis County dispatch at 5:27 PM and told a detective that Officer Wilson acted in self-defense. At 5:45 PM, detectives were stopped near the scene by another unnamed eyewitness who said Officer Wilson was "in the right," and "he did what he had to do." The witness refused to identify himself but added that the statements given by bystanders were false. Later that night, around 10:30 PM detectives spoke to two residents who claimed to have witnessed the incident but were afraid to talk about it. They told detectives Brown had the upper part of his body in the driver side window of the police vehicle. They reported that Brown was moving toward the officer in the street when the shooting took place, not surrendering with his hands up or running away. These witnesses refused to give recorded statements out of fear.

On August 11th, another unnamed witness agreed to speak to detectives. She said she had heard talk among her neighbors in the complex; they were upset by what they believed had happened, but she stressed that their beliefs were not consistent with what she saw.

On August 12th, an unnamed local pastor contacted detectives. The pastor had been contacted by a member of his church that claimed to be a witness to the shooting. The witness told his pastor that "Dorian Johnson did not see what he claimed to have seen during his television interviews."

On August 14th, police contacted another witness to get a statement. The unnamed witness told detectives he saw the incident in its entirety, but would not be speaking with them about it due to fear of retaliation from the neighborhood. He did offer, however, that the info being broadcast by the news media was not accurate and there were "blatant lies from those giving accounts of what they saw."

All of these eyewitness accounts, documented in the St. Louis County Police report, are in line with Officer Wilson's statement. The thing about witness statements is, in order to be credible they have to match the story told by the physical evidence. As it turns out, Dorian Johnson's story didn't add up.

The Evidence

The most compelling evidence against Johnson's fabricated

story is the autopsy reports. Three separate autopsies were conducted: one by St. Louis County, one by the Department of Justice, and an independent autopsy conducted by Brown's family. All three reports stated Brown had no gunshot wounds in his back. When Brown fell, he was face down, so if Officer Wilson had stood over Brown and shot him, he would have had gunshot wounds in his back. That is not what Dorian Johnson saw. It's what he fabricated. And, though evidence disproved it, the news media took that fabricated story and turned it into an indictment of public opinion, not just against Officer Darren Wilson, but against American police officers in general.

The problem with fabricated stories is that they are difficult to prop up. There are no witnesses to a fabricated story, only accomplices. However, the truth is supported by witnesses and evidence. The investigation revealed both. Dorian Johnson's unwitting accomplices took his story and ran with it, including the part about Officer Wilson standing over Brown and emptying his gun into his body. Of course, several "eyewitness" testimonies changed when the autopsy reports emerged. Some even admitted they didn't actually witness the shooting, they just repeated what they had heard. According to the Prosecutor's statement, there were even people who originally claimed to have witnessed the incident, but when later confronted with the inconsistencies in their stories, admitted they didn't see anything. They were just giving an account of what they "assumed" happened. People who knowingly lied about what they saw or didn't see are culpable in the conspiracy sparked by Johnson and peddled by the mainstream media against the police. They are responsible for the violent and destructive aftermath of a false narrative.

The grand jury heard more than 70 hours of testimony from approximately 60 witnesses over a 25-day session (non-consecutive). They examined every piece of physical evidence, reviewed hundreds of photographs, listened to hours of recorded police interviews, and were presented with every document pertaining to the investigation. The most convincing evidence of the truth of Officer Wilson's account was the blood and DNA evidence.

Michael Brown's blood and/or DNA was found on the outside of the driver door, the outside of the rear passenger door, inside the driver door, on the upper left thigh of Officer Wilson's pant leg, the front collar of Officer Wilson's shirt, and—wait for it—Officer Wilson's gun. This evidence puts Michael Brown's hands everywhere Officer Wilson said they were, especially on the gun! In support of that, the autopsy confirmed Brown had a grazing gunshot wound to his thumb that contained gunshot residue, proving his hand was in contact with the gun when it was fired. Low and behold "the autopsy, ballistics report and the trajectory of the bullets that caused Michael's death" did not support an execution-style murder of Michael Brown, as the family claimed it would.[15]

On November 24th, after thorough and independent investigations conducted by the St. Louis County Police and the FBI, and a lengthy grand jury proceeding, Prosecutor Robert McCulloch made an official statement on the findings. Among his remarks were these:

> *"Physical evidence does not change because of public pressure or personal agenda. Physical evidence doesn't look away as events unfold… All decisions in the justice system must be determined by the physical and scientific evidence and the credible testimony corroborated by that evidence; not in response to public outcry or for political expediency."*

When he announced Officer Darren Wilson would not be charged in the shooting of Michael Brown, the mob—lawless BLM thugs and their media accomplices—demanded justice. But, justice is not what they wanted—they wanted a racially motivated murder of an unarmed African American man by a white police officer. They wanted the investigation to justify their hatred of the police, but the prosecutor wouldn't give it to them. Ferguson Police command staff, St. Louis County Detectives, Grand Jury members, and Prosecutor Robert McCulloch all did the right thing. They did not skew the truth to match the politics. They stood behind their officer.

The Officer

Five years earlier, Darren Wilson was taking his oath of office and pinning on the badge of a Ferguson Police Officer. As with any cop's swearing-in ceremony, it was probably a proud and happy moment shared with family and friends. It's a noble accomplishment that only comes through hard work and determination. Like most, Wilson probably became a police officer because he had an inner calling to serve and protect. He was a sheepdog.

What society asked of Officer Darren Wilson—what we ask of all law enforcement officers—is to hold the line between good and evil. We ask them to stand watch in the darkness of night so we can sleep safely and peacefully, and to shield our eyes and ears from the wickedness of vile and vicious humanity. We ask them to defeat the wolf we don't see but do it in such a manner that no one is offended. We ask them to endure the ridicule of the foolish, the scrutiny of the pious, the hatred of the studied ignorant, and the malice of the Marxist. We ask them to give up the rights they fight to protect, to give up the safety we so vehemently expect, to be spit upon, assaulted, and yes, even murdered, all while lawless mobs march against them, shouting anti-police slogans like, "Pigs in a blanket, fry them like bacon!" And, "What do we want? Dead Cops! When do we want it? Now!" We ask police officers to do an underappreciated, underpaid, and misunderstood job, without which anarchy would rule. And then, when they do their jobs, we punish them after armchair quarterbacking a decision they had a split second to make in good faith. Yet, they get up every day, put on the uniform, and do it all over again, anyway.

Unfortunately for Darren Wilson, he would never be able to put on the uniform again. The media and the government made an example of him, not by charging him criminally, but by using the incident as an opportunity to call for police reform in the face of "systemic racism." Darren Wilson survived physically, but his character, reputation, and integrity were assassinated. His dream of being a police officer was cut short. The fall-out from the shooting rendered him "unemployable" in the field of law enforcement,[16] a profession to which he had dedicated his life. He resigned from the Ferguson Police Department, having come to the realization that the controversy surrounding his deadly force encounter put his peers, and himself, in danger.

It wasn't just that he would never have the distinction of serving as a police officer again, but that he had to go into hiding. He and his family received multiple death threats by phone, e-mail, and social media. On December 1, 2014, the FBI arrested Jaleel Tariq Abdul-Jabbaar on three counts of Interstate Threats after he posted a death threat on Facebook—a charge for which he was later convicted.[17] The post read:

> *"Are there any REAL BLACK MEN that would love to go down to Ferguson Missouri to give back those bullets that Police Officer [D.W.] fired into the body of Mike Brown. If we're unable to locate Officer [D.W.] then We'll return them to his wife and if not her then his children."*[18]

According to the federal criminal complaint against him, Abdul-Jabbaar contacted an acquaintance on Facebook for the purpose of acquiring a handgun, specifically a "9mm or .40 caliber," indicating he was "going to Ferguson."[19] As a result of this and other threats, members of the area Fraternal Order of Police (FOP) rallied around Wilson, donating their time off to provide security. Nevertheless, Wilson and his family were forced to move more than once when his home address was circulated around the internet, for fear it would fall into the hands of would-be retaliators.

There's an additional aspect of Officer Darren Wilson's life that most haven't considered—indeed most wouldn't understand. Col. Grossman puts it this way:

> *"Killing comes with a price, and societies must learn that their soldiers [and police officers] will have to spend the rest of their lives living with what they have done."*[20]

Officer Darren Wilson did not escape this incident unscathed.

Every day, he must wrestle with the psychological and emotional consequences of taking human life.

The Second Investigation

Six years after a grand jury exonerated Officer Darren Wilson, The family of Michael Brown appealed to a new prosecutor to reopen the investigation, possibly hoping they had a better chance of getting an indictment with an African American prosecutor in office. Wesley Bell, elected to succeed Robert McCulloch, spent five months re-investigating the case. At a press conference on July 30, 2020, he announced that he arrived at the exact same conclusion as his predecessor.

> *"After an independent and in-depth review of the evidence, we cannot prove that [Wilson committed murder or manslaughter under Missouri Law]. I would violate my ethical duties if I, nonetheless, brought charges."*[21]

Of course, Bell couldn't leave it at that. He had to soften the blow for those pressuring him to undo the justice meted out by a St. Louis County Grand Jury and the United States Department of Justice in 2014. He continued,

> *"The question of whether we can prove a case at trial is different than clearing [Wilson] of any and all wrongdoing. There are so many points at which Darren Wilson could have handled the situation differently, and if he had, Michael Brown may still be alive."*[22]

Bell is right. Had Darren Wilson handled the situation differently, Michael Brown may still be alive, but Officer Wilson may have died in the line of duty. Notice that personal responsibility on the part of Michael Brown is not mentioned. To borrow Bell's words, there are so many points at which Michael Brown could have handled the situation differently, and if he had, he may still be alive.

More than five years after the incident—five years after Dorian

Johnson was caught in a lie, after so-called eyewitnesses supporting Johnson recanted their stories and even admitted they lied, after the physical evidence destroyed any and all claims that Brown was executed, after the rioting, looting, death and destruction in America's largest cities—the false narrative of Ferguson was still alive and well. In August 2019, presidential candidates were still riding the cop-hating rhetoric like a stallion across the campaign countryside. Senator Kamala Harris tweeted:

"Michael Brown's murder forever changed Ferguson and America. His tragic death sparked a desperately needed conversation and a nationwide movement. We must fight for stronger accountability and racial equity in our justice system."[23]

Senator Elizabeth Warren similarly tweeted:

"5 years ago Michael Brown was murdered by a white police officer in Ferguson, Missouri. Michael was unarmed yet he was shot 6 times. I stand with activists and organizers who continue the fight for justice for Michael. We must confront systemic racism and police violence head-on."[24]

Senator Cory Booker tweeted:

"5 years ago, Michael Brown was killed by a police officer ... I have been thinking all day about Mike and his family, and my prayers are with them. I am also thinking about the everyday citizens who stood against this police violence and racism and were tear-gassed for their patriotic acts. Ferguson called to the conscience of our nation and inspired a movement that rightly continues."

Senator Kirsten Gillibrand said:

"5 years ago, a Ferguson police officer killed Michael Brown, an unarmed teenager. He shot him 6 times. Nothing will bring Michael back, but we can't stop fighting the injustice done to his family and so many others."

Mayor Bill DeBlasio said:

> *"Michael Brown should be here today. My city knows the pain of Ferguson all too well ... no one should die due to the color of their skin."*[25]

The Myth Debunked

The myth, fabricated by Johnson and repeated by his accomplices, is that Michael Brown was standing with his hands up, begging Officer Darren Wilson for his life when he was subsequently executed in cold blood by this racist murderer in uniform. The mainstream media repeated this mantra nationally until protesters all over the nation were chanting, "Hands up! Don't shoot!" It was the anthem of justice for the Black Lives Matter organization. There was only one problem. It never happened. The myth was debunked flatly by a fair and impartial investigation.

The man who fed the media their first account of the incident, Dorian Johnson, lied to them, to the police, to the federal government, and to the grand jury. In the Department of Justice report on the shooting, Johnson's testimony is listed under the heading, *Witnesses Whose Accounts Do Not Support a Prosecution Due to Materially Inconsistent Prior Statements or Inconsistencies With the Physical and Forensic Evidence.* The DOJ report debunks the myth as follows:

> *"Witness accounts suggesting that Brown was standing still with his hands raised in an unambiguous signal of surrender when Wilson shot Brown are inconsistent with the physical evidence, are otherwise not credible because of internal inconsistencies, or are not credible because of inconsistencies with other credible evidence."*

With a decent grasp of the English language, it's hard to misunderstand this. So, why were democratic presidential candidates, especially former prosecutor Kamala Harris, still repeating this debunked myth in 2019 as if it were an established fact? As Sharyl Attkisson wrote in The Hill, it's "time to retire the Ferguson narrative."[26]

Chapter 5
Baton Rouge, Louisiana

*"And maybe remind the few, if ill of us they speak, that we are all
that stands between the monsters and the weak."*
—*Michael Mark*

Just shy of two years after the Ferguson incident, Baton Rouge,
Louisiana erupted in civil upheaval following the shooting of
Alton Sterling, a 37-year-old African American man, by Baton
Rouge Police Officer Blane Salamoni.[1] There were two stark dif-
ferences in the Baton Rouge shooting—the suspect was armed
with a handgun and there were multiple videos of the incident.
However, by this time the Black Lives Matter (BLM) organization had become a larger, more socially and politically dangerous
machine and, like a firestorm feeding on every molecule of available oxygen, BLM capitalized on Baton Rouge to continue the
vacuum of hate speech and violence upon which it was founded.

Another difference in the Baton Rouge shooting was that the
facts were generally undisputed, but that didn't stop the media
or the mob from ironically demanding "justice for Alton Ster-

ling." As is true of Ferguson, those who can look beyond the racism narrative and examine the evidence for themselves could easily conclude that the officers' actions were justified. But the narrative of Ferguson was still alive and well. "Hands up! Don't shoot!" was still the mantra, only now Michael Brown's face was replaced with that of Alton Sterling. BLM had christened a new martyr and they were upping the ante.

The Original Call—Aggravated Assault with a Firearm

Louisiana Revised Statutes §14:36. Assault is an attempt to commit a battery, or the intentional placing of another in reasonable apprehension of receiving a battery. §37.4 Aggravated assault with a firearm is an assault committed with a firearm.[2]

Moments after midnight on July 5, 2016, a 911 call was made by John Young to the Baton Rouge Police Department. He reported to dispatchers that he was panhandling outside the Tripple S Food Mart on North Foster Drive when an African American male wearing a red shirt brandished a handgun and threatened him. He was describing Alton Sterling who stood about 6'1" and weighed over 300 pounds. Sterling was selling bootlegged CDs and DVDs outside the store; he told Young to get out of that area, presumably because Young's panhandling would dip into Sterling's sales.

This threat, according to Louisiana state law, constituted *Aggravated Assault with a Firearm*. The wording of the statute—to attempt to commit a battery, or the intentional placing of another in reasonable apprehension of receiving a battery—simply means to assault a person or cause one to believe he would be assaulted. If Sterling was trying to scare Young away and brandished a handgun while doing so, it would be reasonable for Young to believe that if he didn't leave he would be shot. He was convinced enough that he moved to the other side of the street. He called police a second time to give them more information and stress to the dispatcher that Sterling had a gun in his pocket.

The Confrontation

Officer Salamoni and his partner, Officer Howard Lake arrived within seconds of each other at the Tripple S Food Mart. Young had given a good description of Sterling's appearance, clothing, location, and activities, making it easy for the officers to quickly locate and identify their suspect.

There are several things to consider when analyzing this situation: the information the officers have been given by dispatchers, their response to that information, their investigation of any violations of law, and the final disposition of the call. They respond to a problem, they deal with the problem, and they try to solve the problem. If they can't solve it, they refer it to someone who can (mental health professionals, medical professionals, civil courts, etc.). Police officers go through this process repeatedly every shift, solving problem after problem, with priority number one always being officer safety. This is basic police work in a nutshell.

Police interactions always begin with a conversation. As the officer, I need to find out who you are, what the problem is, who's involved, etc. But the conversation must take place on my terms, my first priority being *officer safety*—which is drilled into every police officer from the very first day they report to the academy. If I have reason to believe you have a weapon, we have to deal with that first. The U.S. Supreme Court (Terry v. Ohio, 392 U.S. 1. 1968) gives me the authority to do just that.

> *"Where a reasonably prudent officer is warranted in the circumstances of a given case in believing that his safety or that of others is endangered, he may make a reasonable search for weapons of the person believed by him to be armed and dangerous."*[3]

It is my experience that a law-abiding citizen who is legally in possession of a firearm is more than happy to inform a police officer they are armed, and usually do so immediately. Cops aren't concerned—nor do we feel threatened—by an honest citizen with a gun. It will be those citizens whom we believe will stop and help when they see us in trouble. Therefore, if you have a problem with me checking you for weapons before we talk, then we might have a bigger problem. Because it is also my experience that armed people who don't want me to know they're armed, are not up to anything good. When the officers approached Sterling, it became obvious very quickly that he had a problem with being searched—that's because he was armed with a loaded .38 revolver in his right front pocket.

This incident could've easily been resolved at the conversation level. This is what that scenario could've looked like. The officers arrive and approach Sterling. They ask him to put his hands on the vehicle so they can conduct a Terry search for weapons, and he complies. They cuff him for safety and search him, finding a loaded revolver in his right front pocket. The gun is secured and Sterling is effectively detained without incident and now the conversation can begin. One of the officers interviews Sterling while another officer locates and interviews John Young and any witnesses. Officers weigh all statements and any other evidence to determine whether probable cause exists to believe a crime has been committed. If so, Sterling is informed he is under arrest, taken to jail and the gun is seized as evidence. The appropriate charges are filed, but Sterling is innocent until proven guilty, and will have his day in court in a couple of weeks. That scenario is an investigation that never escalates beyond a series of conversations. No one is hurt and everyone goes home safe. Problem reported, problem confronted, problem investigated, problem solved.

Unfortunately, that's not even close to what happened. I can guarantee you, with a relatively high level of certainty, that Officers Salamoni and Lake did not go to work that night with the desire or intention to use deadly force and subsequently have their careers and lives turned upside down. Alton Sterling made the decision to escalate the incident from conversation to physical altercation to armed confrontation.

Officers approached Sterling in front of the store, interrupting one of his bootleg transactions. Officer Lake's first priority is *officer safety*; he, therefore, asks Sterling to put his hands on the car that is parked in front of him. Victim John Young's report of an Aggravated Assault with a Firearm, his description of the suspect, and his assertion of the firearm's exact location on the suspect's person provided more than enough cause for Officers to believe Sterling was armed. Naturally, they wanted to control the movement of Sterling's hands; at the very least to keep Sterling's hands visible. From the very beginning, Sterling refused to comply with Officers' instructions. When someone is armed, this is BAD!

There are several reasons someone might resist a Terry search, not the least of which are: they intend to run, fight, or obtain a weapon. Any one of those actions would require the officer(s) to use a force option. Contrary to popular belief, police officers don't want to use force—especially now. If they do, they will be subjected to investigation, departmental discipline, civil litigation, or even prosecution. Before left-wing political and social pressure canceled reality police television shows, you probably watched COPS or Live PD a time or two. If so, you may have seen the infamous pause just before the fight or flight action of a suspect. You've probably also heard an officer admonish that suspect, "Don't do it, man," as they seemingly read the suspect's mind in that split-second pause. I've done it many times. Why do cops do that? Because they don't want the situation to escalate; they don't want to use force. Officers Lake and Salamoni did *not* want to use force.

The entire encounter was caught on the officers' body-worn cameras and store surveillance cameras. With information that Sterling possibly had a handgun in his right front pocket, the officers tried to control Sterling's arms to direct him to the hood of the car. He is seen pulling his arms away from the officers while spinning around, which effectively breaks their grasp on him. Then, Sterling is seen placing both hands toward his right side. Both officers disengage, and Officer Salamoni draws his weapon, all the while, both officers are heard giving repeated, loud, and clear commands for Sterling to put his hands on the car.

Officer Salamoni ordered Sterling, "Put your hands on the car or I'm going to f—— shoot you in your head, you understand me!?" Obviously, the officer was criticized for this tactic. In his interviews with detectives, the FBI, and the Attorney General's investigators, he was asked to explain his use of harsh language. Officer Salamoni stated he believed the aggressive tone and language would convince Sterling that they "weren't playing" and would make him think twice before further resisting. At first, it seemed to work as Sterling was seen momentarily placing his hands on the car.

When the officers moved in to cuff Sterling, he is seen tensing up his body and again refusing to comply. Both officers are seen struggling to get Sterling's arms under control. At this point in the confrontation and with the knowledge that Sterling is armed with a gun, the officers had used repeated verbal commands—that didn't work. They moved up the force scale to hands-on physical force to gain compliance—that didn't work. They were unable to overpower Sterling and get him under control, yet he still posed a threat of serious physical harm or death to the officers. The next force option they employed was a conducted electrical weapon (CEW), commonly referred to as a "Taser," the original name of the manufacturer of the model most police departments carry.

Less-than-lethal Force

Joe Public often mistakes a CEW as an alternative to a firearm. I've heard people ask, "Why didn't the cops *taze* him instead of shooting him?" The easy answer is that a CEW is a less-than-lethal weapon and a gun is a lethal weapon. They serve different purposes. They represent different levels of force. Movies and television shows depict someone being *tazed* after which they become unconscious and unresponsive. That's not how it works. The purpose of the CEW is to achieve *neuro-muscular incapacitation* (NMI), which is what allows the police the opportunity to get the suspect under control. A CEW, if effective, gives an officer five seconds to get someone cuffed. That's how long the CEW is activated for each trigger pull.

Cops have a saying: "You don't bring a Taser to a gunfight." The reason for that is the possibility of a CEW being ineffective. It doesn't always work. Any cop who has used a CEW more than once has probably had an ineffective deployment. Sometimes it's because of the angle of the shot. Sometimes it's because the barbs—which conduct the electricity into the skin—don't penetrate through the outer clothing (Sterling's autopsy showed no punctures in his skin from a CEW barb). This is why it's not a fail-safe alternative to a lethal weapon.

Here's a personal example with some comic relief. Several years ago, I went on a domestic violence call. My backup officer was Matt, a K-9 handler, and his partner, Jinx. We get there and observe a young man in his twenties holding his girlfriend down on top of a picnic table in the back yard, as she screamed and struggled. He sees us and runs toward us, pulling his shirt off, and taking a classic fighting posture. After verbal commands and a hands-on approach failed, Matt and I backed up a few steps and pulled out our Tasers, seeming to play ring around the Rosie with him as we ordered him to the ground. This gentleman wasn't going to comply with our requests; he wanted to fight. Just as he was about to swing on Matt, I pulled the trigger. When I did, the bad guy went down—and so did Matt! For a brief second, I panicked. I had no idea how, but I tazed both of them. Then, I remembered I only had 5 seconds to get this guy under control—I couldn't pull the trigger again because Matt was attached! So, I hurried up and got him cuffed. Matt was slowly getting up on his knees as he muttered, "Son of a B——! That hurt!" He may have used my name in vain a few times.

As it turns out, Matt and I had both fired our Tasers at the same time. Matt hit the bad guy. Apparently, due to my gangster grip, my barbs went sideways hitting the bad guy *and* Matt, completing a circuit between the two. He will never let me live it down. Matt has a side gig, breeding and training working dogs. We got a family German Shepherd from him, and I named the dog, Tazer, in Matt's honor. The moral of the story is, CEW deployments don't always go as planned and, unfortunately, the incidents don't always end well.

Officers Salamoni and Lake disengaged from Sterling, putting several feet of distance between them and Sterling, and Officer Lake deployed his CEW. At first, it seemed to take effect as Sterling can be seen dropping to his knees, however, he reached around to his back, as if to remove the barbs, and got back up. Officer Lake "hit him again," (meaning he pulled the trigger to activate the CEW a second time) which had no effect at all.

The Shooting

As we walk through and analyze this story, you have to keep in mind that Alton Sterling was an armed felon actively fighting two police officers. At this point, the officers were not trying to arrest him as much as they are trying to keep him from getting his hands on his gun and shooting both of them. They were in grave danger. Anyone who would argue that Alton Sterling was in the most danger should understand that he initiated the fight and had the ability to stop the fight—immediately. All he had to do was give up. The officers gave Sterling plenty of opportunities to stop resisting and comply with their instructions.

When Sterling got up off the ground after the failed CEW attempt, Officer Salamoni decided to holster his weapon and try another tactic. He tackled Sterling into a vehicle and they went to the ground. Sterling was lying face up with Officer Salamoni on top of him, "belly to belly," as the officer put it. Sterling wrapped his left arm around Officer Salamoni's head and was pulling him into his chest in a head-lock type move. Officer Lake immediately got control of Sterling's left arm, forcing him to release Officer Salamoni's head.

While Officer Salamoni was still fighting to control Sterling's right hand, he saw the butt of a revolver sticking partially out of Sterling's right front pocket. He announced to Officer Lake, "He's got a gun!" (As an aside, even though the officers already knew Sterling likely had a gun, cops are repeatedly trained to call out, "Gun" to other officers when they encounter a gun on someone's person.) As Sterling tried to get his right hand in his pocket, Officer Salamoni continued to fight to prevent that from happening. In his interview with investigators, the officer said he was in fear for his life, knowing that Sterling didn't have to get the gun out of his pocket to kill him with it, he only had to get his finger on the trigger, because the gun was pointed in the direction of his thigh. The officer told investigators he believed that if the gun was fired it would possibly hit his femoral artery, causing his death.

This account from Officer Salamoni was in line with his next words to Officer Lake. As Salamoni drew his gun and pointed it at Sterling he shouted, "he's going for the gun!" Salamoni fired three times into Sterling's chest and rolled off of him. As Sterling sat up, the officers ordered him to get on the ground. Instead, he rolled away, his hands still out of the officers' view, his gun still unaccounted for. It is drilled into police officers during training that they are to shoot until the threat is over. Because Officer Salamoni perceived that Sterling was still a threat, Sterling was getting up, he couldn't see Sterling's hands and didn't know where the gun was, he fired three more times into his back, which effectively stopped him. From beginning to end, this incident occurred in only 90 seconds.

The officers' actions after the shooting are important. Officer Lake notified dispatch of the shooting and requested emergency medical services. He then recovered a .38 caliber revolver from Sterling's right front pocket, locking it in his patrol car. Officer Salamoni was clearly upset. He got up off the ground and is heard breathing heavily, trying to catch his breath. He then began to search Sterling's pockets for the gun. He asked Officer Lake, "where's the gun," obviously not realizing Lake had already retrieved it and locked it in his patrol car. According to the Louisiana Department of Justice report, this corroborates Officer Salamoni's belief that Sterling was armed with a gun, in addition to both officers' statements that they saw the gun sticking out of Sterling's pocket.

The Investigation

The shooting was investigated by the Obama Justice Department and the Louisiana Attorney General's Office, respectively. It's important to note that the Department of Justice is limited in its investigations into police actions. They are strictly examining cases for civil rights violations, such as a violation of the 4ᵗʰ amendment right against unlawful and unreasonable searches and seizures—a use of force is considered a seizure under the law. These cases are scrutinized by federal prosecutors who must *"prove that an officer's actions willfully broke the law and were not simply the result of a mistake, negligence or bad judgment. To prove a crime, prosecutors would need to convince a jury that the force used was more than what would be reasonably necessary to arrest or subdue a suspect, meaning convincing jurors that, in the middle of an arrest, the officer made a clear and willful decision to cause someone's death."*[4] The DOJ could not meet this bar in the Ferguson case.

To put it plainly, in order for a police officer to be convicted of a civil rights violation in the use of deadly force, prosecutors must prove that the officer acted maliciously—that they willfully and knowingly violated the law by using deadly force. However, If an officer reasonably believes their life is in danger and subsequently makes the decision to use deadly force to defend themselves, you can't call it willful—which means *an intentional illegal act* in legal speak. There's no malice in the decision to defend one's self. It simply comes down to, *"it's either you or me, and it's not going to be me."*

The DOJ hired two use of force experts to review the evidence: Kenneth Sanders and Charles Key. The case evidence examined by these experts, FBI agents, and federal prosecutors consisted of video footage from police vehicles, officers' body-worn cameras, surveillance cameras, and cell phones, witness statements, autopsy reports, toxicology reports, EMS reports, police reports, physical evidence collected by the Baton Rouge Police Department (BRPD) Crime Lab, personnel files and prior use of force reports for the involved officers, BRPD policies and training records, dispatch recordings, forensic evidence reports, scene photographs, and all other pertinent evidence.[5]

The independent experts differed in their opinions of some of the tactics used. One of the tactics in question was that of Officer Salamoni when he employed the use of aggressive and harsh language to persuade Sterling to comply with commands. While it is expected that police officers maintain composure under stress, the human element must be considered in a deadly force encounter. Again, keep in mind that when Officers Lake and Salamoni confronted Sterling, they had reason to believe he was armed with a handgun and had already threatened someone, therefore, they proceeded with the mindset that they were approaching someone with the intent and means to use deadly force against them. When Officer Salamoni reacted to Sterling's refusal to comply by pointing his gun at Sterling and saying, "Put your hands on the car or I'm going to f—— shoot you in your head," he was doing what Lt. Col. Grossman calls *posturing*.

In his book, *On Killing*, Grossman builds on the common "fight or flight" responses to danger, adding "posturing and submission" when the danger comes from one's own species, citing evidence throughout the history of armed conflict. He argues that in "intraspecies conflict" the first decision to be made is whether to flee or posture.[6] Posturing, simply defined, is the display of aggression without violence, which has often been proven in conflict to persuade an opponent to give up rather than face violence. As a police officer, without the option of fleeing, Salamoni decided to display aggression in a manner that he believed would persuade Sterling to comply. The Louisiana Attorney General conceded that this *posturing* seemed to be effective, as Sterling's response was to momentarily place his hands on the vehicle as instructed.

I don't think anyone would disagree that posturing—the display of aggression without violence—if effective, is better than violence itself. The purpose of posturing is to avoid violence. Officer Salamoni's statement in every interview he conducted was consistent, that he was attempting to give Sterling a reality check—these police officers aren't playing. One argument is that pointing a gun at Sterling at this stage of the incident constitutes excessive force. However, this argument is defeated by court precedent establishing that police are justified in pointing a gun at a suspect (or *displaying* deadly force) when there is a reasonable belief of danger to officers.[7] This belief was established when John Young told police dispatchers Sterling was armed with a handgun.

Another tactic over which Sanders and Key disagreed was Officer Salamoni's decision to tackle Sterling to the ground. Sanders called it "a proper and effective destabilization technique," while Key said it was "the dumbest thing [he] did." The difference in opinion between the two represents the minutia of personal preference between veteran officers in a given situation. Both Sanders and Key are considered experts, but their different interpretations were subjects of policy rather than the law. When it came down to brass tacks, however, both agreed that the officers' use of force was both reasonable and justified.

Déjà Vu All Over Again

Alton Sterling's autopsy revealed he had several illegal drugs in his system, including Cocaine and Methamphetamine. The level of Methamphetamine in his blood was 280 ng/mL, a level known to contribute to violent and irrational behavior. As it turns out, this wasn't the first time Alton Sterling had a violent, armed confrontation with police. Seven years earlier, an incident occurred which was almost identical to this one, aside from the outcome.

On May 29, 2009, Anthonia Anderson called 911 and reported that Alton Sterling had approached his vehicle on Rosenwald Street and pointed a gun at him. Baton Rouge Police Officer Timothy Daigre responded and encountered Sterling in front of Scotlandville Grocery Store where he was selling bootlegged CDs. The Officer asked him if he had any weapons and he ignored the question. The officer then instructed him to put his hands on the hood of his patrol car. This time he complied, until the officer tried to conduct a Terry search. Sterling took his hands off the hood and the fight was on. While fighting Sterling on the ground for control of his hands, a black semi-automatic 9mm handgun fell out of Sterling's waistband. Sterling continued to fight Officer Daigre until a Deputy Sheriff arrive and helped subdue him.

Alton Sterling was not an innocent victim of racist police violence. He was a wolf, a predator. He conducted a criminal lifestyle with a history of perpetrating violence against others. His criminal record included public intimidation, domestic abuse, illegal possession of a stolen firearm, resisting arrest, and aggravated assault. He had a history of fighting police while armed with a gun. Likely the only reason the 2009 incident did not turn deadly was that Sterling's gun fell out of his pants and he was overpowered by officers, which ended the threat.

The pot is calling the kettle black when gun control activists lecture the country on the need for stricter laws and stopgap measures to keep convicted violent criminals from obtaining guns, and in the next breath cry, "Justice for Alton Sterling!" Sterling was a textbook example of the failure of the radical gun control agenda, and the necessity of law-abiding citizens to have their second amendment rights protected. Stricter gun laws do not take guns away from those who use them for criminal activity. Sterling had already once been convicted of unlawful possession of a firearm, arising from the 2009 incident, but that didn't stop him from carrying a gun. If gun control laws worked, Sterling would not have been able to use a gun to threaten Young, may not have encountered police on July 5, 2016, and certainly wouldn't have been shot by police for trying to get a gun out of his pocket while resisting arrest.

Alton Sterling's death was indeed a tragedy—a tragedy for his children, his family, his friends, and humanity itself. But he was not "murdered" by a racist white police officer. His death was not the result of systemic racism in law enforcement. It was the proximate result of his criminal lifestyle and his refusal to obey lawful police commands while posing a threat of deadly force.

Lives That Didn't Matter

After a ten-month investigation, the DOJ published the following findings on May 3, 2017:

> *"Although Sterling's death is tragic, the evidence does not meet...substantial evidentiary requirements. In light of this, and for the reasons explained below, the federal investigation concluded that this matter is not a prosecutable violation of the federal statutes...Given the totality of the circumstances – that the officers had been fighting with Sterling and had attempted less-than-lethal methods of control; that they knew Sterling had a weapon; that Sterling had reportedly brandished a gun at another person; and that Sterling was much larger and stronger than either officer – the Department cannot prove either that the shots were unconstitutional or that they were willful. Moreover, two different, independent experts opined that this shooting was not unreasonable given the circumstances."*

This decision was met with animus—as one can imagine—and it was Ferguson all over again. The "advocates" demanded justice. Their message inferred that the color of Alton Sterling's skin gave him a pass on personal responsibility, and made him the victim of racially motivated police violence. Again, Sterling's death was the proximate result of his criminal lifestyle and his refusal to obey lawful police commands while posing a threat of deadly force. The narrative—fabricated by Dorian Johnson two years prior, syndicated by BLM, and repeated by every race-baiter—again dominated the streets of dozens of major American cities in protest. This time—inside of two weeks—it would escalate to the murder of eight police officers in Dallas, Texas, and Baton Rouge.

On July 7, 2016, just two days after Alton Sterling was killed, a peaceful rally was held in downtown Dallas. When the rally was over, at approximately 8:58 PM, Micah Xavier Johnson opened fire on police officers from a sniper's nest. He shot twelve cops, killing five. When a police negotiator was able to make contact with him, Johnson claimed he was upset about the recent police shootings in Louisiana and Minnesota and wanted to kill white police officers. He claimed to have placed improvised explosive devices (IEDs) around the city, but none were ever found. After more shooting, police took him out by robotically delivering and detonating an explosive device near his location.[8] For those who believe this was excessive, I would remind them that this man had already shot twelve police officers, killing five of them. It was the deadliest day in law enforcement since 9/11.

On July 12, 2016, Baton Rouge Police uncovered a plot to ambush and murder police officers. Three people were arrested for breaking into a pawn shop and stealing guns, one of whom informed police the guns were being obtained to use against cops. A 17-year-old, a 20-year-old, and a 13-year-old boy were charged with burglary and theft of firearms after a surveillance video showed them climbing a ladder to the roof of the business to get inside. A fourth suspect evaded apprehension. Of the eight firearms that were stolen, only six of them were recovered.

Baton Rouge Chief of Police Carl Dabadie defended his department's show of force in the face of fierce protesting and rioting following Sterling's death, citing the "substantial, credible threat" uncovered by the burglary investigation. He said, "We have been questioned repeatedly over the last several days about our show of force and why we have the tactics that we have. Well, this is the reason, because we had credible threats against the lives of law enforcement in this city."[9]

On July 17, 2016, twenty-nine-year-old Gavin Long, dressed in black fatigues and armed with a rifle, opened fire on officers near Baton Rouge Police headquarters on Airline Highway. He shot six officers, murdering three of them: Officer Montrell Jackson, Officer Matthew Gerald, and Deputy Brad Garafola. A former Marine and Iraq War veteran, Long had been vocal on his website about the recent police shootings of African American men, and stated he planned to stand up to the "injustice."[10] He was ultimately shot and killed in an ensuing gun battle with members of the BRPD Special Response Team.

Five days earlier, Gavin Long had come to Baton Rouge after attending the Dallas protest. He stayed in a different hotel each night leading up to the day of the shooting. He had armed himself with a black, Stag arms SAG-15 semiautomatic rifle, a 9 millimeter Springfield XD-9 semiautomatic pistol, and an Israel Weapon Industries (IWI) Tavor semiautomatic rife—the one he would use to assassinate three police officers. Police would later discover his reasons for the attack in a suicide note he had left in the front passenger seat of his Chevy Malibu rental car. It read, in part:

> *"I know most of you who personally know me are in disbelief to hear from media reports that I am suspected of committing such horrendous acts of violence. You are thinking to yourself that this is completely out of character of the man you knew who was always positive, encouraging, and wore a smile wherever he was seen...I know I will be vilified by the media and police, unfortunately, I see my actions as a necessary evil that I do not wish to participate in, nor do I enjoy partaking in, but must partake in, in order to create substantial change in America's police force, and judicial system... Condolences to my people and their loved ones who have been victims at the hands of bad cops for decades. And condolences to the good cops and their families as well."*

Long's three-page note clearly articulated his plan to murder police officers in retaliation for the shooting of African American men, and his expectation that he would not survive. Long's toxicology report stated he had alcohol and methamphetamine in his system. Before the shooting was over, Long would fire more than fifty rounds at responding officers (at least 43 casings were recovered.) It was discovered that he had used green tip steel penetrator rounds, which are made for increased penetration at long distances. One of the special response team members observed, "[Long] had skill. He honed in on us immediately... He laid effective fire." In addition to murdering three officers, Long wounded three others.

Baton Rouge Police Corporal Chad Jackson was one of the first responding officers and was shot in the head just above his ear before he could even exit his patrol vehicle. Despite his wound, he was able to stay in the fight; he exited his vehicle and fired multiple rounds in Long's direction. The officer most severely wounded was Deputy Nicholas Tullier of the East Baton Rouge Sheriff's Office. Deputy Tullier, who was checking Long's rental vehicle, was shot in the stomach. As he struggled to get back into his vehicle, Long shot him twice more in the head and shoulder. Sergeant Bruce Simmons of the East Baton Rouge Sheriff's Office, who had arrived right behind Deputy Tullier, was shot in the arm while trying to get to him to render aid. According to a federal lawsuit later filed against Black Lives Matter on Deputy Tullier's behalf, his wounds rendered him permanently disabled. After 19 surgeries, he had lost a large portion of his intestines, suffered a shattered skull, and lost brain matter from the left side of his brain, which affects his communication. Additionally, Deputy Tullier lost the use of his left eye due to a "blown" optic nerve and suffered severe chronic pain due to his injuries. Unfortunately, the lawsuit was dismissed on September 28, 2017, by Judge Brian Jackson of the U.S. District Court of the Middle District of Louisiana. That decision was upheld by the 5ᵗʰ Circuit of the U.S. Court of Appeals, who later reversed part of its decision and remanded the case back to the District Court for further discovery.

The irony of a man who claimed to seek justice, committing an evil and heinous *injustice* to deliver his message, escapes all logic and sensibilities. In his note, Long called it a "necessary evil" to "create substantial change" in policing. This is the modus operandi of radical groups such as BLM; they perpetuate injustice on the innocent to demand justice as they see it. This is a textbook definition of terrorism. The murder of innocent cops to scare the nation into "substantial change" in policing is nothing less than domestic terrorism.

Micah Xavier Johnson and Gavin Long, both military veterans, denied being affiliated with any radical groups, yet the violent atrocities they perpetrated were attributed—by their own admissions—to retaliation for the death of African American men at the hands of white police officers. These two monsters, whose evil drove them to collectively murder eight cops and attempt to murder several more, may not be claimed as the faces of radical activist groups, but they did embody the hypocrisy upon which their movements are built. Hypocrisy is an African American man (Long) killing an African American police officer (Officer Montrell Jackson) to avenge the death of African American men killed by white police officers. Did Officer Jackson's life not matter? Was his skin too blue? Did retired St. Louis Police Captain David Dorn's life not matter when he was shot and killed outside a pawn shop during the BLM riots of 2020? Perhaps the Black Lives Matter organization is more baited to destroy American law enforcement and undermine the rule of law than they are to champion the cause of African American men and women whom they have decried as victims of a racist system of policing. If Black Lives Matter truly carried the standard of the unjust oppression, abuse, and murder of "their people," where is the same national outrage—at the retaliatory killings of innocent African American police officers—that has upended several American cities with riots, looting, and destruction?

What about Reserve Deputy Constable Martinus Mitchum, who was shot and killed outside of a New Orleans High School by a disorderly subject he was escorting out of a basketball game? What about Lieutenant Michael Boutte, of the Hancock County, Mississippi Sheriff's Office, who was shot and killed on a suicidal call before he could even get out of his cruiser? Or, Police Officer Travis C. Wallace, of the Helena-West Helena, Arkansas Police Department, who was shot and killed while attempting to arrest a shooting suspect? Or, Police Officer Marshall Walters, of the Mangham, Louisiana Police Department, who was shot and killed on a traffic stop? Or Sergeant Harold Preston, of the Houston Police Department, who was gunned down on a domestic violence call? What about Detective Kevin Dwaine Collins, of the Pine Bluff, Arkansas Police Department, who was shot and killed conducting an investigation? Have you ever heard of Wildlife Officer Julian L. Keen, Jr., of the Florida Fish and Wildlife Conservation Commission, who was shot and killed during a traffic stop? Or, Officer Breann R. Leath, of the Indianapolis Metropolitan Police Department, who was gunned down on a domestic violence call? All police officers. All African American. All murdered by gunfire in 2020 and 2021, yet there were no marches, no protests, no rallies demanding an end to violence against African American law enforcement officers.

Guilty After Being Proven Innocent

Officer Salamoni was cleared by the United States Department of Justice and The Louisiana Attorney General's Office, both ruling that his use of deadly force against Alton Sterling, given the circumstances, was justified and reasonable. But that didn't keep the new Baton Rouge Police Chief from "publicly sacrificing him on the altar of political expediency."[11]

Chief Carl Dabadie, who served the Baton Rouge Police Department for more than thirty years, retired on October 2, 2017. In his letter of retirement, he said:

"My hope is that the men and women of the Baton Rouge Police Department will be allowed to perform their jobs according to state law, without prejudice, and that politics will not prevail over public safety."

Chief Dabadie's hopes were short-lived. His replacement, Chief Murphy Paul, wasted no time in terminating Salamoni, citing violations of use of force and command of temper policies. It would be naive not to suspect that this termination was an unwritten condition of his offer of employment. That's not to imply Paul was chosen *because* he was African American, but that fact certainly would not hurt community-police relations.

Chief Paul didn't just terminate Salamoni, he publicly humiliated him and apologized to the family of Alton Sterling and the citizens of Baton Rouge for hiring him, stating Salamoni displayed, "a pattern of unprofessional behavior, police violence, marginalization, polarization and implicit bias by a man who should have never ever wore this uniform."[12] Chief Paul went on to say:

"We're sorry for our failure not to discipline an officer who demonstrated unprofessional behavior and violated our code of conduct consistently, escalating incidents."[13]

Paul's statement contradicted the Department of Justice report which cited "no prior incidents involving substantiated allegations of misconduct by Officers Salamoni or Lake." Salamoni appealed his termination to the city's civil service commission, which he likely would have won due to the failure of the police department to document or substantiate any of the claims Chief Paul made about his performance. The city eventually struck a deal with Salamoni that would reverse his termination and allow him to resign, instead of facing the possibility that the civil service commission would give him his job back.

John McLindon, Salamoni's attorney, called the chief's public statement "inappropriate," rebuking him for his "inflammatory" and "extraneous accusations" during what was supposed to be a call to bring closure to the city.[14] The harsh reality is that closure *has* never and *will* never come until we begin seeking justice for all, not just those upon whose misfortune we can capitalize for political and financial gain (such as Michael Brown and Alton Sterling). This will never happen until society stops taking the bait of—what author Taleeb Starkes calls—the racial grievance industry.[15]

Chapter 6
Black Lies Matter

"Terrorism is a psychological warfare. Terrorists try to manipulate us and change our behavior by creating fear, uncertainty, and division in society." —Patrick J. Kennedy

#Blacklivesmatter started as a social media trend after Trayvon Martin, an African American high school student from Sanford, Florida, was fatally shot by a white man who was acquitted of his murder in 2013. Black Lives Matter rose to national prominence after Michael Brown's death in Ferguson and emerged as the organization now known as the Black Lives Matter Global Network Foundation (BLMGNF). Before discussing this any further, it's important to make a sharp distinction here between "Black Lives Matter" the *organization* and "Black Lives Matter" the *movement*—these are two distinct groups of people—lest the reader mistake my opposition to the activist organization for opposition to justice for African Americans. I possess a strong moral conviction that African Americans are children of God and deserve equal justice under the law, and I support the movement, just as my parents and grandparents believed in the Civil Rights movement in the 1960s. In short, I believe Black lives matter—period. But I am absolutely convinced the Black Lives Matter organization is corrupt. What began as a movement—to seek legitimate justice for all African Americans—has been hijacked by opportunistic, gang-minded thugs that have propagandized racial hatred and incited violence and destruction upon major cities across the country in the aftermath of high-profile fatal police encounters. In short, BLM is not as pro-Black as it is anti-police.

This propaganda of racial hatred has vilified the police. Isn't it ironic that while police officers are trained to reject an "us versus them" mentality in policing, BLM is preaching a racial doctrine of "us versus them?" Their goal is not police reform and unity, but fear of police, division of race, and ultimately abolishment of law enforcement as we know it. Fear of police is taught and the lesson plan is to throw the spotlight on every African American death at the hands of police, create a list of facts—I mean, lies—and repeat those lies until they are accepted as facts. The list of lies will always include an African American innocent victim, a white racist officer, and the "I told you so" scolding that systemic racism is to blame. That's exactly how the "hands up, don't shoot" lie became a nationally recognized protest mantra.

In his book, Black *Lies* Matter, Author Taleeb Starks agrees. He writes:

> *"BLM and its media allies are the driving forces behind today's anti-cop climate, ignoring the normality of black-on-black homicide to chase the anomaly of blue-on-black homicides. This BLM-induced avalanche of destructive propaganda — such as cops are hunting black men — is demonstrably false, but still has effectively appealed to peoples' emotions instead of critical thinking."*[1]

The same twisted logic that gave us common core math is apparently used to run the numbers in police racial disparity arguments. The Proceedings of the National Academy of Sciences (PNAS)—the same journal that published the article denying racial disparity in police shootings, and then retracted it—published another study claiming, "About 1 in every 1,000 Black men can expect to be killed by police."[2] They can *expect* to be killed by police? Aside from being false, you tell me if that statement isn't intended to create fear and racial division between the African American community and the police. On the other hand, The Bureau of Justice Statistics said there were 6.5 million police interactions with African American citizens in 2018. Twenty-two of them were killed by police. According to these numbers, an African American has a higher chance of being killed by lightning than by a cop.[3] However, I must acknowledge that to those who have lost a loved one to a deadly force encounter with police, their loss is not a statistic. At the same time, in the words of African American Judge Valerie Roller, "We have made poster children out of thugs when we wouldn't bring them home for dinner."[4]

In 2015, The Washington Post began tracking fatal police shootings across the country. This was in response to incomplete numbers from the FBI due to a percentage of law enforcement agencies not submitting their stats. It is likely the Post believed they would discover a massive plot to cook the books, but they have inadvertently proven that white cops are not killing Black people at an alarming rate, as many headlines would lead the public to believe. As of the date of this writing, the Post reports 6,355 people have been shot and killed by police since January 2015. Only 2% of them were African American and unarmed.[5]

In a *USA Today* op-ed, Heather MacDonald maintains "the evidence does not support the charge that biased police are systematically killing African Americans in fatal shootings." She points out that about 1,000 civilians are killed in police shootings each year, most of them armed with a weapon, but only about 23% of them (both armed and unarmed) are African American.[6] One of the reasons this data is rejected by race-baiters is because it doesn't support the narrative of fear. Consider that medical error claims more than a quarter of a million American lives each year and is the third leading cause of death in the nation. Some even argue there are racial disparities in healthcare. Where is the demand for medical practice reform? Where are the activists? Where are the signs that say, "Doctors Are Murderers?" When and where do we riot?[7]

The truth is, if police use of force deaths are isolated incidents, then African American citizens have nothing to fear as long as they don't try to seriously injure or kill a police officer. After all, public action drives police reaction. But, if police are systematically killing African Americans, then fear is justified. This is where Black Lives Matter Global Network Foundation, Inc. comes in. They are selling hate and fear in bulk, and unfortunately—whether due to historical context or reverse racism—people are buying it.

In 2020, 12% of social media users said that what they have seen on social media has changed their views about Black Lives Matter, police brutality, and the need for police reform, so says the Pew Research Center.[8] The Black Lives Matter organization relies heavily on social media to spread its poison. Their 2020 impact report[9] boasts 750,000 Facebook followers, 1 million Twitter followers, and 4.3 million Instagram followers. They raised $90 million in 2020 alone, giving them the resources to run mass television and social media ads. They reported more than 51 million total impressions for their digital ads. An "impression" is the number of times an ad was displayed on someone's computer or mobile device (such as a phone or tablet). Their "defund the police" ad alone received 177,000 impressions and more than 10% engagement (percentage of impressions that like, comment, or share). In short, BLM is pouring a fortune into social media to "sell" their propaganda–the Blue Lie.

#Blacklivesmatter is no longer just a hashtag on Twitter, it is a large, wealthy, and dangerous domestic terror organization whose mission is to *"eradicate white supremacy and build local power to intervene in violence inflicted on Black communities by the state and vigilantes."*[10] *State* is code for government and *vigilantes* is code for police. They go on to proclaim their intention to *"combat and counter acts of violence"* against Blacks by police. Interpretation: "We will use violence to retaliate against the government and police in response to Blue-on-Black deaths, regardless of the circumstances." And they have done just that.

Domestic Terrorism

The mission of BLM reads like an antithesis of the mission of a far-right extremist organization. It sounds like a "Black supremacist" manifesto. In order to recognize this, you have to read between the lines and decode the politically correct language they use to define themselves, which is in sharp contrast with their actions on the streets. They seek to *build local power to intervene* in violence inflicted on Black communities by the *state and vigilantes.* They intend to *combat and counter violence* against Blacks. In summary, BLM sounds like a racist, anti-government, militia organization.

The Department of Homeland Security, Federal Bureau of Investigation, the President of the United States, and a hodgepodge of politicians have all declared domestic terrorist organizations to be the number one threat of terrorism to the nation. However, when it was suggested by the International Law Enforcement Educators and Trainers Association (ILEETA) that BLM is one of those organizations, the government and the media lost their collective mind. In December of 2020, ILEETA published a document entitled, *Understanding Antifa and Urban Guerrilla Warfare.*[11] It was intended for law enforcement eyes only as a training tool—because you don't want to reveal your strategy to your adversaries—but it was obtained by the media, which plastered the newsstands with their disdain. Here are a few of the headlines: The Washington Examiner writes, *"International police association with deep Wisconsin ties spreads claim that BLM activists are 'terrorists'."*[12] The Associated Press (AP) reports, *"Police guide that calls BLM a terrorist group draws outrage."*[13] The Majority Report, an online radio outlet warns its listeners, *"Police Association Spreads Paranoia."*[14] How dare someone call out BLM on its domestic terror, right?

Apparently, calling out organizations that condone violence is such a horrible infraction that it merits disqualification from police service. In Hopewell Township, New Jersey, 20-year veteran Officer Sara Erwin was fired when she made a Facebook post calling BLM protesters "terrorists." Her post—which was called *racist*—read as follows:

> *"Last night as I left for work I had my two kids crying for me not to go to work. I don't think I've ever felt the way I did last night. And then I watched people I know and others I care about going into harm's way. I love my police family like my own. So when you share posts and things on Facebook I'd really appreciate if you'd THINK before doing so. I've seen so many black lives matter [sic] hashtags in these posts. Just to let you know — they are terrorists. They hate me. They hate my uniform. They don't care if I die."[15]*

There is nothing racist about this post. Erwin wasn't calling African Americans terrorists, she was calling violent protesters, looters, and vandals, terrorists. And she paid the price for speaking out in opposition to the mobocracy that is BLM. Erwin's attorney is appealing the termination, pointing out that not only has Erwin never been disciplined in her career, she has never been the subject of an internal affairs investigation. She served as a DARE (Drug and Alcohol Resistance Education) officer for several years, making her well known and well-liked in the community. A fellow officer, Sgt. Mandy Gray was suspended and demoted for "liking" Erwin's post. At the time of this writing, lawsuits are underway seeking reinstatement for both officers.

ILEETA was asserting the same opinion as Officer Erwin. Their 176-page report—that raised such a fuss—is a historical study of the guerrilla organizations that attempted to overthrow governments in Algeria in the 1950s and 60s, Northern Ireland and Germany in the 1970s, Egypt in 1996, and others. The author compared the tactics used in these "revolutions" to those used by activist groups such as Antifa and BLM. The similarities are concerning, to say the least. Read the following carefully.

> *"Their basic goal is control of men's minds...They are, in the*

words of one observer: '...political partisans for whom success or failure will hinge...on their capacity to get their message across, to erode the morale of the forces of order, and to induce a general 'climate of collapse'."

"The first step along that road is to separate the loyalty of the target constituency from the governing authorities by creating an 'us versus them' mentality."

"[They] seek to break down the existing social structure and encourage a general feeling of insecurity and disorientation... [they] discredit governmental authorities..."

"[They] seek to sap the morale and break the will of the authorities through a strategy of psychological leverage."

"[They] demoralize the local [police]...it discourages members of minority ethnic groups from cooperating..."

"[These} groups and the media are locked together into an inexorable symbiotic partnership of mutual need and benefit because violence is news. Sometimes it is difficult to distinguish which is the instigator and which the respondent."

"The exploitation of riots is an especially important tactic... Large-scale rioting can quickly exhaust police resources thereby enhancing [protesters'] freedom of action. [They] can also encourage demonstrators to commit acts of violence...Riots offer an excuse to erect barricades and to create defacto 'no go' areas where government authority is suspended if only temporarily." (Sound familiar?)

Now, let me ask you a question. Was the author speaking of guerrillas and terrorist organizations or Black Lives Matter and

Antifa? Take your time. Read it again if you need to. Doesn't it alarm you that at this very moment you're not sure—that it could go either way? While you were reading, did your mind go to scenes from Minneapolis, Seattle, Portland, New York City, and other major U.S. cities? Line by line, the tactics of the Black Lives Matter Organization mirror those of terrorist organizations abroad that have overthrown governments.

Oklahoma County District Attorney David Prater also called BLM and its supporters, domestic terrorists. In the Summer of 2020, he charged several rioters with violation of an Oklahoma anti-terrorism law who were engaged in the destruction of property during riots in Oklahoma City. Dozens of protesters staged a sit-in at his office demanding that he drop the charges and resign. The local BLM chapter supported those demands, circulating an online petition with the following statement:

> "To conflate acts of vandalism against property with acts of terrorist violence against human beings is a moral and legal equivocation without compare. It is an insult to survivors of terrorism and it is a sacrilege to its victims. Please join us in condemning these charges and demanding that District Attorney David Prater dismiss them without delay."[16]

Prater responded by stating "When you employ these tactics [inciting violence and destruction in the streets] for a political purpose, you are a terrorist."[17] He did, however, agree to a plea deal for at least one of those defendants, who pleaded guilty to Arson in exchange for dropping the Terrorism charge.[18]

Terrorists don't just fly planes into towers and detonate car bombs and suicide vests. Terrorists use acts of destruction and violence to wage psychological warfare on people who don't agree with their beliefs. Terrorists spread propaganda to infect society with the viruses of fear and hate toward those of different values, convictions, and skin color. Terrorists are not fighting for control of territory, they are fighting for control of minds in order to coerce change.

The Terrorists' Demands

Terrorist organizations always have demands. The Black Lives Matter Global Network Foundation, Inc. has seven demands listed on their website. *1. Convict and ban Trump from future political office. 2. Expel Republican members of Congress who attempted to overturn the election and incited a white supremacist attack. 3. Launch a full investigation into the ties between white supremacy and the Capitol Police, law enforcement, and the military. 4. Permanently ban Trump from all digital media platforms. 5. Defund the police. 6. Don't let the coup be used as an excuse to crack down on our movement. 7. Pass the BREATHE Act.* All seven of these items are political in nature and are aimed at delegitimizing the government—especially the police. The specific demands I will focus on are 3, and 7. I will deal with *defund the police* in its own chapter.

Demand #3: Launch a full investigation into the ties between white supremacy and the Capitol Police, law enforcement, and the military.

The corrupt BLM organization and their surrogates—the mainstream media and many democratic politicians—were aghast at the very notion that BLM was a domestic terror organization, but demand that law enforcement as a whole is investigated thoroughly for its ties to white supremacist domestic terror organizations. The hypocrisy is dissonant. To be clear, there is no place in law enforcement for racism and bigotry. Far-right, white supremacist, extremist groups are no place for police officers. Police officers who belong to such and participate in explicitly racist speech or behavior should be removed and prohibited from ever again serving in law enforcement. Having said that, this issue has already been investigated and, despite the effort to summarily condemn all of law enforcement as systemically racist, the evidence is just not there.

At a town hall meeting in February 2021, when President Joe Biden said that the greatest threat of terror to the United States was domestic terror, he proceeded to brazenly insult the men and women of the thin blue line by implying white supremacy organizations are full of U.S. military veterans and former police officers.[19] Therein, the President of the United States labeled cops as racist, legitimizing the propaganda of hate and violence against police that has driven groups like BLM—which ironically has not been acknowledged as a domestic terror organization, despite damning evidence that it has incited and/or failed to condemn riots causing millions of dollars in property damage, numerous assaults, and even murders carried out by those lauding, "Black Lives Matter!"

Case in point: During the trial that convicted former Minneapolis officer Derek Chauvin of killing George Floyd in 2020, BLM activist and model Maya Echols—with half a million followers on TikTok (a social media video platform)—posted a video stating,

> *"If George Floyd's murderer is not sentenced, just know that all hell is gonna [sic] break loose. Don't be surprised when buildings are on fire. Just sayin'."*

Ashley Gantt, a prominent BLM leader in Rochester, New York, told reporters in the summer of 2020,

> *"If there was looting, if there was things [sic] on fire, that is not what is important. What is important is why these things happen…I don't care if the whole city burned down. We need justice."*[20]

Ismaaiyl Brinsley, a 28-year-old BLM supporter, executed NYPD officers Rafael Ramos and Wenjian Liu while they sat in their patrol car eating lunch. Before committing these cold-blooded murders, Brinsley posted the following on Instagram.

> *"I'm Putting Wings On Pigs Today. They Take 1 Of Ours... Let's Take 2 of Theirs #ShootThePolice #RIPEricGardner #RipMikeBown This May Be My Final Post I'm Putting Pigs*

In A Blanket"[21]

The President's statement also stems in part from information disseminated by FBI and Department of Justice reports on domestic terrorism. In 2006, the FBI conducted an intelligence assessment into white supremacist infiltration of law enforcement. The report outlined the various concerns and dangers of extremist groups having police officers in their ranks, as well as a sampling of isolated incidents of such occurring. However, the report offers no evidence of an active connection between law enforcement and far-right, white supremacist, violent, extremist organizations.[22]

In 2009, the Department of Homeland Security published an intelligence study. The report made the assumption that the election of America's first African American President would prompt the resurgence of right-wing extremist violence. Daryl Johnson, the report's lead researcher, seemed to zero in on disgruntled and returning veterans as likely candidates for right-wing extremist organizations. The report reads:

"The possible passage of new restrictions on firearms and the return of military veterans facing significant challenges reintegrating into their communities could lead to the potential emergence of terrorist groups or lone wolf extremists capable of carrying out violent attacks."[23]

Conservatives didn't take too kindly to Johnson's implications toward veterans and pushed back. Under political pressure, Secretary of Homeland Security Janet Napolitano disavowed the report and apologized to veterans.[24]

In 2020, an independent report on this topic was released by Michael German, a former FBI Special Agent and current fellow with the Brennan Center for Justice's Liberty & National Security Program. The report, entitled, *Hidden in Plain Sight: Racism, White Supremacy, and Far-Right Militancy in Law Enforcement* cites the FBI's Counterterrorism Policy Directive and Policy Guide (2015) which alleges:

"Domestic terrorism investigations focused on militia extremists, white supremacist extremists, and sovereign citizen extremists, often have identified active links to law enforcement officers."[25]

German further alleges that these "active links" to law enforcement officers have been discovered in fourteen states. One of the incidents he cited was a 2018 rally at the California State Capitol building, in Sacramento, held by the Traditionalist Worker Party (TWP), a Neo-nazi extremist group. The members clashed with "anti-fascist" (Antifa) counter-protesters and things took a violent turn. Seven people were stabbed including a TWP member who suffered a perforated artery. German's report implies that the TWP launched an unprovoked attack on counter-protesters, but that is terribly misleading. German asserts that local law enforcement charged several of the anti-fascists but failed to prosecute any TWP members for the bloody confrontation, deducing that there must be a connection between the police and the far-right, white supremacists.[26]

What German doesn't tell you is that the Neo-Nazi group, which had the proper permit, only had 30 members at their demonstration, while Antifa showed up to crash the party with 400 counter-protesters. He also doesn't tell you that the California Highway Patrol had to bring the Neo-Nazi members into the capitol to keep them from being further attacked. Make no mistake, I am firmly opposed to white supremacist extremists, but it's pretty clear who the assailants were in this brawl. The investigation revealed that members of the TWP were not the instigators. That's why their members were not criminally charged, not because the cops had an active link to their organization.

Though some of his research hints at a bias against police, German—who spent time undercover infiltrating white supremacist groups—cites several specific cases of law enforcement officers with ties to extremist organizations. Such cases include: two Texas officers who were fired in 2001 when their KKK membership was discovered; A Nebraska officer who was fired in 2006 when authorities discovered he was on a KKK members-only chat room; three Florida officers were fired or resigned between 2009 and 2014 over their discovered KKK affiliations; a Louisiana officer was fired in 2015 after he was seen in a photograph giving a Nazi salute at a KKK rally; A Michigan officer was fired in 2019 when he was reported for displaying a Confederate flag and a framed KKK application at his home; In 2020, three North Carolina officers were fired after a random audit of dashcam recordings captured them making racist statements, including threats of shooting African Americans, including an African American police officer.[27] These examples reveal what we've already conceded: law enforcement has problem children who need to be rooted out, just as these disgraceful cops were. But, this isn't evidence of systemic racism. That these racists behind the badge are being eliminated from the profession is evidence that law enforcement has evolved with its country since the days of the civil rights movement. It is growing, improving, and learning from its mistakes.

The President's generalized statement that white supremacist organizations are fueled by military and police is also fed by information alleged by the Department of Justice investigation into the January 6, 2021 riot at the U.S. Capitol Building. Among the 465 protesters arrested, 16 were members of Oath Keepers, an organization that has been labeled by the media as a far-right, white-supremacist, anti-government militia group. Oath Keepers, singled out by the DOJ report in 2009, invites active and former military services members and law enforcement officers to join. Their name reflects the collective commitment to keep their sworn oath to protect and defend the Constitution of the United States against all enemies, foreign and domestic. Because the organization's membership appeals to former and current law enforcement, and because they are labeled by the media as a racist organization, the narrative becomes: racist organizations are full of police officers. Of course, that's no more true than saying all African Americans or those who believe that all Black Lives Matter are anti-police. It's important to note, of the 16 Oath Keepers charged in the Capitol riot, none of them were former or active law enforcement officers. However, this incident was exploited to make an "active connection" between white supremacy and law enforcement.

The problem with this is that Oath Keepers—according to founding president Stewart Rhodes—is not racist, anti-government, or a militia group. The organization's bylaws and code of conduct support that assertion.

> *Section 8.02 (a) No person who advocates, or has been or is a member, or associated with, any organization, formal or informal, that advocates the overthrow of the government of the United States or the violation of the Constitution thereof, shall be entitled to be a member or associate member.*

> *Section 8.03 (b) No person who advocates, or has been or is a member, or associated with, any organization, formal or informal, that advocates discrimination, violence, or hatred toward any person based upon their race, nationality, creed, or color, shall be entitled to be a member or associate member.*

> *Section 8.04. Code of Conduct. "…Oath Keepers shall have a zero tolerance policy for actions that bring disrespect, dishonor or disrepute on Oath Keepers or the military, law enforcement, fire fighters and first responder community.[28]*

The Oath Keepers—and similar organizations such as Three Percenters[29] —describe themselves as patriots, people who love and support their country. The first Americans to be called patriots were soldiers—Black and white—in the American Revolution who fought for Independence from British rule in 1776. The greatest generation—Black and white—that freed the world from the tyranny of Hitler in 1945 were patriots. Unfortunately, the word *patriot* has become the politically correct way of describing someone as a white supremacist.[30] I suppose it's only a matter of time before the New England Patriots are forced by political pressure to change their name. Nevertheless, being a patriot does *not* make someone a white supremacist. Being a member of a group of patriots who denounce white supremacy, racism, and violence—like those favored by cops such as Oath Keepers and Three Percenters—also doesn't make someone a white supremacist, especially since both organizations have African American members. But, that doesn't stop the hypocritical mob from pointing the finger to take the attention away from themselves.

In Orange County, California, a deputy sheriff working a protest in the summer of 2020 was photographed wearing a morale patch on his ballistic vest which depicted the logos of Oath Keepers and Three Percenters. He was reported to the sheriff's office. Sheriff Don Barnes released a statement that the deputy was placed on administrative leave and is being investigated for his possible affiliation with an "extremist group."[31] Similar incidents were reported in Costa Mesa and Chicago. Frankly, that BLM supporters feel they have the moral authority to call someone else out as a hate group is laughable, least of all veterans who fought for our country and police officers who continue to do so on a daily basis.

So, what do Oath Keepers do? The group surfaced in 2014 during the riots in Ferguson. Several members converged on the protest-torn city, dressed in fatigues and carrying long guns. They climbed up on rooftops on West Florissant Avenue, the epicenter of the unrest, to stand watch over businesses and those living in apartments above them. Ferguson resident Greg Hildebrand, who lived in one of those apartments, told the St. Louis Post Dispatch about his interaction with an Oath Keeper member who was on his rooftop. When he asked the armed man what he was doing, the Oath Keeper said he was protecting Hildebrand's apartment block and business. Hildebrand said, "I am in the middle of a difficult spot. I feel a lot better having those guys up on the roof." They were later forced out of town by the police under threat of arrest for operating without a license.[32] A small group of Oath Keepers also went to Louisville, Kentucky in September of 2020 to protect businesses in the aftermath of the grand jury's decision not to indict officers in the death of Breonna Taylor.[33]

The Oath Keepers organization was labeled a far-right, white supremacy group by the Southern Poverty Law Center (SPLC), an organization that claims to monitor the activities of domestic hate groups and other extremists across the country. It should be noted that many religious organizations are listed on their "hate map"[34] as well, due to their moral standing on certain politicized issues. How can a group of cops and veterans, who vehemently deny being racist and anti-government, be classified as a domestic terror organization, but not the Black Lives Matter Global Network Foundation, whose behavior would seem to be just as racist as what they argue against, and whose actions make clear that they are anti-government? Ironically, in the aftermath of the violence against police in 2015, Lecia Brooks, Director of Outreach for the SPLC, was asked if BLM would be added to their list of hate groups. She replied, "We're very much concerned about the killing of police officers. That said, Black Lives Matter is not on our radar."[35]

Social media is a popular method of recruiting and indoctrinating members for extremist organizations. We have already established the effort and money BLM has put into its social media standing. White supremacist organizations also rely on social media. The "active links," that are alleged by the federal government, between white supremacist extremist organizations and law enforcement, include investigations into the social media activity of law enforcement officers. Michael German's article cited a 2019 study called, *The Plain View Project*, claiming to have identified more than 5,000 racist social media posts and comments from 3,500 accounts connected to former or current law enforcement officers in only eight jurisdictions.[36]

The Center for Investigative Reporting conducted a 2019 study entitled, *To Protect and Slur,* to "find cops with connections to extremist groups." The study describes how they arrived at their results. They cross-referenced membership lists of pro-police Facebook groups and extremist Facebook groups. They accomplished this by writing software that would download the lists directly from Facebook (which has since shut down the ability to do so). They searched for users who were members of at least one pro-police group and one extremist group. They reported getting 14,000 "hits". The study explains they conducted months of further research to verify the users who were actual law enforcement officers, including calling police departments to ask if the user was a former or current employee. The final result is as follows:

> *"We confirmed that almost 400 users were indeed either currently employed as police officers, sheriffs or prison guards or had once worked in law enforcement."*[37]

Ultimately, Michael German admits, "Only a tiny percentage of law enforcement officials are likely to be active members of white supremacist groups." It seems he's right. As I noted earlier, there are approximately 800,000 law enforcement officers in the United States. If we are to assume that the 400 "verified" police officers in *The Center for Investigative Reporting* study are in fact members of white supremacist groups, that percentage is 0.005% of all cops. If we accept that those 400 *and* all 3,500 users identified by *The Plain View Project* are racist, that percentage is still less than 0.05% of all cops. Even if 7,200 cops in the U.S. are racist (an egregious number that no study has ever come close to), that would still be less than 1% of all cops.

Does racism exist in law enforcement? Yes. Are there cops who sympathize with and join extremist groups? Yes. But, fortunately, those cops represent a tiny fraction of the law enforcement profession. The other 99.99% don't deserve to be called racist cops by the President of the United States. No investigation into this issue has ever revealed evidence to even loosely support a theory of systemic racism in modern American law enforcement. Period.

In our discussions about the small minority of cops who are racist, Judge Roller asked me, "How do we identify those bad apples? When I come in contact with a police officer, I don't know if they are one of the small percentage of racists." It's a question being asked by many in the African American community, and it merits discussion. From a road cop's perspective, my first three words of advice in any encounter with police are, comply, comply, comply. Court is where we fight the police, not on the street. Hear me out. When a minority is contacted by a police officer, respectful compliance will do two things. Firstly, it may *reveal* an officer's racism. Secondly, it will give a racist officer no justification for mistreatment. Racism in law enforcement is not acceptable. Therefore, a racist cop may disguise racism behind a justifiable use of force, so removing the justification takes away their excuse. Resistance, however, is only a guarantee that force will be used. If unlawful force is used, report it.

Demand #7: Pass the BREATHE Act

The Breathe Act is legislation that has been authored and proposed by the Movement for Black Lives and embraced by the Black Lives Matter Global Network Foundation.[38] At first read, this bill is not "pro-Black lives," as much as it is "anti-police". It is drastic, radical, and has no basis in reason. Basically, it is a laundry list of demands that would destroy what's left of law and order in the United States, not to mention it would severely hurt low-income black communities. You can read the entire bill on BLM's website. Here are just a few highlights.

Eliminate the Edward Byrne-Justice Assistance Grant Program.[39] This is not money that is just handed out by the federal government to police agencies with no strings attached. This grant is highly competitive and sought mainly by smaller law enforcement agencies that don't have the resources to replace old and outdated equipment, such as radios, body armor, in-car computers, and other much-needed tools. This is just another way to defund the police but is focussed on smaller agencies, whose budgets are already lacking.

The grant is named in honor of NYPD Officer Edward R. Byrne, who was executed in 1988 at the age of 22 with only seven months on the job. He was sitting in his patrol car, guarding the residence of a witness when members of a drug organization ambushed him, shooting him in the head five times. The location of the murder, 91st Avenue in South Jamaica, Queens, was renamed Edward Byrne Avenue in 2018.[40]

Eliminate community oriented policing services. Community Oriented Policing Services or COPS is a U.S. Department of Justice program responsible for resourcing law enforcement agencies across the country to further the practice of community policing. The DOJ defines community policing as a "philosophy that promotes organizational strategies that support the systematic use of partnerships and problem-solving techniques to proactively address the immediate conditions that give rise to public safety issues such as crime, social disorder, and fear of crime." In short, community policing focuses on partnerships with the community to solve the problems that give rise to crime. Why would BLM, an organization that claims to seek community solutions, want to erase a time-tested, nationwide initiative that has proven to improve the relationship between police and the communities they serve? Even Joe Biden, while campaigning for President, proposed putting $300 million into the COPS program.[41]

One of the main components of the COPS program is "Collaborative partnerships between the law enforcement agency and the individuals and organizations they serve to develop solutions to problems and increase trust in police." The reason the legislative agenda of BLM includes eliminating community policing is that they don't want to increase trust in police; they want to vilify and delegitimize police. Creating trust in police takes the wind out of their sails, the words out of their message, and the hate out of their plot. No, we can't have that. We have to stick to the propaganda: police are racist murderers and, therefore, must be disarmed, defunded, and dismantled.

Abolish the Drug Enforcement Administration (DEA) and Immigration and Customs Enforcement (ICE). The DEA has more than 10,000 employees. Of those, almost 5,000 are special agents (sworn federal law enforcement officers). In the first five months of 2021, the DEA seized almost $20 billion worth of illegal drugs.[42] Similarly, ICE has a workforce of more than 10,000, of which, more than 7,000 are special agents. In addition to enforcement activities, ICE manages more than three million immigration cases daily. This legislation includes ending state and local police cooperation with ICE until it is dismantled, meaning, stopping the flow of intelligence between federal and local agencies which helps to create a united front against the criminal activity that comes with illegal immigration and drugs. Do supporters of such madness realize that these two problems are the foundation upon which most crime rests? They probably do, but a rise in crime doesn't influence their agenda in the least.

Decriminalize drugs. This issue has been compared with the prohibition era of the early twentieth century in the many arguments for and against. Those who err on the side of legalization seem to have this illusion that decriminalizing drugs will eliminate the black market. That is an absurdity and has already proven to be a farce.

As a police officer, I have always had a strong opinion about this matter—my professional opinion is that drugs breed crime. While some argue drug abuse is a victimless crime, I can point you to hundreds of cases over a career that prove otherwise. Street-level drug crime creates victims of theft, burglary, identity fraud, robbery, assault, and even homicide. Decriminalizing drugs will not make a dent in, let alone eliminate, the collateral damage that comes with it. Whether an addict's drug of choice is legal or illegal, they need to get their fix. When they don't have the money, they'll do whatever they have to do to get it. That includes stealing grandma's jewelry to pawn for a few dollars, stealing blank checks from mom and forging her signature, breaking into cars and homes to rummage for cash or items that can be turned into cash like guns and electronics, stealing a friend's prescription pain medication to either use or sell on the street, falsifying a police report that one's own medication is stolen so the doctor will write a new prescription, robbing and assaulting someone for their drugs, or even killing someone over drugs.

Addicts are not motivated by the legality of their actions, but by the psychological and physical need for their drugs. Making it legal to possess and use drugs will not stop an addict from stealing, assaulting, or worse, in order to get them. If their addiction is strong enough to compel them to victimize their family, it is not likely to be affected by the legality thereof.

Our best information on the results of decriminalization comes from states like California and Colorado, which have had several years of experience with legal marijuana. Heavy state-imposed regulations on the sale of legal marijuana in these states cause overhead to increase and profits to plummet, driving "retailers" back to selling on the black market. There goes the logic. Governor Gavin Newsom has even resorted to deploying the California National Guard to the northern counties where black market marijuana and its problems are the highest.[43] At the top of the list is Humboldt County, called the illegal marijuana capital of the United States, producing approximately 60% of the black market inventory in the country. It is also a place where people have gone to make money and were never seen again, making it the county with the most missing persons cases, per capita, in California. In early 2013, 29-year-old Garret Rodriguez moved to Humboldt County to work in the medical marijuana trade. After several failed attempts to reach him, Rodriguez's father reported him missing in April 2013. Following an investigation, his body was found in a shallow grave in Harris, Humboldt County on December 1, 2013. It was ruled a homicide.[44] It became a high-profile case when Netflix released its documentary series, *Murder Mountain*, in 2018. California is a case study that proves decriminalization does not end the war on drugs.

Impaired driving is a highly ignored problem in this debate. Many are the motorists I have arrested for driving under the influence of marijuana who would, at some point in our visit, defiantly exclaim, "Marijuana is eventually going to be legal, anyway," inferring that I should leave them alone and go find a real criminal. I would then have to explain that driving under the influence of marijuana will never be legal—just as in the case of alcohol. The legal limit of alcohol in every state is .08 grams of alcohol per 210 liters of breath. Likewise, marijuana has a legal limit. In Ohio, 10 or more nanograms (ng) of marijuana per milliliter of urine is considered impaired. In many of my cases, defendants would test over the legal limit as many as 12 hours after they admitted to last using marijuana.

The State of Colorado decriminalized recreational marijuana in 2012. According to the National Institute on Drug Abuse, more than 38% of all impaired driving arrests in 2018 were drug-related, most of them due to marijuana.[45] Mothers Against Drunk Driving (MADD) reports that marijuana-impaired driving arrests in Colorado increased 373% between 2009 and 2017. Additionally, 69% of marijuana users admitted to driving after use in 2018. It's also important to note that Colorado's black market activity has increased. Seizures of Colorado marijuana in the U.S. mail system have increased 1,042% since recreational marijuana became legal.[46]

Using California and Colorado as microcosms for the national debate on marijuana legalization alone, the numbers are definitely not favorable, let alone the other widely used illicit drugs such as heroin, cocaine, methamphetamine, etc. The aforementioned are just a few of the issues in this debate. But, once you take the lid off of pandora's box, you'll never get it back on.

In addition to the above highlights, the Breathe Act, supported by Black Lives Matter Global Network Foundation, Inc. is committed to defunding, disarming, and dismantling the police—which will be discussed in the *Defund the Police* chapter—making it, quite possibly, the most egregious piece of legislation ever proposed. Mike Gonzalez and Andrew Olivastro called it a *blueprint for misery*, in a New York Post op-ed.[47] Fortunately, it is so outrageous that it is not likely to ever be considered, much less become law. Nevertheless, any part of it is bad for the peace and safety of Americans.

Political Influence by Force

Influencing government policy is as American as baseball and apple pie. The political positions of lawmakers are very rarely without external influence. This is just politics 101. In a "civilized" political system—such as ours—lobbyists, political action committees (PACs), special interest groups, public advocacy, all have the potential to shape policy. Industries, businesses, and activist organizations are always eager to snatch up former political appointees and Washington insiders in order to use their knowledge, influence, and connections to further an agenda. The Black Lives Matter Global Network Foundation, however, is a 501(c)(3) non-profit organization and is therefore prohibited from supporting a political party, agenda, or candidate—financial or otherwise. Prior to receiving 501(c)(3) approval from the IRS in December of 2020, BLMGNF was under the umbrella of fiscal sponsor Thousand Currents, also prohibited from taking a political stand.[48] So how does that work? Well, in 2020 the Black Lives Matter Political Action Committee (BLM PAC) was formed.

Again, politics 101. Political action committees aren't limited to fundraising for candidates. They also fund events, programs, and media buys to educate the public about their agenda. In the 2019-2020 fiscal year, the BLM PAC raised approximately $1 million. Most of the money spent was for media buys and production costs, including more than $330,000 in support of the campaigns of Georgia Democratic Senators Raphael Warnock and Jon Ossoff.[49] This pales in comparison, however, to the $90 million raised by BLMGNF in 2020, and calls are increasing for the financial transparency of the organization.[50] This year (2021) BLMGNF will be required to file its first public financial disclosure since obtaining 501(c)(3) status, which will likely answer many of its supporters' questions. The policy "demands" of BLM are certainly no secret. Their attempt to influence policy, however, is being accomplished by fear and intimidation, not by their PAC.

On June 15, 2021, The White House released a fact sheet on "The National Strategy for Countering Domestic Terrorism."[51] It states that "In a true democracy, violence cannot be an acceptable mode of seeking political or social change." It quotes Chapter 18 of United States Code, Section 2331(5) which defines domestic terrorism as,

> *"Activities that involve acts dangerous to human life that are a violation of the criminal laws of the United States or of any State; appear to be intended to intimidate or coerce a civilian population, to influence the policy of a government by intimidation or coercion, or to affect the conduct of a government by mass destruction, assassination, or kidnapping; and occur primarily within the territorial jurisdiction of the United States."[52]*

In my career, I've filed hundreds of criminal charges. They consist of a complaint documenting the elements of the offense, and a sworn probable cause affidavit that those elements were present in the commission of the offense. In my estimation, 18 USC § 2331(5) reads like a probable cause affidavit charging BLM and its advocates with domestic terrorism. Still not convinced? Let's use as an example the sustained protests in Seattle, Washington following the death of George Floyd in 2020. Seattle remained in national news for several months due to the escalating violence by "peaceful protesters." Nightly, for months, businesses were destroyed and looted, vehicles and buildings were set ablaze, and several police officers were injured from assault. It was in Seattle where police abandoned an entire precinct building due to the ongoing violence against police officers and widespread destruction of property. Seattle became known for its CHOP (Capitol Hill Occupied Protest) zone which was seized by protesters, barricaded, and the entrances guarded by armed protesters. Business owners inside the CHOP zone were extorted, there was mass property destruction, assaults, at least four shootings, and two homicides. After a month-long standoff, Black Lives Matter protesters "negotiated" with the police over the release of the CHOP zone. The police went in on July 1ˢᵗ and took it back. Here is what happened the previous month that led to the police retreating from an entire area.

Assault on Seattle East Precinct

According to the Seattle Police Blotter,[53] on Friday, May 29, 2020, one of the first nights of protest after George Floyd's death, Five protesters were arrested for assault on a police officer. At a demonstration at Westlake Park on the morning of May 30th, the crowd—consisting of about 5,000 people, became violent and began throwing bottles at police officers, and some threw fireworks at other demonstrators, causing injury to officers and citizens. After the order to disperse was ignored, the protest was declared a riot. The crowd began using incendiary devices, including Molotov cocktails, to set several police and private vehicles on fire. As the day progressed, businesses were set on fire, police headquarters was under siege by hundreds of protesters, more officers were injured, more city vehicles were set on fire, and at least one patrol rifle was stolen from a police vehicle. There were multiple reports of persons armed with guns, shootings taking place, and hundreds of buildings or businesses damaged and/or set on fire. More than twenty officers were assaulted. This was only the first weekend; it got worse from there.

Chief Best acknowledged the presence of a peaceful element in the crowds, however, the peaceful crowd was drowned out by violence and lawlessness, supporting my contention that the cause of the sincere was hijacked by violent thugs. She asserted early on, "The Seattle Police Department will continue to support the peaceful exercise of First Amendment rights. We will not, however, tolerate violence and property destruction."[54]

After a week of similar protests, on June 7, 2020, a group of almost 10,000 protestors surrounded the East Precinct of the Seattle Police Department (SPD). Despite the officers' efforts to maintain a perimeter, they were attacked by rocks, glass bottles, fireworks, and other projectiles. The massive crowd began dismantling fencing to use as weapons and moving concrete barriers. The Chief declared it a riot and called in mutual aid, including deployed Nation Guard troops. At approximately 9:20 PM, protesters were heard making announcements to burn down the precinct. For the next two and a half hours, police struggled to hold their perimeter around the precinct, as rioters continued to take ground away from them inch by inch. Some of them mimicked police tactics, creating barricades with bicycles to hold the ground they took. The crowd passed large sections of plywood—with embedded nails—to the front of the crowd to use as shields, presumably to push the officers back. Some were shining flashlights in officers' eyes, others used laser pointers, attempting to blind them. Rioters threw plastic bottles containing chemical irritants at officers.

Several times throughout the night, police announced that they would not retreat from their line and ordered the crowd to disperse, warning that non-lethal force—such as OC spray, pepper balls, CS gas—would be used if they got within five feet of the police line. The crowd ignored the warnings and pushed on. In the face of an all-out assault on their precinct, Seattle Police officers maintained unbelievable restraint, even moving their red line back, to avoid using force until absolutely necessary. It wasn't until after several hours under siege—12:14 AM to be exact—that police made the decision to push back. SWAT officers were authorized to deploy CS gas to disperse the crowd. It worked. Officers were able to regain their perimeter and hold their line but they were still not out of the woods. Rioters continued to throw projectiles. It was reported that improvised explosive devices (IEDs) were being placed in dumpsters, which would be pushed toward the precinct and detonated. A block away from the precinct, a man was trying to set up an IED, but blew himself up instead, according to Seattle radio traffic. Throughout the night, officers continued to fight back pockets of rioters until after 4 AM. The next day, the Seattle City Council would order Chief Carmen Best to instruct her officers to abandon the East Precinct. She later posted a video claiming that it was not her decision.

After reading this brief recap of the assault on Seattle's East Precinct, let's compare it to the elements of the federal definition of domestic terrorism. *"Activities that involve acts dangerous to human life,"* Check. *"Intended to intimidate or coerce a civilian population."* Check. *"To influence the policy of a government by intimidation or coercion."* Check. *"Or to affect the conduct of a government by mass destruction, assassination, or kidnapping."* Check. (The murder of cops had already taken place in the name of Black Lives Matter in Dallas and Baton Rouge four years earlier.) The only thing missing is kidnapping. And this is just in Seattle! Without even taking into account the protests and riots that spanned across the nation, this incident alone, organized by, encouraged by, and in support of BLM meets all the necessary elements to call it an act of domestic terrorism. This was not a peaceful protest and it was not just a riot. It was a coordinated, violent assault on a police precinct by a far-left extremist group. It was a war zone.

It is a fair argument that Black Lives Matter is not responsible for the actions of rogue protesters who turn to vandalism and violence. However, there is more than enough circumstantial evidence to implicate BLM for inciting imminent lawless action that occurred during these protests. Such incitement is not protected by the 1ˢᵗ Amendment, according to the U.S. Supreme Court in Brandenberg v. Ohio, 395 U.S. 444 (1969).

> *[T]he constitutional guarantees of free speech and free press do not permit a State to forbid or proscribe advocacy of the use of force or of law violation except where such advocacy is directed to inciting or producing imminent lawless action and is likely to incite or produce such action."*[55]

Two days after the East Precinct was attacked, Black Lives Matter Seattle-King County, in conjunction with six individual plaintiffs, filed a lawsuit against the City of Seattle in United States District Court, Western District of Washington, over the police department's use of force in the protests of the previous week. The complaint reads like a fairy tale in which a large group of peaceful demonstrators gathered around the Seattle East Precinct, held hands, and sang Kumbaya, while the police attacked them with rubber bullets, flashbangs, and tear gas, thereby egregiously violating their civil rights. It's melodramatic and spurious at best. Here is a sampling of the claims made in the complaint.

"With limited exceptions, these protesters have been overwhelmingly peaceful."

"On an almost nightly basis, the SPD has indiscriminately used excessive force against protesters, legal observers, journalists, and medical personnel."

"The purpose and effect of this excessive force…has been to restrict, frustrate, and deter protesters from exercising their rights under the First Amendment to the United States Constitution to peacefully assemble, petition for redress of grievances, exercise freedom of speech, and exercise freedom of the press."

"Plaintiffs have been, and want to continue to be, part of the protest movement to protect black lives. They want to participate in demonstrations against police brutality in Seattle without being exposed to the less-lethal weapons regularly deployed by the SPD against protesters as a method of crowd control. Plaintiffs bring this action to restrain the City of Seattle from continuing to respond to peaceful protest with unconstitutional and indiscriminate force."

"The use of other less-lethal weapons that cause panic and injury also create the potential for increased COVID-19 spread by compressing large groups of people as protesters and bystanders attempt to flee from the use of force."

"Seeking medical care for injuries caused by police presents another opportunity for COVID-19 spread, as injured people and people delivering medical care come into close physical contact with one another."[56]

The complaint makes obviously false representations on both

sides. Calling these protests "overwhelmingly peaceful" with "limited exceptions" is ridiculous. This was their M.O. in protests all over the nation; they—BLM or protesters in support of BLM and other similar organizations—filed similar lawsuits against Los Angeles, Santa Monica, San Jose, Phoenix, Chicago, Detroit, Rochester, New York, Fredericksburg, Virginia, Toledo, Ohio, Las Vegas, Austin, Des Moines, New York, Omaha, Cleveland, and others. While creating mayhem in the streets all over the nation, they exhausted the city governments with lawsuits alleging indiscriminate excessive force against "peaceful protesters," costing local governments millions of dollars. These were more than just protests, they were multi-pronged coordinated assaults on our nation, physical attacks against our communities, financial attacks against local governments, and psychological attacks against our police—domestic terrorist attacks!

In the case of the assault on East Precinct, Seattle Police were not using force randomly and haphazardly. The mob was not peacefully assembling or petitioning for "redress of grievances." All you have to do is watch a few YouTube videos to come to those conclusions. Perhaps the most revealing statement in the entire complaint is that protesters wanted to protest—more specifically, rioters wanted to riot—without being exposed to less-lethal weapons (pepper spray, flashbangs, tear gas, etc.) In other words, "We want to be able to attack police with glass bottles, rocks, plastic bottles containing chemical irritants, metal poles, and whatever other weapons we possess, but we don't think the police should be allowed to use crowd control weapons in response." Nope, that's not how it works. You don't get to attack police officers without consequences.

Of course, the plaintiffs' attorneys added a few COVID-19 claims for good measure. If someone gets COVID-19 it won't be because they're gathered in large crowds and ignoring all of the social distancing guidelines, but because the police used less-lethal weapons that caused the spread, or because they sought medical treatment for injuries caused by police. It's quite laughable. Even if we assume the complaint in this lawsuit was already written when the assault of East Precinct went down on June 7ᵗʰ, the protests had been going on in that intersection all week long, which likely accounted for a majority of the claims made.

On June 12, United States District Court Judge Richard A. Jones granted a Temporary Restraining Order (TRO) enjoining the SPD for 14 days from "employing chemical irritants or projectiles of any kind against persons peacefully engaging in protests or demonstrations."[57] The judge conceded, however, that the court "recognizes the difficulty in drawing an enforceable line that permits police officers to use appropriate means in response to violence and destruction of property but that also does not chill free speech or abuse those who wish to exercise it." This is legal-speak for, "When peaceful protestors are intermingled with a mob of domestic terrorists, the peaceful protesters bear the risk of breathing the tear gas, as well, so a compromise has to be reached. Chief Best had already compromised—as a result of an open letter signed by several city and county council members claiming the police were not playing nicely enough—by announcing a moratorium on the use of CS gas for 30 days except in certain situations. It is possible that the 14-day order was issued to appease the plaintiff's mob. Judge Jones said that the evidence "leaned" in the direction of the plaintiff, meaning, he likely had seen evidence supporting isolated incidents when a few peaceful demonstrators—the individual plaintiffs—were affected by CS gas, blast balls, and pepper spray because they were in close proximity to the violent mob.

The TRO was extended several times, as far out as September. BLM filed multiple motions for contempt, alleging SPD was violating the order in protests sparked by the fatal police shooting of Brianna Taylor. In his ruling, the Judge stated, "To be sure, the protests were much more complex and dynamic than set forth in this Order. Hundreds of protestors, dozens of police officers, and countless projectiles exchanged between them make it nearly impossible to render a comprehensive factual account." Nevertheless, after arguments examining several specific uses of less-lethal force that were alleged to be in violation of the TRO,

Judge Jones found the city in contempt based on one use of pepper spray and three uses of blast balls that were not in compliance with his original order.

Basically, BLM was using violence on the street, then challenging the police response in court. The TRO took away the tools of the police to respond to these riots, effectively tying the hands of officers in dealing with the violent and sustained riots throughout the last half of 2020. The mob refused to play by the rules, then accused the police of not playing by the rules. Chief Best and the Seattle Police were overwhelmed by the constant war on their department. Morale was low among the rank and file. And, to add insult to injury, in the middle of all of this, the Seattle City Council voted in August 2020 to cut the police budget. Chief Best resigned shortly thereafter, followed by 44 officers in September.[58] By May of 2021, 260 officers—almost 20%—had left the police department.[59]

Seattle, Washington was victimized by the domestic terror of Black Lives Matter. BLM succeeded in getting its message of hate and division across, eroding the morale of the forces of order, and inducing a general "climate of collapse." They succeeded in creating an "us versus them" mentality, discrediting governmental authorities, and demoralizing the police. BLM encouraged large-scale rioting, quickly exhausting police resources, encouraged demonstrators to commit acts of violence, and created the lawless CHOP zone. BLM and its supporters engaged in activities dangerous to human life in violation of the criminal laws of the United States and the State of Washington; this activity successfully intimidated and coerced the civilian population and affected the conduct of the local government to defund its police and change its policies. Seattle's City Council, King County's Council, and many other local politicians and leaders bowed down to the demands of BLM. As a result, the city ended 2020 with the highest homicide rate in two decades.[60]

Seattle is a case study of what has happened in major cities all across America. Our entire nation has been victimized by domestic terror, not at the hand of conservatives or patriots, not at the hands of police officers, but at the hands of an organization that has demonstrated its hatred of our great nation.

The most accurate depiction and analysis of the Black Lives Matter organization was written by David French in the National Review. The following is the sound of the hammer hitting the nail squarely on its head:

> *"They advance narratives every bit as inflammatory as the worst white-nationalist rhetoric—repeating known lies such as it's "open season" on black men or "hands up, don't shoot"—and they aggressively launch lawless protests, excuse (and sometimes foment) violence, and traffic in conspiracy theories... But now—as the violence escalates—Black Lives Matter is really about peace and justice... [It] has been playing a double game. It harbors, shelters, and empowers true radicals, people who not only have no problem seeing our cities burn, they're also fanning the flames. Yet it also counts as sympathizers the millions more who want no part of riots or police shootings."*[61]

I would add, if there were ever a bipolar organization—one which can be manic and depressive at the same time—it's BLM. If you are not yet convinced they are a domestic terror organization—bent on destroying our nation from within—consider these remarks about the American Flag, posted on the BLM Utah Chapter Facebook page.

> *"When we Black Americans see this flag we know the person flying it is not safe to be around. When we see this flag we know the person flying it is a racist. When we see this flag we know that the person flying it lives in a different America than we do. When we see this flag, we question your intelligence. We know to avoid you. It is a symbol of hatred."*[62]

Chapter 7
Deadly Force En-
counters

"There is within most men an intense resistance to killing their fellow man. A resistance so strong that, in many circumstances, soldiers on the battlefield will die before they can overcome it."
—Lt. Col. Dave Grossman, (ret.)[1]

Despite the very small percentage of deadly force encounters with police, the mobocracy has been systematically crafting and polishing the oppressive, violent characterization of police officers as cold, heartless human beings that are empowered by the state to kill, and perpetually prowling for minorities upon whom they can mete out their barbaric street justice. Every use of force—no matter how justified—that is perceived to lend credence to this characterization is manipulated and exploited to further the cause. This conspiracy to discredit America's law enforcement officers has gone all the way to the top of our federal government. Presidents Obama and Biden have conspicuously and repeatedly thrown their political weight behind it. At the memorial service for the five slain Dallas Police Officers in 2016,

Obama used the opportunity to insult the families of the fallen cops by standing over the caskets of their beloved and inferring that they were agents of a racially violent system.

> *"[W]hen mothers and fathers raise their kids right and have "the talk" about how to respond if stopped by a police officer – "yes, sir," "no, sir" – but still fear that something terrible may happen when their child walks out the door, still fear that kids being stupid and not quite doing things right might end in tragedy…We wonder if an African-American community that feels unfairly targeted by police, and police departments that feel unfairly maligned for doing their jobs, can ever understand each other's experience."[2]*

The funeral of cops killed in the line of duty by an African American homicidal maniac was certainly not the time or place for a partisan political speech. It was disgraceful.

President Joe Biden echoed Obama's anti-police rhetoric almost four years later after the tragic and senseless death of George Floyd. On May 29, 2020, President Biden said,

> *"Imagine if every time your husband or son, wife or daughter left the house, you feared for their safety from bad actors and bad police. Imagine if you had to have that talk with your child about not asserting your (sic) rights, taking the abuse. Imagine having police call[ed] on you, sitting in Starbucks or renting an Airbnb or watching birds. This is the norm black people in this country deal with."[3]*

Statements like these, generalizing all police contacts as troublesome, are designed to play to the narrative of disproportionate policing carried out by racist police officers. They do not, however, accurately or fairly represent the multiplied millions of annual contacts police officers have with citizens, writes Heather MacDonald in a WSJ June 2020 op-ed. "A solid body of evidence finds no structural bias in the criminal justice system with regard to arrests, prosecution or sentencing. Crime and suspect behavior, not race, determine most police actions."[4]

A Diametric Narrative

The truth is much less controversial. There is a diametric narrative that is not given proper acclaim. It plays out daily, as police officers across the nation put on their uniforms, load their gear into a patrol car, sign on the radio, and report for duty. On any given shift, the American police officer invariably crosses paths with a citizen who is in need, down on their luck, without answers to life's daily problems and needs help. The police officer doesn't say, "that's not my job," or "I'm sorry I can't help you," but rather makes that person-in-need their immediate priority, finding solutions to problems. The American police officer will change a flat tire, give a ride to a stranded motorist, shovel snow, take someone's garbage can to the curb, buy someone's meal, cut someone's grass, play basketball with a group of kids, and an unending list of other acts of service for the members of their community.

Buried under all of the negative press aimed at today's law enforcement, there are positive stories highlighting this other narrative. But, because these stories paint the police in a positive light, they very rarely get much traction. Headlines like *Ohio Officer Delivering Meals to Needy Residents During COVID-19 Pandemic,*[5] *New Jersey Officers Give Away 300 Pizzas to Needy Families,*[6] *Alabama Officers Help Truckers Buy Drive-Through Fast Food,*[7] and *Idaho Officer Gives Man a Bicycle to Help Him Get to Work,*[8] tell the real story—an altogether different story—of our unsung heroes.

In January 2020, South Fulton, Georgia police officers were dispatched to a local Walmart for a shoplifting complaint. When the officers arrived, they discovered the perpetrators were a homeless woman and her four children who had been living in their car. The items they had taken were food and hygiene products. Rather than arrest them, the police officers worked with the retailer to drop the charges and allow the woman to keep the items. They also took the family to a local restaurant and fed them. The restaurant owner picked up the tab and paid for them to stay in a local hotel for a week. The story doesn't stop there.

These police officers went beyond the badge, reaching out to the community and local businesses to raise money for the family. Through the community's collective generosity, the woman and her children were able to get much-needed medical and dental care. The officers were later honored by the city for their actions. Chief Keith Meadows praised their compassion saying, "Deeds like this help to restore faith and legitimacy in the future of law enforcement."[9]

Our friends, Joel and Jenn, live out in the country. In April 2021, their two boys, Joel (9) and Jacob (6), were playing in the front yard when a drunk driver swerved off the roadway and plowed through their front yard—narrowly missing the boys. The truck hit one of their vehicles, their house, and killed the family dog before hitting a tree and coming to rest. Little Joel was lauded as a hero for getting his brother out of the path of the truck as it came barreling through, right where they had been playing. Troopers from the Ohio State Highway Patrol wanted to recognize little Joel for his bravery and quick actions, so they got together and bought the boys a new basketball hoop to re-place the one damaged in the crash.[10]

In July 2021, a 22-year-old DoorDash driver was stopped and arrested in Jonesboro, Arkansas for driving under a suspended license and a warrant for failing to appear in court on a previ-ous traffic charge. A police officer delivered the food, explaining to the customer what had happened. She gratefully responded, "Thank you, you're awesome!"[11]

These are the kind of acts of service performed by American law enforcement officers on a regular basis. *To Protect and Serve* is not just an empty, generic slogan. It's a commitment, a mis-sion, a conviction in the heart of every man and woman who wears the badge. Police officers are the embodiment of the best of us; they are human empathy and compassion on display. They are people who deeply love their fellowman, have a calling to protect the sheep from the wolf, and a capacity for righteous violence in the event it is necessary. Police officers do not initiate violence, they respond to violence. This anti-police notion that

cops are systematically hunting down minorities and indiscriminately executing them is not only absurdly false but contrary to
primal human nature. Nevertheless, as long as there are wolves
among the sheep there must be sheepdogs ready to do violence.

The Human Resistance to Killing

Actually, it is not as easy to kill another human being as Dirty
Harry and John McClane make it look, so says Col. Grossman
in his book, *On Killing: The Psychological Cost of Learning to Kill
in War and Society*. He quotes Brigadier General S. L. A. Marshall, who said,

> *"The average and normally healthy individual—the man who
> can endure the mental and physical stresses of combat—still has
> such an inner and usually unrealized resistance toward killing
> a fellow man that he will not of his own volition take life if it is
> possible to turn away from that responsibility."*[12]

Gen. Marshall came to this conclusion after conducting very
eye-opening research into the firing rates of soldiers in combat
during World War II. He used a team of Army historians to
conduct interviews with thousands of infantry soldiers in hundreds of companies after they had been in firefights. His research
showed that only 15% to 20% of riflemen actually fired their
weapons at the enemy.[13] Those who did not fire at the enemy
would engage in various other tasks including ammo supply, re-
laying messages, or tending to the wounded. What Col. Grossman has dubbed the *conspiracy to miss*, are in fact the psychological and emotional "safety catches" built into most human beings
that keep them from killing another human being. Man is just
not wired to kill.

If this is true for soldiers on the battlefield—who have been
trained and tasked with killing the enemy—how much more true
it must be for law enforcement officers on the streets. The DOJ
Office of Justice Programs published a report of 7,512 arrests
conducted in six urban police agencies. The participating agencies were the Charlotte-Mecklenburg (NC) Police Department,

Colorado Springs (CO) Police Department, Dallas (TX) Police Department, St. Petersburg (FL) Police Department, San Diego (CA) Police Department, and San Diego County (CA) Sheriff's Department. The report showed that only 18 of those arrests involved officers discharging their weapons. Conversely, 17 of those arrests involved a suspect using a gun, making it relatively parallel in comparison.[14] This confirms my assertion that police officers do not initiate violence, but respond to violence. The Bureau of Justice Statistics reported 61.5 million contacts between police and U.S. citizens (16 years of age and older) in 2018. Contacts with police in which an officer pointed their weapon at someone and/or discharged their weapon only accounted for 0.3%[15] of those contacts. This doesn't support a narrative of killer cops. It more closely supports the truth—the diametric narrative—that most cops never have to use their guns.

In Ferguson, the false claims made by Dorian Johnson sounded like something right out of an action movie or violent crime drama. Ask yourself this question. Can a normal human being shoot someone who poses no threat, then stand over that person, laying helplessly on the ground, and shoot them several more times, executing them in cold blood? No, a *normal* human being cannot. To accept anything to the contrary would be to deny the existence of the psychological and emotional safety catches built into every normal human being. To deny that existence is to believe that every human being is capable of merciless and barbarous acts, making us all sociopaths, with no empathy for our fellow man. This train of thought does not stop at the station of logic and reason, yet this is what Johnson wanted the world to believe about Officer Darren Wilson. Not only is Officer Wilson not a sociopath, but he is also not criminally insane. Executing someone in cold blood in the middle of the street, in broad daylight, with potentially dozens of eyewitnesses, would require that he either, one, doesn't understand the consequences of his actions, or two, doesn't care about the consequences. If either of those were true, Wilson would be classified as a sociopath. If he is a sociopath, how did he pass thorough psychological exams in the hiring process of not one, but two law enforcement agencies? The truth is, Wilson was a *normal* human being, an exemplary officer, and had no red flags in his personal history to suggest otherwise.

Col. Grossman writes,

> *"There can be no doubt that this resistance to killing one's fellow man is there and that it exists as a result of a powerful combination of instinctive, rational, environmental, hereditary, cultural, and social factors. It is there, it is strong, and it gives us cause to believe that there just may be hope for mankind after all."*[16]

The resistance to killing is so strong that it prevented 80% to 85% of World War II infantrymen from firing their weapons at the enemy. Going back to the American Civil War, the resistance to killing is illustrated by the recovery of more than 27,000 muskets from the battlefield at Gettysburg after the battle. Of those, 24,000 were still loaded. 12,000 of them were found to be loaded more than once, meaning there were multiple projectile in the barrel. One weapon was found to be loaded 23 times! This discovery suggests that many soldiers opted to keep loading their weapons rather than firing them at their fellow countrymen.[17]

Use of Restraint in Deadly Force

Everybody talks about police using excessive force—which is both unethical and illegal, to be sure—but nobody is talking about officers using restraint in the use of deadly force, even when it's justified. Except, Dr. Anthony Pinizzotto, a retired FBI senior scientist, clinical forensic psychologist, and law enforcement consultant, and Edward Davis, a retired police lieutenant and FBI Academy instructor. Their collective research has discovered that a large number of police officers have been in situations when deadly force was justified, but they chose to resolve the incident without deadly force. This further corroborates Col. Grossman's theory on the resistance to killing.[18]

Their study surveyed 295 law enforcement officers with an average of 17 years of experience. 197 participants (70%) responded that they had been involved in at least one situation where they legally could have discharged their firearm in the performance of their duties but chose not to fire. Officers in the survey were involved in 1,189 situations where deadly force was legally justified. Officers used deadly force in only 7% of these situations. In other words, officers in the survey used restraint 93% of the time even when not legally mandated to do so. Additionally, 80% of the officers said they have been assaulted at least once in their careers.[19]

Dr. Pinizzotto asks a very good question. "If officers risk their personal safety by using restraint in deadly force, why has this phenomenon largely gone unnoticed in the media and research?"[20] These findings succinctly contradict the claim that police violence is a public health crisis in America. They unambiguously reverse the mobocracy's desired perception of police officers. The story told by this largely ignored data is that police officers are not only risking their lives to protect others, they are also needlessly risking their lives to avoid having to *take* lives 93% of the time!

Despite the lack of research regarding restraint in the use of force, there are plenty of well-documented occasions when a police officer was clearly justified in using deadly force, but took alternate actions instead, or hesitated—sometimes at their own peril. Every time it happens it proves that a natural resistance to killing is ingrained into normal, healthy human beings. However, it is also indicative of a potentially deadly, tactical error of hesitation.

Incident One

Travis, an Ohio deputy sheriff, told me his first-hand account of a warrant attempt that could've turned deadly in a split second. He and his partner knocked on a wanted man's front door to serve an arrest warrant. After receiving no answer, Travis walked around the perimeter of the residence to ascertain whether or not there were signs of anyone home (it's pretty normal for folks to refuse to answer the door for police, especially when they have an outstanding warrant). Believing the man was inside, they decided to knock on the door once more before leaving. Suddenly, the front door swung open and the man—with an obvious death wish—thrust his hand toward Travis's partner, pointing a gun inches from his face. The deputy reached up and grabbed the gun, and they fought for control. Fortunately, this story has a positive ending and nobody got hurt. But the potential was certainly there for cops and/or the suspect to be seriously hurt or killed.

I think we can agree there was more than enough justification for the use of deadly force here. My question is, why didn't the deputy draw his weapon and fire? This situation happened in mere seconds; obviously, the deputy felt his best chance for survival was to grab the muzzle of the suspect's gun and get it away from his face. It's fair to say that no one knows exactly what their first reaction would be unless they were in the deputy's shoes. Whatever his reasons for not using deadly force, it obviously worked out for him in this case. He lived to tell about it and the bad guy lived to go to jail for his warrant, with a bonus of new charges. My intention is not to second guess or Monday morning quarterback how this incident was handled, only to make the point that police officers don't always use deadly force, even when it's clearly justified.

Incident Two

On June 5, 2021, College Park, Georgia police officer Ivory Morris spotted a stolen vehicle in a hotel parking lot. When Officer Morris approached the vehicle it took off; meanwhile, Morris attempted to detain a 15-year-old male accomplice who had been outside the vehicle. While struggling with the male, the 17-year-old driver came back around to where they were struggling. The 15-year-old jumped on the hood of the vehicle and yelled to his accomplice, "Go, go, go!" The driver accelerated, throwing both the accomplice and the officer to the pavement. Both were run over by the stolen vehicle. At the hospital, Officer Morris' body cam recorded his conversation with his Sergeant as he recounted his thought process during the incident.

> *"When I was on top of that car, I had my other hand free to reach for the gun, but I said 'I don't want to reach for it, I don't want to pull it,' Sarge, I was like I don't want to hurt this kid, I don't want to take nobody's kid away."*

Chief Tom Kuzniacki confirmed that Officer Morris would've been justified had he used deadly force. Fortunately, Officer Morris only suffered a broken leg, underwent surgery, and was released to recover at home.[21] He risked his own life and suffered serious injury to avoid taking human life. That isn't the action of a cold-blooded killer, but of a human being struggling with the decision to take human life, even if restraining himself may result in his own death.

Incident Three

The resistance to kill is confirmed by the immediate display of remorse after the use of deadly force. In June 2021, a Flint, Michigan police officer was working a Juneteenth parade when he was ambushed by a woman with a gun. As he stood his traffic post, 19-year-old Briana Skyes pulled up next to him and started shooting at him. The officer returned fire, killing the woman. A bystander's video captured the incident and shows the officer collapsing to the pavement after the shooting, appearing to break down sobbing. A witness said the officer had no choice. Although the officer quickly returned fire, his immediate reaction to the shooting shows his overwhelming remorse for having had to use deadly force to defend himself.[22] This is not the behavior of a cold-blooded killer, but a normal human being.

Incident Four

March 29, 2016. In a suburb of Cincinnati, Officer Josh Hilling was on his way to grab some lunch, either Popeye's or Chipotle, as he recalled. Driving southbound on Interstate 75, he observed a man walking on the shoulder. Hilling hadn't passed any disabled vehicles and wondered where this guy had come from. He decided to stop and see if he could help.

Walking on the Interstate is a minor misdemeanor in the State of Ohio, but Officer Hilling didn't have enforcement action in mind. He figured he'd just give him a ride to the next exit. When he stopped to talk to the man, he asked the usual questions, "How are you doing?" "Where are you coming from?" "Where are you going?" "What's your name?" That's the question that raised Hilling's suspicions. The man started to give him a name, then stopped and gave him a different name. The, now suspicious, male was unable to produce an I.D. and began stumbling over his answers to Hilling's questions.

Anytime I gave someone a ride, I always explained to them I had to pat them down and search any belongings for weapons before they could get in my car. I also explained that they were free to decline a search, but I wouldn't be able to give them a ride and would call someone to come pick them up if they wished. This policy is just good officer safety. Officer Hilling was going to do just that, only his "spidey senses" were going crazy and he knew something was off.

What Officer Hilling didn't know was that twelve days earlier, Pablo Javier Aleman had stabbed his landlord to death in Baltimore County, Maryland, and was on the run. Hilling walked Aleman over to his cruiser and asked him to put his hands on the trunk. When he began to pat him down, Aleman suddenly swung around with a long, fixed blade knife in his hand—likely the same one he had used in the homicide—and started screaming, "Kill me!"

I asked Officer Hilling what was going through his mind at that exact moment. He said he honestly couldn't recall, but his training instantly kicked in. He drew his gun and shot Aleman once in the abdomen, while simultaneously creating distance between him and his knife-wielding attacker. Aleman went down when he was shot, but got back up and continued to scream, "Kill me!"

Hilling said he started thinking, "What do I need to do to

bring this situation to an end!" While watching Aleman, he knew he had to watch the highway traffic as well. He said as he created distance, a vehicle had already stopped in the slow lane, which gave him room to move. Then a semi stopped and blocked the other lanes, so he knew he had the whole highway and could focus on his attacker. Despite being shot, Aleman was still armed with the knife and closing the distance to Officer Hilling, only he was slower now and having trouble moving. Hilling knew if he kept his distance he would be okay.

Officer Hilling yelled into his radio, "Shots fired," and the cavalry started coming. Within a matter of minutes officers from every neighboring jurisdiction, the Sheriff's Office, and the Highway Patrol were on scene. One of the responding officers was able to get close enough to Aleman to deploy a Taser, which allowed officers to disarm him and get him into custody. And just as quickly as it started, Officer Hilling's deadly force encounter was over. From the time he stopped until the threat was over, less than four minutes had elapsed.

At the time of the shooting, Officer Josh Hilling had just recently been promoted from part-time to full-time and was only three months into his probationary period. Understandably, he was shaken up by what had happened. He said, "I pulled over to give this guy a ride and he tried to kill me!" Hilling knew he had acted justifiably, but in the back of his mind, he was thinking about the high-profile Ray Tensing case that was in progress at the time. Tensing was a University of Cincinnati Police Officer who was indicted for murder after fatally shooting Sam DeBose on a traffic stop. Hilling didn't sleep for a week. When the prosecutor officially cleared him, a weight lifted off Hilling's shoulders. He was ready to put the uniform back on and go to work.

Pablo Javier Aleman recovered from his wounds and was convicted of felonious assault on a police officer. He will serve a sentence of eleven years in an Ohio prison, before being extradited back to Maryland to face the consequences of murder, for which he plead guilty.

This 31-year-old probationary police officer was just on his way to grab some lunch when he stopped to help a pedestrian and came face to face with a murderer. During this deadly force encounter, Pablo Javier Aleman had yelled, "Kill me" more than forty times. He wanted Officer Hilling to shoot him again. The question I wanted him to answer was, "With clear justification, why *didn't* you shoot him again when he got up and kept coming at you?" Officer Hilling made a calculated decision to keep his attacker at bay until help could arrive. He didn't want to take a life. He is a perfect example of the human resistance to killing one's fellow man.

Incident Five

Tim, a retired police sergeant, told me about a deadly force encounter that unfolded on a hot summer night in 1992, about thirteen years into his career. It began as a fight call at a local bar. The first officer on scene was met by a large crowd in the parking lot; as his cruiser approached the crowd he heard a single gunshot. In an almost choreographed response, the crowd suddenly parted like the Red Sea and he was facing a man with a gun, directly in front of his cruiser. Before the officer had time to do anything, the armed man leveled the gun at him, compelling him to duck behind the dashboard, calling "shots fired" over the radio. When he looked up, the gunman was running toward the woods behind the bar.

In this situation, the police have to work fast to create a perimeter around the suspect's last known location—in this case, the wooded area behind the bar—to contain his movements. Within minutes, more officers started arriving on scene to set up the perimeter. Tim cut all the lights before coasting in on the adjacent street to the North of the bar. He took a post at the North edge of the woods, opposite from where the gunman had entered. He paused to listen and could hear the rustling of brush—the sound of someone coming toward him out of the woods. He keyed up his portable radio and advised the other officers, "He's coming out on Frederick," loud enough to be heard, but quietly enough so as not to give himself away. The squealing of tires and roaring of engines—as officers raced to get there—spooked the bad guy, nonetheless, and he retreated back into the woods.

The gunman made another attempt to escape, emerging from the east side of the wooded area, behind an apartment complex. He encountered five officers, who all drew down on him and began ordering him to drop the gun. The 19-year-old drunk man raised his pistol, pointed it at the officers, and said, "Five-O don't have the balls to shoot me!" Rather than using deadly force, the officers continued to try to reason with the gunman as he waved his gun around. About this time, Tim had made his way to the other officers who were in the back yard of this apartment complex, behind a small parking garage. Tim came around the east side of the garage, taking cover behind a bush at a 90° angle from the gunman, on his left flank. The K-9 officer present was shouting orders at the man to drop his gun or he would release the dog. He made good on that threat. When the dog got close to the gunman, he pointed his gun at the ground and fired. Then suddenly he raised his gun again and pointed it at the K-9 handler.

Tim told me, "I don't recall making the conscious decision to fire. My training just kicked in." He fired one round from approximately 60 feet away and the gunman went down like someone cut his legs out from under him. The threat was over, but the stress was not. EMS, additional patrol officers, detectives, and command staff—all the way up to the Chief of Police—converged on the scene. Tim's sergeant pulled him aside and asked for his gun, as per procedure. The Sarge then pulled out his own gun, handed it to Tim, and said, "Put this in your holster, you know how all this goes." He was taken to the emergency room where he would have to submit to a toxicology screen—again, common procedure.

While he was sitting in the E.R., Tim could see to the other end where they were working on the man he had shot. He said, "It wasn't until I saw his parents come in that I realized who he was." The gunman—whose face had been obstructed from Tim's view by a ball cap at the time of the shooting—was a young man that he had previously interacted with and knew by name. He used to frequent a local grocery store where Tim had done an off-duty detail. He said, "He was always respectful when he saw me. I felt terrible for what I had to do. I didn't sleep for three days."

The 35-year-old then patrol officer was placed on administrative leave during which he followed the prescribed protocol for officers involved in a shooting—consultation with a union attorney, interviews with detectives, an evaluation by a psychiatrist, interviews before the internal affairs police shooting board, etc. A special grand jury was convened to determine whether the shooting merited criminal charges. All the officers present at the scene testified one by one; Tim was the last. Before his testimony began the assistant prosecutor said, "Officer, I have to read you your Miranda rights because you could be indicted." Tim recalled, "I had never felt so small than I did when he was reading me my rights." Ultimately, Tim was cleared by the grand jury and the internal investigation into his use of force. And, fortunately, the gunman lived to be indicted, convicted, and imprisoned for felonious assault on a police officer.

After the shooting, the gunman spent considerable time in the hospital healing from his injuries. Because he was in custody, a police officer was always posted outside his hospital room. A conversation between the man and his parents was overheard by one such officer. The man's parents were planning to hire attorneys to file a lawsuit against Tim and the police department. He was overheard telling his parents, "I'm not suing anybody. I was drunk, I was stupid, and that officer did what he had to do." No lawsuit was ever filed.

After the investigation was over, Tim wrestled with questions regarding the hesitation of the other officers on scene that night. He didn't know at the time of the shooting that before he came around the east corner of that parking garage, the suspect had already once pointed his pistol at the senior officer in the group. What if he had killed one of them then? Why had they not defended themselves? He had given them clear justification for the use of deadly force. Tim went to the senior man in private to find out. His explanation for hesitating was, "The guy was drunk, he had a small-caliber weapon, and I had my vest on." Tim reminded the veteran officer, "Your vest doesn't protect you from the neck up." The hesitation of the younger officers likely amounted to their deference to the senior man. Either way, if Tim had hesitated when he saw the suspect raise his gun the second time, they could've been having a police funeral instead of this conversation.

Overcoming the Resistance

It is well established that hesitation in the face of evil—whether on the battlefield abroad or the streets at home—costs lives. A better understanding of the resistance to killing that *causes* that hesitation has reshaped how we train soldiers and law enforcement officers. This is why they no longer train by shooting at round bulls-eye targets. They have been replaced with targets depicting a human silhouette. By repetition, it conditions the mind to shoot at the likeness of a person rather than an inanimate object. Shoot-don't shoot training was introduced in the 1970s to condition officers to make target choices—gunman and/or innocent bystander—followed by rewards or consequences[23], respectively.

The best example of this is Hogan's Alley, a tactical training facility at the FBI Academy, named after the comic strip with the same name from the 1890s. The mock small town was built with the help of Hollywood set designers. According to the FBI, *"It's a hotbed of terrorist and criminal activity. Its only bank is robbed at least twice a week. Mobsters, drug dealers, and international terrorists lurk around every corner. Hogan's Alley is exactly the way we want it."*[24] For more than thirty years the facility has been used to train federal, state, and local law enforcement officers in a controlled environment, as close to real-life as can safely be achieved. Officers use modified weapons that shoot non-lethal paint bullets and shoot at role players. This type of training is considered operant conditioning to help officers to overcome the resistance to killing if and when they have a real deadly force encounter.

Operant conditioning has proven to be very successful. When our military began using it to train soldiers in the 1960s, they successfully raised the firing rate from 15%-20% in World War II to 95% in the Vietnam War.[25] Why is it important to condition law enforcement officers to overcome this resistance to taking human life? Because every day a police officer goes to work could be the day he or she is confronted by someone who wishes to do them ill. In the moment, police officers need to be ready to be a warrior; the only way to accomplish that is to maintain a warrior mindset. But isn't that the problem that has created the political and social unrest of today's America? No. The problem is the public is being fed a false narrative that cops are racist killers. We, the sheepdogs, are being compared to the wolves against whom we are sworn to protect the sheep.

The Deadly Mix

Police deadly force encounters are not scripted, choreographed incidents that play out according to an officer's training or experience. They are unpredictable, dynamic situations, that are often unexpected and can turn in favor of the offenders at any moment. There is no playbook, no manual, no lines or moves to memorize. There is no training that can completely and adequately prepare an officer to respond perfectly to every such encounter. They take place in mere seconds, seconds for which every officer must have a warrior mindset.

In our culture of handheld mobile devices, everything is on video. But regardless of the most up-to-date technology, video will never capture everything. Every dashcam, body cam, surveillance, or cell phone video of a deadly force encounter is missing context. Yet, from those videos, officers are judged in the court of uninformed public opinion—and sometimes even fired or prosecuted to appease the mob—before the wheels of due process can even begin to turn.

In their research on police use of deadly force, Dr. Pinizzotto and his colleagues at the FBI identified what they termed, "The

Deadly Mix." The three components of the deadly mix are the officer, the offender, and the circumstances that brought them together. These three components are the context that will always be missing from a video. The relationship between these three explains how the fluid situation of a deadly force encounter unfolds. Despite the increase in training, technology, and resources to equip law enforcement officers over the years, the average number of officers killed or assaulted each year remains constant. Dr. Pinizzotto says the explanation is found in the deadly mix.[26]

Unpacking this idea for people without any law enforcement background is no easy task. In our conversation, Dr. Pinizzotto recalled, even when explaining the deadly mix to the most educated audience, he can almost see their heads spinning on their shoulders. Understandably, Joe and Jane Public generally have the most simple-minded perception of what's going on at a scene and it can keep them from understanding the outcome. Even when watching a police encounter on video, what one cannot see are the thought process of the officer, the thought process of the offender, and how the circumstances that brought them together factor into the equation. These three components often form the deadly mix that leads to a fatal encounter. Dr. Pinizzotto illustrates this using two scenarios involving the same offender being stopped by two different police officers.

Scenario 1

"A lone police officer stopped an offender for a speeding violation but did not check the license plate number of the vehicle or the violator's name in NCIC (National Crime Information Center). Although he normally followed this procedure in every traffic stop, he was due to meet a fellow officer 1 mile away for lunch in 5 minutes. The officer obtained the driver's license and registration and walked to the rear of his police vehicle and proceeded to write the traffic citation. The offender, wanted for a felony violation in a nearby jurisdiction, remained in his vehicle, closely watching the officer in his side-view mirror. At that point, the officer received a radio transmission from

the officer he was supposed to meet for lunch. He answered the radio and confirmed that he was on his way to the restaurant. The officer then finished the citation and approached the offender who shot him several times with a handgun and fled in the vehicle. Although seriously wounded, the officer survived. Authorities captured the offender 2 days later in a neighboring jurisdiction."[27]

The officer was later interviewed and said he was never aware that he was in any danger. He believed the offender had appeared very "cooperative and polite." The offender was also interviewed in prison. He was asked what led to his attack on the officer. He said, "It was nothing personal. The officer seemed like an okay guy. I was willing to take a traffic ticket for speeding; that was the least of my worries. But, when I saw the officer talking on the radio, I thought he discovered I was wanted on a felony warrant. If he had not gotten on that radio, I would have thought everything was okay, taken the ticket, and left."[28]

Do you see how the perception of both the officer and the offender played into the outcome of this scenario? The officer incorrectly believed he was in no danger, and the offender incorrectly believed the officer knew about his warrant and was going to arrest him. Had their perceptions of each other been opposite—according to the offender—this incident would've ended with a traffic ticket instead of the assault on the officer. This is the deadly mix that no video will ever show.

Scenario 2

[The] same offender stated that in the past and under a similar set of circumstances, he had been stopped by another law enforcement officer. In that situation, the professional manner of the officer impressed the offender so much that he did not use the weapon he had under his seat. The offender explained that he believed the officer conducted himself in a professional manner. By this, he meant that the officer's attention was focused directly on him and the movements he made in the vehicle. The offender watched the officer in his side-view mirror and, at one point, made eye contact with the officer who was watching him. He saw the officer touch the back of his car, look in the

rear passenger area, and take a position slightly behind the center post of the car door. He decided, "It wasn't worth taking the chance that I might get over on him. He had his stuff together. I didn't feel I'd be able to get my gun without getting hurt."[29]

In the second scenario, the perceptions of both the officer and the offender were correct. The officer was vigilant and correctly believed that a threat could exist (even though he never knew his life was actually in danger), and the offender correctly believed that the officer was aware of every move he was making and was ready for an attack at any minute. Because of these independent perceptions, the stop was conducted without incident, and both the officer and offender went on their way. The deadly mix is where the three components—the officer, the offender, and the circumstances that brought them together—overlap. Each component affects the other and has the potential to change the outcome of a police encounter.

Let's consider the third component—the circumstances that brought them together. The offender encountered both officers on a traffic stop. Traffic stops are dangerous for many reasons (we'll talk about traffic stops in another chapter). In the second scenario, what saved the officer's life was his vigilance, his attention to detail, and his constant observation of the offender's movements, which ultimately made the offender unsure of his ability to successfully get the upper hand, and thwarted his attack. Now, let's throw another circumstantial element into the scenario, like another motorist who pulls up alongside the officer and divides his attention. Could this potentially have changed the outcome of this police encounter? Absolutely! That might have given the offender a window of opportunity to get his gun from under the seat and prepare to shoot the officer when he approached.

The reason I make this point is that it happens all the time. Standby for a public service announcement: Never approach an officer conducting a traffic stop. It divides their attention, distracts them, and leaves them open to an attack. Hypothetically, had this occurred in scenario 2, an innocent, unsuspecting citizen could've gotten the officer killed simply by distracting him.

A councilman in Frederick County, Maryland did this very thing and went way too far with it. The safety of the officer was the least of his concern—He was worried about the driver. In June 2021, a deputy sheriff stopped a vehicle for a license plate violation. While the deputy was talking to the driver, Frederick County Councilman Kai Hagen stopped his vehicle in the roadway next to the vehicle. The deputy—who recognized Hagen—told him he needed to move on, as he was blocking the roadway. Hagen refused to leave until he could ask the driver if he was okay, informing the deputy, "I'm going to sit here until you're done to ensure this is a safe stop."[30]

Several days later, Frederick County Sheriff Chuck Jenkins brought up the incident during a radio interview, and Hagen called in to the station to address him. He said, "We noticed that a deputy was pulling over a car that wasn't speeding, so we didn't know what that was all about, and obviously it could be a lot of different things. And as we drove past...we noticed that it was a Black driver."[31] During a heated on-air discussion, Sheriff Jenkins explained that Hagen had jeopardized the safety of the deputy, and had no business interfering with the stop.

The Sheriff said the deputy held the high ground and resolved the situation by letting the councilman ask the driver if he was okay, in an effort to get him to move on. The deputy said when Hagen finally pulled away, the driver—who received a warning—said, "That was the weirdest thing, man."[32]

The entire time the deputy was having to argue with this county councilman, he was distracted, his attention was divided, and had the driver wanted to do him harm, he would've had plenty of opportunities. If the councilman was that worried about the safety of the African American driver, he could've legally parked his vehicle nearby and observed until the stop was over—or even recorded it, for that matter—without distracting the deputy.

Although this particular example is on the extreme side, distractions are not all that rare. I have personally had people approach me on traffic stops to ask directions, or want to know what was going on because I was stopping a family member, or some other random question. So, when you see a law enforcement officer conducting a traffic stop, keep in mind they are doing something very dangerous but necessary, and maybe say a prayer for the officer *and* driver.

How does the discussion of the deadly mix fit into the equation of the resistance to killing and restraint in the use of deadly force? It affects the officer's thought process during a deadly force encounter. At the very inception of any officer's career, they join up with a general sense of altruism. They want to make a difference and help people. No officer has ever said they became a police officer because "It gives me the legal authority to abuse people." Therefore, when faced with the threat of deadly force, their thought process is, "I don't want to hurt this person," or "I'm not here to take life but to save it." Additionally, If the officer has already experienced a deadly force encounter and has walked through the process of an internal investigation, grand jury investigation, public and media scrutiny, the threat to his livelihood, his family, and possibly even his freedom, there is another thought process that he is experiencing. In his mind, he is saying, "I don't want to go through that again." All of these thoughts are going through the officer's mind in a matter of nanoseconds as they stare down the sights of their gun at an offender that is risking their life, or the life of someone else. In this split second they have to make a decision that will affect the rest of their lives. This causes hesitation, which in the equation of the deadly mix, can be fatal.

The study goes a step further to suggest that officers often unwittingly sacrifice their own safety.

> "[S]tudies found that officers often neglect their own safety when performing their duties. The[y] also discovered that many officers [that were assaulted] fit the following categories of personal characteristics: hard working; friendly and well-liked; fails to follow all the rules, especially in regard to arrests, confrontations with prisoners, traffic stops, and waiting for backup when backup is available; and feels they can "read" others/situations and will

drop their guard as a result. When officers received calls for service, as well as when they initiated contacts, their mental and physical reactions were geared toward responding, helping, clearing the call, and returning to service for the next call. They often were thinking about the next call before they cleared the current one. Consequently, they sacrificed their own safety for what they perceived as "the greater good: the safety of the community."[33]

To summarize, the officers in the study appear to have a pattern of fast and efficient "customer service," at the expense of their own safety. Sometimes, officers get to a point in their career when they are comfortable and begin to feel bullet-proof. They use the idiom, "It'll never happen to me," to justify cutting small corners on personal safety in the name of expediency. As a sergeant, I felt it was my responsibility to look out for safety issues with my troops and hold them accountable. They would grumble about it, but I thought of them as my own kids and didn't want them to get hurt. I didn't want to have to tell their families that I let them get hurt. It was my job to remind them that every call has the potential to be deadly—even if you've done it a hundred times before—and everyone has the potential to be dangerous.

Everybody is Dangerous

In today's America, open season has been declared on cops. This has always been the case, but never to the present extent. We want to save life, not take it, as I've illustrated above. Unfortunately, the latter is a position into which the wolf forces us. Consequently, survival means vigilance. Even when performing the most frequent, mundane of tasks, cops have to believe everyone is dangerous. That means balancing professional, friendly policing with a warrior mindset, which can be challenging. It takes discipline to strike the perfect mix between customer service and defender. Former Secretary of Defense, General "Mad Dog" Mattis said it best when he told his Marines, "Be polite, be professional, but have a plan to kill everybody you meet."[34] That is exactly what cops have to do.

The phrase cops recite more than any other is, "Let me see your hands." It's automatic, almost like a sixth sense. It's the way we were trained. We must always know what the hands are doing. Watching someone's hands will alert you to an impending attack. Watching someone's hands will tell you if they are carrying a weapon. Watching someone's hands will tell you if they're lying. A person's hands will give them away every time. When cops make minor requests of people in the interest of officer safety, such as, *"Let me see your hands," "Keep your hands where I can see them,"* or *"Could you take a few steps back for me,"* they often react with offense to the request. They say things like, *"I'm not a criminal," "I'm the one that called you,"* or *"Officer So-and-so is a friend of mine."* Please know it's not personal, we're not being rude, we just don't know you and we want to go home safe at the end of our shift.

Because of a culture of complaints in the police field, cops are often reprimanded for failing to maintain a friendly demeanor. Sometimes the complaint is unsubstantiated, and it was the *citizen* who was less than cordial. The general public needs to realize this isn't the retail or foodservice business. The customer is not always right. Yes, we want to be friendly and treat everyone with respect. Yes we want to maintain a positive image, but sometimes the police have to be the police, and that will always be somebody's bad day.

I'll be polite and friendly, but rest assured, if you threaten my safety, Officer Friendly goes out the window. I remember watching a video in training of an officer from a Southern state stopping to investigate a suspicious person. The officer, with the accent and demeanor of a Southern gentleman, spoke very politely until the offender's gun came out. The officer very quickly went from, "Yes, sir. No, sir," to screaming at the top of his lungs, "If you don't put that gun down I will kill you!" He went from customer service to warrior in 3 seconds flat! Knowing when to flip the switch is critical to survival. Going too far in one direction or the other at an inappropriate time will either get a cop in trouble or killed. For example, being friendly is one thing, but being too friendly could have dire consequences. This excerpt from *Violent Encounters* illustrates the violent outcome of an officer letting his guard down.

> *"While a friendly image does much to promote a positive image for the officer and the department, overly friendly behavior at an inappropriate time may cause some offenders to view this as a sign of vulnerability. In one case, the offender seized upon the officer's willingness to discuss non-work-related activities. This appeared to have lulled the officer into a sense of complacency while the offender developed and initiated a plan to attack the officer. Interviewed officers agreed with the basic principle that while officers may appear friendly, they never should let down their guard because no one can know what is in the mind of another person. The officers further agreed that they should maintain a professional demeanor while displaying a friendly manner. As an example, they can smile at a person and exchange a friendly greeting or salutation, but they must remember that the person they are dealing with may be contemplating their assault to effect an escape."* [35]

I was first exposed to this and other research conducted by Dr. Pinizzotto and his colleagues when I attended a training called, "Officer Safety and Street Survival," offered by the *FBI Law Enforcement Officers Killed and Assaulted* program. This is a sample of the ongoing education cops receive to stay ahead of the criminals to either avoid or survive deadly force encounters. My purpose for bringing you into the room to see a few of these things is to show you some of the street stress behind the stone-faced "standoffishness" often perceived about police officers. This job is tough and unforgiving. Cops deserve to be respected for the risk they take and the sacrifice they make to keep the wolf at bay. To borrow the message I read on a t-shirt, "I'm a police officer. My job is to save your a—, not kiss it." It's impossible to do both.

L.O.D.D.

L.O.D.D. is an acronym for line of duty death. On average,

176 law enforcement officers make the ultimate sacrifice each year.[36] No matter how much we train or what we do to mitigate safety risks, we still lose brothers and sisters in blue to the violence of evil predators. Every single officer's murder is a grim reminder of the uncertainty of our profession, that on any given day, a police officer may not come home. It's not something cops really think about; most go to work day in and day out, mentally removed from the danger, until the news of another L.O.D.D.

When a police officer dies in the line of duty, we honor our fallen by escorting them to their final resting place in all the pomp and circumstance befitting a hero. Brothers and sisters in blue from all over the country don their dress uniforms, polish their police cruisers and converge upon the community of the fallen officer for the funeral. A procession of hundreds of cruisers—from agencies far and wide—escorts our fallen comrade to their grave, with red and blue lights flashing for as far as the eyes can see. Grateful citizens line the procession route to pay their respects. Children wave, mothers cry, and veterans stand at attention and salute as a true American hero makes his final pass. With honor guards, twenty-one gun salutes, and the playing of taps in the distance, the law enforcement community makes one last feeble attempt to commemorate the life and service of a cop whose life was taken too soon.

When the eulogies are complete, the songs have been sung, and the tributes have ended, the fallen officer's last call is given. A dispatcher broadcasts the officer's badge number over a live police radio. Following a period of silence, the dispatcher announces that the fallen officer is "out-of-service" for the last time, in a ceremonial "End of Watch." Some are brief, some are lengthy dedications. Regardless, they invoke emotional responses from even the toughest of cops, because they represent a brother or sister who didn't answer the radio, whom we couldn't save, who sacrificed his or her life.

Detective Jorge Del Rio, a 30 year veteran of the Dayton, Ohio Police Department, was shot on November 4, 2019, while serving a search warrant with the DEA task force. As he was descending the stairs into the basement of the residence, a gunman opened fire, striking him twice in the face.[37] He succumbed to his wounds on November 7, 2019. The following is a transcript of the beautifully written last call for Detective Del Rio.

"Dispatch to crew 916, checkup. Dispatch to all crews, hold radio traffic on all channels.

Dispatch to crew 916, Detective Jorge Del Rio, badge number 262, check up on any channel.

Dayton car one, on your written authority, we will show crew 916 out of service, End of Watch.

Dispatch to all crews, Detective Jorge Del Rio, badge 262, will be shown out of service after 30 honorable years with the Dayton Police Department. With the last 18 years, serving as a United States Drug Enforcement Agency Task Force officer. Detective Del Rio was mortally wounded on November 4, 2019, and succumbed to his injuries on November 7, 2019. We observe this end of watch with a moment of silence at this time.

Detective Del Rio, we thank you for your examples of professionalism in your personal and work life, your integrity, being beyond reproach. By you respecting your family, your friends, your fellow law enforcement professionals, and even those that meant to do harm to others, and your example of being fair in all your interactions with loved ones, and with Lady Justice, the citizens of Dayton, and of Ohio, and of the United States are safer because of you. Although you are gone, you will never be forgotten. Your badge number will be permanently assigned to you, as there will be no one that can fill your shoes. Rest in peace, our friend. We will take it from here.

Dispatch to all crews, resume normal radio traffic at 1402."[38]

When the last call has ended there is silence, broken only by the muffled cries of family, friends, and fellow officers. But, when the tears have dried the law enforcement community refocuses its attention on the apprehension, prosecution, and conviction of the officer's killer.

As long as there are wolves who prey upon the sheep, there will always be sheepdogs willing to suit up, put their lives on the line, and endure the scrutiny, hatred, and scorn of the public. And because they are men and women of character, integrity, and honor, they will do it despite the malice of the anti-police, anti-law and order, Marxist mob. They will do it with love in their hearts, smiles on their faces, their uniforms pressed and their brass polished, knowing they do so with a righteous purpose and a valiant mission. They will serve while the unjust call for their prosecution and the riotous mob calls for their murder, without retaliation, and without recourse. For, the police know that their presence is the only way the sheep can successfully coexist with the wolf.

As long as there are wolves in the world, there will always be deadly force encounters. The deterrence factor is the only way to minimize deadly force encounters. We have conditioned police to overcome the "safety catches" to kill when and if necessary, but then presented them with the threat of prosecution if they justifiably do so. Crippling the police by taking away their tools, unjustly prosecuting them, stripping away their protections, and therefore demoralizing them, removes the deterrence factor. If we defund, disarm, and disband the police, who is left to discourage the wolf from attacking the sheep?

Chapter 8
Traffic Stops

"People sleep peacefully in their beds at night only because rough men stand ready to do violence on their behalf." —George Orwell

The disparagement of police has largely centered on the events that unfold during traffic stops. In addition to the deadly force issues, stops have been scrutinized for 4th Amendment rights intrusions when cops ask motorists and passengers to exit a vehicle, conduct searches, etc. Unfortunately, America's cops are often perceived through the lens of U.S. Army 2nd Lt. Caron Nazario, who was a victim of excessive force on a stop in Windsor, Virginia, or the tragic Daunte Wright accidental shooting by an officer in Brooklyn Center, Minnesota. These two high-profile incidents are anomalous—and a black eye and embarrassment to the law enforcement community—but touted by mainstream media as the norm. That simply is not accurate. There is a case to be made in favor of the police, who conduct millions of traffic stops each year without incident.

Americans are mobile. Consequently, law enforcement officers have a large volume of public interaction during traffic stops. Beyond the enforcement of traffic laws and the deterrence factor, an equally large volume of criminal activity is curbed. Crimes—even homicides—have been solved as a result of the investigations that are initiated by traffic stops. They are an essential tool in policing.

There is no such thing as a routine traffic stop, yet the term is repeatedly used to describe the bizarre events that occur during one of the most dangerous police functions. *"Fugitive Wanted In Colorado, Apprehended After Routine Traffic Stop In Johnson City,"* reads a headline in Tennessee.[1] *"Half-ton of marijuana, valued at over $8 million found by dog on routine traffic stop,"* reports ABC News from Indiana.[2] In Michigan, *"Routine traffic stop leads to 50 kgs of crystal meth, value estimated at over $1 million."*[3] Two of these headlines are basically oxymorons. While it is not all that uncommon to arrest a wanted person out of a traffic stop, there is nothing routine about seizing $8 million in marijuana or $1 million in methamphetamine on a traffic stop. However, a new movement threatens to take traffic enforcement away from the police and make headlines like these a thing of the past.

Traffic Without Police?

One of the biggest misconceptions about traffic stops is that they are only about traffic safety. That's why I have to shake my head when I read about academics and politicians suggesting that we entrust traffic enforcement to unarmed "traffic safety employees". What I don't understand is why the people who aspire to create policy want to give one of the top three most dangerous law enforcement activities to unarmed, non-law enforcement paper pushers. Will an unarmed traffic safety employee arrest an armed and dangerous felon wanted from another state? Will an unarmed traffic safety employee detect and seize a half-ton of marijuana or 50 kilograms of crystal meth? No, they will not. These are police actions—interactions between sheepdogs and wolves.

Notwithstanding, this idea has actually been floated and is increasing in popularity among the anti-police malcontents. In July 2020, Berkeley, California became the first U.S. city to move toward the removal of police from traffic stops.[4] The Berkeley Police Department offered no official opinion in response, but the police unions of Los Angeles, San Jose, and San Francisco released a joint statement in opposition to the measure. It stated in part:

> *"We do not believe that the public wants lax enforcement of those incidents by non-sworn individuals. Traffic stops are some of the most dangerous actions police officers take. What happens when the felon with an illegal gun gets pulled over by the parking police? Nothing good, we're sure of that."*[5]

In April 2021, the Minneapolis city council announced its intention to develop an unarmed traffic safety division as a separate entity from the police department. The directive listed four goals for this division—maximize the traffic safety benefits of traffic enforcement, eliminate racial disparities in traffic enforcement, educate the public on safe driving behavior and traffic laws, and earn the trust of communities "harmed" by previous traffic enforcement practices.[6] These goals appear to be exclusively traffic-related and terribly uninformed, thus confirming my belief that even many local government officials don't understand the dynamics of traffic enforcement, let alone Joe and Jane Public. Surely, a police official has explained to the Minneapolis city council that separating traffic enforcement from criminal enforcement doesn't remove the criminal element that is regularly encountered *during* traffic enforcement. They do seem to understand, however, that divorcing the two allows those criminals to easily fly under the radar. That's the idea.

Jordan Blair Woods, a University of Arkansas Law Professor, published a study in the Stanford Law Review in October of 2020 entitled, "Traffic Without the Police." It is riddled with statistics and scholarly opinions as to why police should be removed from traffic enforcement. Woods argues that "People of color and other marginalized communities [are] vulnerable to over-policing and overcriminalization in today's driving regime." In summary, it suggests decriminalization of minor traffic violations (speeding, running red lights, etc.), creating civilian traffic agencies staffed with unarmed traffic monitors to conduct "routine" traffic stops for those violations, looking the other way in the "failed war on drugs" in the framework of traffic stops, giving traffic monitors discretion regarding whether or not they contact the police when they encounter criminal activity on traffic stops, decriminalizing DUI and entrusting traffic monitors to conduct DUI investigations, decriminalizing driver's license revocation or suspension violations, and giving police only narrow authority to stop vehicles in cases of serious traffic offenses, violent crime, and felony warrants.[7]

This study is based on several false premises. First, it assumes the false narrative of systemic racism in law enforcement. Secondly, it infers that the police are inherently violent, therefore, to drastically reduce police-citizen contact is to drastically reduce police violence. Thirdly, it takes a position on "over-policing" without quantifying the term. Where is the line drawn between too much policing, or not enough policing? Fourthly, it insists that the war on drugs in this country has failed, and therefore, any enforcement effort to take drugs off our streets is futile. Throughout, the study hints at the presumption that police are to be feared and avoided whenever possible. "Traffic Without the Police" was written from the perspective of a perfect world where everyone plays by the proverbial rules *except* the police, without a single mention of the personal responsibility of Joe and Jane Public.

A Chicago Tribune column headline reads, "Police traffic stops are a needless danger." The premise of this oped is equally false. "In every traffic stop, the driver and the police officer face the risk of being killed, and too often the risk becomes a reality. Why not take both out of the line of fire?"[8] Wrong. On every traffic stop the police officer faces an unknown threat, but—with few exceptions—a driver or occupant only faces the risk of being killed when they threaten the safety of the police officer. Claiming the police and the public face the same threat of violence during traffic stops infers that the police have malicious intent.

It's a slap in the face to men and women of law enforcement to paint them as violent predators who are patrolling the streets of America, seeking their next victim. This is an example of taking a topic that is not controversial and making it so to push an agenda—the vilification of police.

"Routine" Traffic Stops

Traffic stops are not cut-and-dried encounters between motorists and police, wherein the interaction only involves issuing a citation for a minor traffic violation, after which everyone goes on their way, as if a coupon was handed to them for a free cheeseburger at McDonald's. In many traffic stops, the original violation is only the beginning. The anti-police mob calls these, "pre-textual traffic stops," meaning lawful stops made for traffic violations, for which the police have other motives, such as looking for drugs, guns, etc. This practice is a valuable law enforcement tool and has been upheld by the U.S. Supreme Court.[9] I have conducted hundreds of traffic stops over my career. Only a fraction of them resulted in a citation for a minor traffic violation. Most of the time there is something else going on that requires police action, by an armed police officer as opposed to an unarmed civilian traffic monitor.

Every time a police officer stops a vehicle he or she is assuming a certain amount of risk. Cops are trained to assess and categorize each stop as low-risk, high-risk, or unknown-risk prior to approaching the driver. A low-risk stop is what most are referring to when they use the term "routine." Stopping granny for speeding on her way to church would constitute a low-risk stop. In other words, it appears the risk to the officer's safety is low. Most stops fall into this category. At the other end of the spectrum are high-risk—or felony—stops. Felony stops involve stolen vehicles, persons armed with weapons, violent offenders, etc. An officer who deems a stop high-risk has some information about what and who may be in the vehicle, such as a violent crime that has just been committed by the driver or passenger. In other words, there is a known high-risk to officer safety. Felony stops usually involve several officers. All other traffic stops fall in the category of unknown-risk, meaning, the officer is unaware of the level of risk until he or she gets involved in the stop. Once the officer makes contact with the driver, he or she is usually able to determine what risk, if any, exists.

Contrary to the above-cited op-ed, the motorist has already taken their risk and is now experiencing the consequences of such. If you commit a minor traffic violation, you risk getting stopped by police and receiving a citation. There is a big difference between risk and consequence. Being shot by police on a traffic stop is a consequence of the risk posed to the officer's life, not a risk of merely coming in contact with police. The difference is personal responsibility. Holding the police responsible for actions they take in response to a threat you posed is like holding your mail carrier responsible for the bill you ran up.

Drugs

Every traffic stop is an investigation. It may be simple and result in a warning; it may be complex and result in the seizure of contraband and one or more felony arrests. From traffic stops, I have removed an untold quantity of drugs from the street. This includes marihuana, heroin, methamphetamine, cocaine, crack, morphine, Xanax, hydrocodone, and other scheduled narcotics, possession of most of which is a felony. When a driver is in possession of one or more of these drugs, there is a higher likelihood they are also under the influence, resulting in an impaired driving arrest. Traffic stops also yield drug paraphernalia such as pipes, spoons, scales, hypodermic syringes, snorting straws, and other items used to ingest these drugs. Under the traffic without police idea, if a traffic monitor encounters illegal drugs or paraphernalia on a "routine traffic stop," they would not be required to contact the police, and drug users and traffickers would be given a free pass to conduct their business on public roadways undetected, as long as they are not violating any "serious" traffic laws.

Impaired Drivers

This is not trivial. Most cops take drug enforcement very seriously, especially when it comes to users getting behind the wheel. Driving impaired is more than just a traffic law violation, it's a dangerous—and sometimes deadly—crime. The National Highway Traffic Safety Administration (NHTSA) reports that 65% of drivers involved in serious injury and fatal crashes in the third quarter of 2020 tested positive for at least one drug.[10] Every cop has a niche. Mine was OVI investigations (OVI is an acronym for Operating a Vehicle Impaired, the Ohio equivalent of DUI). In addition to leading my agency in OVI arrests, I was honored to be twice recognized by Mothers Against Drunk Driving (MADD). Operating by a no-tolerance policy, I have removed hundreds of impaired drivers from the streets. The reason I'm so passionate about this issue is that—in addition to the citizens—my family members travel these streets, and every impaired driver that I arrest is one less threat to the safety of my family and the citizens I serve. Traffic without police means impaired drivers would be filtered through a layer of civilian traffic monitors who would be more likely to look the other way.

Moreover, DUI detection is a honed skill that takes training and experience. Evidence of impairment isn't limited to egregiously erratic driving, the odor of an alcoholic beverage, or slurred speech, especially when alcohol is often mixed with drugs. Different levels of impairment have different clues. Law enforcement officers go through extensive training to conduct these investigations. Advanced Roadside Impaired Driving Enforcement (ARIDE) training teaches officers what indicators to look for, how to conduct proper field sobriety tests, what clues to look for in the tests, and how to properly prepare the case for court. In addition, some officers go on to be trained as drug recognition experts (DRE), which is a scientific study of each class of drug, how each affects the body, and how to look for evidence of those effects to determine what a driver has ingested. While DUI investigation is not an exact science, it is a highly technical, specifically structured process—a skill that is honed over time.

I would be remiss to reveal all the tricks of the trade (so to speak), but I'll give you an example of a random observation that led to a DUI arrest. One summer night I was traveling down a state route in front of a mobile home community. Next to the entrance to the community was a gravel pull-off. As I was passing, I noticed a vehicle was coming out of the pull-off onto the road; it then stopped in front of the entrance to make a left turn into the community. It is my experience that impaired divers often overshoot their intended turns, usually putting their vehicles in a ditch or someone's front lawn. I decided to pull over to observe the vehicle further. As the driver was waiting for traffic to pass, he suddenly turned left, cutting off a vehicle coming the opposite direction, which required the oncoming vehicle to take evasive action to avoid a crash. With clear probable cause, I stopped the vehicle and discovered the driver was obviously intoxicated.

Detecting impaired drivers is an important job in law enforcement. It's not as simple as looking for obvious signs, like a swerving vehicle. I've dealt with people who have been driving drunk for so long they can drive as straight as an arrow. How are they detected by law enforcement? Minor traffic or defective equipment violations (a headlight out, no license plate light, etc.). If police were prohibited from making traffic stops for those minor things, we would miss a lot of impaired drivers. Delegating "routine traffic stops" or even DUI investigations to traffic monitors would remove a deterrent effect, increase impaired driving, and subsequent crashes that occur as a result. Let's not forget that in most states DUI is an escalating offense, meaning with every conviction the next violation is a more serious charge. DUI is not just a serious traffic offense, it escalates to felony status for career drunk and drugged drivers. The first time a traffic monitor was to let an impaired driver go—either due to ignorance or neglect—and that driver went down the road and caused a fatal crash, people would be hanging traffic monitors out to dry and calling for more police.

Suspended Drivers

Suspended drivers are another big problem. People don't seem to understand that driving is a privilege, not a right. When their driving privileges are taken away—usually as a penalty for habitually violating traffic laws—a Judge has ruled they have lost the privilege of driving because they have abused it through unsafe driving practices. The notion that civilian traffic monitors could administer "roadside sanctions," such as suspending someone's license for a serious traffic violation, has no teeth. Why? Because most people already ignore their suspensions and drive anyway. According to NHTSA, between 60% and 80% of drivers with suspended licenses continue to drive. This results in more suspensions. It is not unusual for an officer to stop someone with multiple suspensions on their driving record, usually from multiple courts in multiple jurisdictions. What most don't realize is that a suspended driver can be cited for every open suspension on their record.

Cops have an uncanny ability to memorize names and faces of people in their patrol area with suspended driver's licenses and warrants and can identify them on sight. After a quick verification of the suspension on their mobile data computer, the officer has clear probable cause to stop and cite the driver. I don't give much credence to the argument that citations cause an undue financial burden upon violators, because a fine is a consequence of behavior. If one wants to stop the fines, then one should stop the illegal behavior. It really is that simple. Habitual suspended drivers are careless, dangerous, are thumbing their noses at the law.

Warrant Arrests

From traffic stops, I have made hundreds of warrant arrests. They range from drivers who didn't show up to traffic court, all the way up to out-of-state fugitives from justice. So what is a warrant? It's a court order signed by a Judge that orders any police officer that comes in contact with the person named, to physically bring them in front of said Judge. There are different types of warrants. Arrest warrants are issued when a criminal charge is filed based on probable cause. Bench warrants are issued when someone charged with a crime fails to appear in court. Commit warrants are issued when someone has been sentenced to jail time. These warrants are issued for both misdemeanors and felony cases. In my experience, people with misdemeanor bench warrants are generally people who are ignoring their problems, hoping they will eventually go away. Sometimes it's an isolated mistake, but most of the time it's a lifestyle. It always amused me when I would ask someone, "Do you have any warrants?" And they would say, "I don't know." I would respond, "If I had a warrant for my arrest I would know about it," meaning it's kind of a big deal. To people who lead a criminal lifestyle, however, it's just another proverbial can they are kicking down the road as far as possible. The police eventually catch up with those folks, and they are forced to face the music. By the way, just because a warrant is for a misdemeanor offense doesn't mean the arrest poses a low-risk to officer safety.

Felony warrants, especially those for violent crimes, up the ante in the risk department, though. Some felons will use any means necessary to avoid being caught and sent to jail, up to and including assaulting or killing a police officer. I've watched many videos of traffic stops that turned violent against the officer because the driver had a warrant and was willing to kill a cop to avoid being caught. It's not logical, but unfortunately, it happens.

Other Benefits of Traffic Stops

From traffic stops, I have removed illegal and stolen guns from the streets, preventing them from being used in other violent crimes. From traffic stops, I have recovered missing persons, kidnapped persons, and runaway children. I have saved the lives of people having medical emergencies while driving, such as heart attacks and diabetic emergencies. If a diabetic's blood sugar gets dangerously low while driving, they can present as impaired. I stopped one such woman on a state highway in the middle of a sunny day; she was varying her speed and swerving. It took her a while to finally stop, but when I approached her window, it was immediately obvious that something was wrong. My daughter is a juvenile diabetic, so I recognized the signs of low blood sugar and called EMS. We got the woman's blood sugar back to normal, then called a friend to come and drive her away.

Traffic stops are an enforcement tool vital to the police officer's ability to curb crime, violent and otherwise. If you think some city worker in a hybrid compact car with a yellow light and a clipboard can replace the role of the police officer in traffic enforcement, you have checked your intelligence at the door. What will happen when a traffic monitor stops a vehicle for a minor violation, unaware that the occupants have drugs in the vehicle that they don't want to be discovered? Or, unaware that an occupant is armed and has a warrant for which they aren't ready to go to jail? Or, unaware that an occupant has just committed a violent crime and doesn't want to be caught? What will happen when the wolf doesn't want to face the sheepdog? He will not care whether it's a police officer or an unarmed traffic monitor with no arrest powers. He will not care if the civilian with the clipboard is not obligated to report suspicious or even criminal activity to the police. The wolf will strike, and the civilian will find himself in an unequal fight for his life, having no way to protect himself. Traffic stops are dangerous for *cops*, so why put unarmed civilian lives in danger by giving them the job?

Pretextual Traffic Stops

Pretextual stops are under scrutiny from anti-police activists and legislators across the country. Their disdain for the police—and more specifically, their disdain for personal responsibility and law and order—motivates them to influence and create policies that cripple our ability to do the job effectively. Most of the enforcement activities I discussed above are considered pretextual stops, even when a police officer is unaware of looming criminal activity. The argument against pretextual stops has been going on since long before the "traffic without police" idea surfaced. Its motivation, however, is similar: cripple the cops.

For instance, the Maine Legislature is in the process of enacting Legislative Document 417, "An Act To Protect Maine's

Drivers from Pretextual Traffic Stops."[11] A summary of the bill reads as follows.

> "*This bill prohibits a law enforcement officer from stopping a motor vehicle an occupant of which the law enforcement officer suspects is engaging in criminal activity for a motor vehicle violation not related to that criminal activity. The bill also provides that evidence obtained in a traffic stop in violation of this provision may not be used in any criminal proceeding.*"[12]

That means, for example, if an officer stops someone for a minor traffic violation—with no other suspicions—then encounters the driver with drugs or guns in plain view, the officer cannot use that evidence to prosecute the driver for the violations that arise out of possessing drugs and guns illegally. It's a free pass. In a nutshell, this bill would remove a valuable proactive policing tool used to locate wanted persons, recover illegal guns, discover missing and kidnapped persons, seize illegal drugs, remove impaired drivers from the streets, and so on. Furthermore, the bill treats evidence obtained during pretextual stops the same as "fruits of the poisonous tree," a fourth amendment doctrine that eliminates evidence obtained by an illegal search. The bill should be called, "An Act to Protect Maine's Criminals from Apprehension."

In San Diego, California, a Citizens Advisory Board on Police/Community Relations reviewed a proposed "pilot moratorium on pretextual stops" in 2019. Board member and president of the San Diego Police Officers Association Jack Schaeffer wasn't having it. He wrote in a San Diego Union-Tribune op-ed that he supported the use of pretextual stops by police, stating,

> "*San Diego has been identified as one of the safest big cities in the nation. That recognition does not happen without one of the best police departments in the nation. We are located just a few miles from one of the most violent places in the world, which reportedly had over 2,000 murders last year. San Diego averages around 40 murders annually. SDPD officers and detectives solve over 90%*

of the murders that occur here. Catching violent offenders quickly prevents them from hurting additional victims. Proactive police work, including pretext stops, can keep our residents safe. When officers stop vehicles for observed violations of the vehicle code and identify the occupants, detectives can solve violent crimes."[13]

Schaeffer went on to point out that the Oklahoma City Bombing case was solved out of a pretextual stop. Timothy McVeigh was stopped for a registration violation (no license plates) and was arrested for having an illegal weapon. While in custody, investigators successfully tied him to the bombing. Additionally, serial killer Randy Kraft was apprehended during a traffic stop; officers found the dead body of a marine in the passenger seat of his car after stopping him for a violation.[14] Ted Bundy's first arrest in 1975 began with a traffic stop when a Utah police officer observed him driving in the early morning hours with no headlights. During the stop, the officer discovered a gym bag containing a ski mask, ice pick, and handcuffs. This pretextual traffic stop is what led police to connect Bundy to unsolved murders in Oregon and Washington State.[15] Bundy escaped custody and continued his killing spree. His reign of terror came to an end in 1978 due to *another* pretextual traffic stop. While driving a stolen vehicle, he was stopped in Pensacola, Florida for an expired license plate[16] and subsequently apprehended.

In addition to these high-profile cases, pretextual stops continue to enable police to bring fugitives to justice. In April 2021, a Nashville officer stopped a vehicle for mismatched license plates, unaware that the passenger was Marvin Veiga, a murderer on the Massachusetts State Police most wanted list. He pulled two knives and attempted to attack the officer, who was forced to fatally shoot him.[17] In October 2016, a Berkeley County, West Virginia deputy sheriff stopped a vehicle for a traffic violation, discovering passenger Jarhod Kearney was wanted in Union County, N.J., with nationwide extradition on charges of robbery conspiracy, kidnapping, unlawful possession of a weapon, and aggravated assault.[18] In January 2016, An Arizona Trooper stopped a vehicle in Casa Grande for swerving out of its lane. After being given false information by the occupants, he discovered the driver to be Keith Rogers, the subject of a nationwide manhunt with homicide and armed robbery warrants out of Louisiana. Rogers and his accomplice, Antoinette Wong—who had a warrant for armed robbery—had kidnapped a 7-year-old boy at gunpoint during a home invasion and Wong's 2-year-old son, who were both also safely recovered from the vehicle.[19] In December of 2012, police stopped a vehicle on I-95 in Ridgeland, South Carolina for following a vehicle too closely. The driver was identified by officers as Nelson Vargas, wanted in Florida for first-degree murder, aggravated battery with a firearm, and use of a firearm during the commission of a felony. He was arrested without incident.[20] Every single one of these traffic stops, resulting in the apprehension of violent fugitives, was a pretextual stop. If these officers had been prohibited from making stops based on traffic violations, these wolves would've been free a little longer to potentially victimize more sheep.

Most cops would agree, some of the best police work, such as the above examples, comes from pretextual traffic stops. Opponents argue that there is no correlation between traffic problems and crime. Among those who disagree is Marcus Felson, a sociology professor at USC and Rutgers University School of Criminal Justice. He believes, "traffic violations are an extension of criminals' lack of self-control."[21] Enforcing minor traffic laws is the broken windows policing of public roadways, the theory of which is the reduction of crime by means of addressing minor offenses.

Tying the Hands of Police

Banning pretextual traffic stops is not just an incredulous idea. It's actually already law in Washington State and New Mexico. A common argument among its proponents is that pretextual stops lead to racial profiling. Once again, the premise of this argument hinges on the false narrative of systemic racism in American law enforcement, against which we have already made a solid argument. Courts cannot determine that an officer has a racist state of mind just because it is "possible" in the case of a pretextual stop, which is exactly what the argument is trying to establish.

State of Washington v. Ladson, 1997

State v. Ladson was the case that banned pretextual stops in Washington. On October 5, 1995, Richard Fogle and his passenger Thomas Ladson—both African American—were stopped by gang unit officers Jim Mac and Cliff Ziesmer in Thurston County, Washington. While conducting routine patrol, the officers recognized Fogle; they had heard a street rumor that he was involved in drugs. They made a traffic stop based on a registration violation; Fogle's license plates had been expired for five days. Once the vehicle was stopped, the officers discovered Fogle was driving on a suspended driver's license, for which they placed him under arrest and secured him in their patrol vehicle. They conducted a search of the vehicle incident to that arrest. Because police officers do not search vehicles with occupants still inside, they instructed Ladson to exit the vehicle. He had left his jacket on the passenger seat when he got out. While searching the vehicle the officers located a stolen handgun in Ladson's jacket pocket, along with several baggies of marijuana and approximately $600 in cash. Ladson was charged with unlawful possession of a controlled substance with intent to deliver while armed with a deadly weapon, and possession of a stolen firearm.[22] This was excellent police work.

Ladson's attorneys filed a pretrial motion to suppress the evidence against him on the grounds that it was obtained during a pretextual traffic stop. The court agreed, ruling "Pretextual stops by law enforcement officers are violative of the [State] Constitution."[23] Between the time of this ruling and the appeal that was later filed by the prosecutor in this case, the U.S. Supreme Court ruled in favor of pretextual traffic stops in Whren v. United States (1996).[24] The Appellate Court, therefore, reversed the lower court's decision based on the newly decided Whren (1996) case. The case ultimately went to the State Supreme Court in 1999, which ruled in favor of Ladson, declaring that pretextual traffic stops are a violation of the state's constitution, which the court contended provides broader protections.

State constitutions remain within the boundaries of the U.S. Constitution, meaning, the state cannot increase power beyond that of the U.S. Constitution, but it can further limit power. In other words, it cannot get larger in scope, but it can get smaller. That is the case in Washington. Article 1, Section 7 of the State Constitution, is its counterpart to the Fourth Amendment of the U.S. Constitution. The State Supreme Court's interpretation of the difference in language is what has informed their rulings against pretextual traffic stops. The Fourth Amendment's language is quite clear.

> *"The right of the people to be secure in their persons, houses, papers, and effects, against unreasonable searches and seizures, shall not be violated, and no warrants shall issue but upon probable cause, supported by oath or affirmation, and particularly describing the place to be searched, and the persons or things to be seized."*

Article 1, Section 7 of the Washington State Constitution is more vague.

> *"No person shall be disturbed in his private affairs, or his home invaded, without authority of law."*

Despite its ambiguity, the State Supreme Court determined in State of Washington v. Simpson (1980) that Article 1, Section 7 provides greater protection to Washington residents than its federal counterpart.[25]

The ruling in State v. Ladson is another point in the column of the lawless. Ladson was carrying prepackaged drugs, large amounts of cash, and a stolen gun, which is typical of drug traffickers. He was the passenger in a vehicle that was lawfully stopped, whose driver was lawfully arrested, prompting a lawful search of the vehicle incident to arrest. The cops did everything right. They protected the sheep from a wolf, but liberal interpretations of law, that give more rights to criminals, released the wolf back into the fold.

Ironically, the State Supreme Court walked back their Ladson decision, without actually reversing it, in State v. Arreola in 2012, by ruling on "Mixed-Motive" traffic stops. The decision states,

> *"So long as a police officer actually, consciously, and independently determines that a traffic stop is reasonably necessary in order to address a suspected traffic infraction, the stop is not pretextual in violation of article I, section 7, despite other motivations for the stop."*[26]

State of Washington v. Gilberto Arreola, 2012

On October 10, 2009, Officer Tony Valdivia of the Mattawa Police Department responded to a possible DUI in progress. Officer Valdivia located a vehicle matching the description from the report and followed behind the vehicle for approximately half of a mile to observe driving behavior. The officer did not observe any signs of impairment but did observe that the vehicle had an altered exhaust in violation of state law. Therefore, the officer initiated a traffic stop. Upon approaching the vehicle, the officer detected an odor of alcohol, observed the driver's eyes to be bloodshot and watery, and observed several open containers of alcohol in plain view inside the vehicle. Gilberto Arreola was ultimately determined to be intoxicated, was cited for the muffler violation, failure to show proof of insurance, and arrested for driving with a revoked license, DUI, and outstanding warrants. Again, this was excellent police work.

But, wait a minute. Isn't this a pretextual traffic stop? According to the Washington Supreme Court, it sure is! However, the trial court stated, because Officer Valdivia testified that he often stopped vehicles for muffler violations and because the muffler violation was an "actual reason for the stop," that the officer "would have stopped the vehicle, once following it, even if he wasn't suspicious of a DUI, and even though his primary purpose for stopping the vehicle was to further investigate a possible

DUI." Therefore, it was a "mixed-motive" stop, and not necessarily pretextual. The State Supreme Court upheld Arreola's conviction, stating in part,

> *"A mixed-motive stop does not violate article I, section 7 so long as the police officer making the stop exercises discretion appropriately. Thus, if a police officer makes an independent and conscious determination that a traffic stop to address a suspected traffic infraction is reasonably necessary in furtherance of traffic safety and the general welfare, the stop is not pretextual. That remains true even if the legitimate reason for the stop is secondary and the officer is motivated primarily by a hunch or some other reason that is insufficient to justify a stop. In such a case, the legitimate ground is an independent cause of the stop, and privacy is justifiably disturbed due to the need to enforce traffic regulations, as determined by an appropriate exercise of police discretion. Any additional reason or motivation of the officer does not affect privacy in such a case, nor does it interfere with the underlying exercise of police discretion, because the officer would have stopped the vehicle regardless...a police officer cannot and should not be expected to simply ignore the fact that an appropriate and reasonably necessary traffic stop might also advance a related and more important police investigation."[27]*

This is the sound of a court talking out of both sides of its mouth. A traffic stop for a legitimate traffic violation is unconstitutional if the officer has other motives—such as investigating suspicions of criminal activity—unless the officer would've stopped the vehicle for the traffic violation anyway.

State of Iowa v Scottize Brown, 2019

Other State Supreme Courts have likewise heard cases and made determinations regarding pretextual traffic stops, Such as the State of Iowa v Scottize Brown. Brown, an African American woman, was stopped in Waterloo, Iowa in 2017 for an improper turn and a license plate light violation. Before initiating the stop, the officer ran the license plate, discovering the owner of the vehicle—not Brown—was tied to local gang activity. When the officer activated his emergency lights to signal the vehicle to stop, Brown did not immediately stop. It wasn't until a moment later when the officer activated his siren that Brown finally brought the vehicle to a stop. As a side note, a driver taking an unusually long time to stop when the blue lights come on is a huge red flag. There are several reasons a driver may not stop right away. They may be looking for a more populated or lighted area for safety reasons, they may be intoxicated and have a delayed reaction to the blue lights behind them, or they may be stalling to hide something—like a gun or drugs—so the officer doesn't see it when he walks up to the vehicle. This delay would have caused the officer to be suspicious something else was going on. It's also a detail an officer might document in his report to support a DUI arrest.

When the officer approached the vehicle, he observed an open container of alcohol in the driver's cup holder and smelled an odor of alcohol coming from the vehicle. When he asked for her driver's license, Brown was unable to produce one and gave the officer her name and date of birth. With this information, the officer discovered she was driving on a suspended license. He transported her to the police station, where he conducted field sobriety tests which resulted in several clues of intoxication. Brown subsequently refused a breath test and was charged with OWI, Operating a Vehicle While Intoxicated (Iowa's version of DUI). Brown had a prior OWI conviction, which made this an escalated charge of aggravated misdemeanor under Iowa law. This was yet another example of good police work.

From a road cop's perspective, there is absolutely nothing unusual about this traffic stop. This is a textbook DUI arrest. Dare I say, every stop that results in a DUI arrest is pretextual. Unlike other crimes that occur in motor vehicles on public roadways—such as drug or gun offenses—Impaired driving occurs *only* in motor vehicles. Apprehending drunk or drugged drivers would be impossible without the investigative tool of pretextual stops. Cops observe driving behavior to detect impairment. In other words, if someone is driving drunk, every minor traffic violation—driving outside their lane, failure to use headlights at night, driving too slow, swerving, etc.—is a direct result of their impairment. A good cop will recognize these indicators and stop the vehicle with the probable cause created by the traffic violation. The DUI investigation that follows is clearly the pretext, but the traffic violation is what gives an officer reasonable suspicion that the driver is intoxicated. Probable cause for a DUI arrest cannot be established without physical contact with that driver and proof of vehicle control. Without pretextual stops, how will police fight the crime of driving impaired? Pretextual stops are not only supported by the U.S. Supreme Court, they are necessary to do our jobs.

Brown appealed her conviction, challenging the stop as pretextual, claiming the pretext was the result of racial profiling. However, according to the Iowa Supreme Court's decision, she made no claims nor presented any evidence that the officer was even aware she was African American when he made the decision to initiate the traffic stop.[28] To be clear, her license was suspended; she shouldn't even have been driving, let alone driving drunk. And this wasn't just a one-time thing; she had a history of driving drunk shown by her prior conviction. Additionally, there is a high likelihood that Brown's two arrests do not represent the only two times she has driven drunk. MADD reports the average drunk driver has driven drunk 80 times before their first arrest.[29] Brown was engaged in criminal behavior that put lives in danger and, like many others, attempted to hide behind a racial profiling defense instead of taking responsibility for her actions. Just because she's African American and is caught breaking the law doesn't mean the cop is racist. It means she's a criminal and the cop was doing his job. Fortunately, her conviction was upheld by the Iowa Supreme Court.

The cases we have examined don't even represent the tip of the iceberg as it relates to the censure of traffic stops. This is just a sampling to illustrate another rope being used to tie the hands of police and embolden the lawless. Every time we unravel their rope, the anti-police dissidents—whether they come in the form of liberal politicians, activist prosecutors, radical media, or the riotous mob—will always create a new one. Perhaps the most devastating—the "defund the police" movement—will be the rope that hangs us.

Chapter 9
Defund the Police

"A true police officer fights not because he hates what's in front of him, but because he loves who stands behind him."
—Unknown

In the aftermath of the death of George Floyd at the hands of Minneapolis police officers, the call to defund the police became a major theme of nationwide protests, given momentum by organizations such as the Movement for Black Lives, Black Lives Matter, and Black Visions Collective. Many believed it would not go beyond an outcry of public anger; little did we know it would go from protest to policy in a matter of a few months, as cities began to drain much-needed financial resources from their police budgets to appease the mobocracy. This crusade dominated the news cycle for weeks, overlaid with images and videos of police vehicles being burned, businesses being looted, and police officers being assaulted. While American cops were fighting a battle against lawless mobs in the streets of our major cities, politicians were selling them out to public opinion—albeit minority public opinion—in city hall. This is the very definition of mob rule.

By August 2020, several major U.S. cities had either cut their police budgets or diverted funds from the police to various social services. Austin, Texas cut $150 million from the police budget, Seattle cut $3.5 million and diverted another $17 million. New York City cut nearly $1 billion from its police budget for 2021, reallocating some to mental health programs. Los Angeles cut its police budget by $150 million. San Francisco cut $120 million from the police and sheriff's departments. Oakland, California cut $14.6 million from their police budget. Washington, DC cut $15 million, Baltimore cut $22 million, Portland cut $16 million, Philadelphia cut $33 million, Newark, New Jersey cut $12 million, Hartford, Connecticut cut $1 million, Norman, Oklahoma cut $865,000, and Salt Lake City cut its police budget by $5.3 million.[1] These deep gouges in police budgets across the nation resulted in departments laying off cops and canceling academy classes.[2] Late to the ball game was the mayor of St. Louis, who in May 2021 proposed cutting $4 million from the city's police budget and eliminating approximately 100 vacant police officer positions.[3]

The Police Executive Research Forum in Washington, D.C. surveyed its membership of approximately 800 law enforcement agencies in July 2020 about the effects of the defund the police movement. Of the responding 258 agencies, 48% reported their budgets had been or likely would be decreased. About half of those agencies reported the budget cuts to be in the five to ten percent range. The survey showed the budget cuts would have the greatest impact on equipment, training, hiring officers, and overtime spending.[4]

PERF's survey also revealed that not everybody was defunding their police. 16% of respondents indicated their budgets would increase. Cities like Roanoke, Virginia, were seeking to increase their police manpower to deal with a rise in crime rates. Local activists tried to pressure the city to slash its police budget, but city leaders responded to their community's plea, hiring more police and giving raises to existing officers. Nonetheless, the city has struggled to maintain its force, having lost 20% of its department in 2020. Several smaller Texas agencies were also trying to increase their police roster. One sheriff's office offered signing bonuses for jail deputies.[5] Even some of Michigan's larger cities were increasing their police protection. City council members in Lansing, Grand Rapids, and Detroit all proposed measures to cut massive numbers from their police budgets, but in all three cities, the cuts failed.[6]

Defunding the police has much harsher consequences the farther down the food chain you are. The policing situation in America's largest cities—such as New York City, Los Angeles, or Seattle—is not representative of most of the country. The Bureau of Justice Statistics says 88% of the nation's law enforcement agencies have less than 50 officers. Many of these small agencies are already struggling to fill vacant positions and keep officers on the streets to meet collective bargaining manpower minimums. Small agencies sometimes have to get creative to fund equipment needs, such as applying for grants and putting tax levies on their local ballots, illustrating the constant competition for available resources just to maintain the status quo. When these agencies lose funds, the first thing to be sacrificed is usually safety. When fewer officers have to carry more of the workload—working overtime shifts, handling more calls per shift—their inevitable exhaustion puts their safety at greater risk. Additionally, for agencies with less than 20 officers—factoring in vacation time, sick leave, etc.—a jurisdiction can be left with only one or two officers on the road at a time, often with the closest available back-up being miles away. In small-town and rural America, defunding the police doesn't make us safe—as the ACLU opined—it puts us in danger.

The majority of Americans—including African Americans—understand this. A Gallup poll released in the summer of 2021 says that 81% of African Americans do *not* want a decrease in police presence. Additionally, 79% of African Americans who have had an interaction with police in the last year want police presence in their neighborhoods to remain the same or increase.[7] It is clear that the demands to defund the police contradict the opinion of American citizens. A Pew Research poll says more Americans want to increase police funds than those who want to decrease police funds.[8] If organizations like Black Lives Matter are genuinely fighting for justice for African Americans, why are they relentlessly fighting to effectively cripple the police protection wanted by a majority of their alleged constituents? This supports an earlier assertion that BLM doesn't represent African Americans, but the mob of lawless thugs rallying to dismantle the country's criminal justice system.

Paying the Price in Blood

Why do we want to defund our police in a society plagued by a virus of violence? While the murder rates in America may have decreased over the last several decades, the aggravated assault rates—incidents of people *trying* to kill someone else—have skyrocketed. So, to what do we credit the decrease in murder rates? A large factor is medical technology. A 2002 study published in the journal *Homicide Studies,* by scholars from Harvard and the University of Massachusetts, concluded that the advances in medical technology since 1970 have prevented about 75% of would-be murders. Meaning, with 1970s-level medical technology, today's murder rate would be approximately three times higher than it is.[9] The fifty-year decrease in the murder rate is not due to less violence, but due to medical science outrunning the violence, in addition to advances in policing and increases in incarceration rates of violent criminals.

The rising violence rates in our society boil over from a brewing cauldron of ingredients including drugs, gangs, poverty, racism, and guns. Add to the pot the ever-increasing dissemination of media violence, and the result is a 150% increase in the homicide rate for males fifteen to nineteen years of age between 1980 and 2000. Homicide is the number two cause of death in that age group, and number one among African American teens.[10]

Despite this rise in violence across the nation, "woke" local government officials are personally, financially, and professionally crippling the police, using them as political pawns. When these people play politics with their police—submitting to the demands of domestic terrorists—their citizens pay the price in blood. One year after the "defund the police" movement began, the FBI reported a 10% increase in murders nationwide, but that doesn't even account for cities like New York, Los Angeles, Chicago, and others that did not report any stats to the federal government. To get a better picture of the nation's crime trends, you have to dig into Compstat reports and other independent reporting systems and thread them together. They tell a grim tale of an obvious spike in violent crime across the nation in the wake of these irresponsible financial policies.

Comparing the trends from 2020 to 2021–just in agencies that were first to jump on the "defund the police" bandwagon–reveals an increase in murder rates almost across the board. Los Angeles experienced a 23% increase, San Francisco and Salt Lake City doubled their murder rates, Oakland, California saw an 84% increase, Portland's murders skyrocketed 1,100%, Philadelphia was up 25%, Newark, New Jersey increased by 38%, Hartford, Connecticut jumped 64%, and homicides increased in Baltimore and Washington, D.C. Other cities with notable increases in their murder rates in 2021 are Mesa, Arizona up 100%; Little Rock up 62%; Denver up 69%; West Minster, Colorado up 300%, Minneapolis up 50%; Albuquerque up 126%; Akron, Ohio up 150%; Columbus, Ohio up 103%; and Toledo, Ohio up 71%. New York City, which has been considered the epicenter of the rise in crime, has experienced a significant increase in violent crime including rape, felonious assault, shootings, and a 103% increase in hate crimes.[11]

These grisly numbers are not an anomaly. They are not due to an increase in gun sales to law-abiding citizens, they are not the result of stress related to the pandemic, and they are not the result of less belief in police legitimacy due to protests of police violence.[12] They are the proximate result of intentionally weakening the nation's police agencies and draining their financial resources at the demand of an anti-police, riotous, Marxist mob.

As if these facts are not egregious enough, local governments continued to drain their cities' police budgets while the victims were stacking up. Oakland–with its 84% increase in homicides–took an additional $18.4 million away from their police department in the Summer of 2021. The impact of this cut cost the city 50 police officers. Chief LeRonne Armstrong took to the airwaves to speak out against the crippling of his police department.

> *"Today, we find ourselves in a crisis…It now has us currently at 65 homicides for the year. That's a 90 percent increase compared to last year. Our shootings are up over 70 percent this year. Our robberies are up 11 percent this year… Our carjackings are up nearly 88 percent. So, we see clearly that crime is out of control in the city of Oakland, and our response was for less police resources."[13]*

As Chief Armstrong struggled to staff his department to deal with the skyrocketing crime rates, the city put the money they took from him into new initiatives like the Department of Violence Prevention (DVP) which employs life coaches and "violence interrupters," and the Mobile Assistance Community Responders of Oakland, or MACRO. Under the MACRO project, alternative crisis responders will handle mental health issues and firefighters will respond to non-violent 911 calls, instead of police officers. Oakland Mayor Libby Schaaf praised the city council for making bold and progressive moves to re-imagine public safety, but in the next breath said the cut would "destroy" the city's public safety structure.[14] In her July 1, 2021, weekly briefing she said,

> *"Unfortunately, it also cuts 50 police officers and much-needed future academies, which will significantly reduce police staffing, delay 911 response times, and force our officers to work even more overtime shifts, which are expensive and unsafe for officers and residents alike."[15]*

President Barry Donelan of the Oakland Police Officer's Association predicted that the senseless cuts in the police budget would increase the number of unanswered 911 calls.

What Oakland did is a growing trend in the so-called police reform movement. The logic behind it is that lower police contact with citizens will decrease police use of force incidents. Again, this idea is based on the false narrative of systemic racism in law enforcement. The local politicians making these policies are doing so without counting the cost, treating the police as an enemy of the people instead of the valuable resource that they are.

Here's why it won't work. Police officers undergo hundreds of hours of continued training throughout their careers. The topics range from understanding autism, to recognizing human trafficking, to responding to mental health emergencies, to crisis intervention, to missing persons, and any other non-emergency situation you can imagine. I was a trained member of a county-wide Crisis Intervention Team, geared toward dealing with the mentally ill. The point is, there is no agency or department better trained to deal with non-emergency calls than the police. Why, then, do we want to divert funds away from the police to create separate agencies to deal with the same things police are equipped and trained to deal with? Notice these programs tend to emphasize "unarmed civilian public safety employees" in the place of police. Those who have underestimated the need for police and overestimated the effectiveness of counselors or interventionists in volatile situations we face will eventually come back around when they are repeatedly confronted with the reality that the police had to be called anyway.

Let me tell you a story about an elderly lady who called 911 to report her adult grandson was talking out of his head and claiming to be the messiah. I was working an off-duty detail but was requested by road officers to respond due to the sensitivity of the situation. The young man they made contact with was very clearly mental, but also confrontational, and his actions had his poor grandmother terrified. He had not violated any laws, but we were confident he needed a mental health evaluation. In order to sign an emergency order, he needed to meet one of four criteria. The officers on scene were undecided if what they had was enough. I talked to the young man briefly; he was very hostile toward us, and even got verbal with his grandmother in our presence. We asked him to go to the hospital voluntarily, but he wasn't having any of it. After our conversation, I was confident we had met the standard of state law to take him to the hospital against his will. Fortunately, we were able to talk him into getting into a police cruiser, and no force was necessary. He was transported to the hospital without further incident, and placed on a 72-hour hold for evaluation.

But even the mental health system is not foolproof. Cops frequently transport suicidal persons to the hospital for an emergency admission. According to Ohio law, a 72-hour hold doesn't mean the patient will be held for 72 hours, it means the behavioral health professionals can only keep them involuntarily for 72 business hours before a hearing is required. Most of the time, in our case, the hospital would release them before we could finish the paperwork. That's what happened with this young man. The next day, officers received another 911 call from his grandmother stating he had claimed to be the son of God and set himself on fire. When officers arrived he was walking down the street in flames, his skin melting off his body. This young man had obvious mental problems; if the hospital had kept him, he likely wouldn't have been able to hurt himself. If a civilian counselor or violence interrupter had been sent to handle this call, they would've had to call the police due to the confrontational and defiant nature of the patient. Sending civilians to do the job of the police will only delay the inevitable and put people at risk. It won't work.

They—the proponents of *defund the police*—got what they wanted. Unfortunately, the people paying the highest price for it are communities already plagued with poverty, drugs, gangs, and violence, the majority of whose citizens want the same or *more* police presence.[16] But while lawmakers—such as Representative Cori Bush who advocates against police—pay tens of thousands of dollars for private security[17], those communities who need it the most get less police presence. While many cities are moving to reverse course and correct their mistakes, there are cities like St. Louis that are still barreling down the path of self-destruction.

Bush, elected in 2020 to Missouri's First District, went viral for her television interview with CBS on August 4, 2021, during which she insisted she would not back down from her *defund the police* demands. The former Ferguson BLM protester defended her expensive security detail, inferring in the interview that it was necessary to protect her from those who have threatened her life, including police officers. When pressed to clarify her accusation against officers, she changed the subject[18] and wouldn't provide any specific examples. She has brought her anti-police activism from the streets of Ferguson to the halls of Congress, frequently making statements that appear to be statistically unsound and premised on the false Ferguson narrative previously discussed.

> *"I don't care if you don't like the words, [defund the police]. How much more should you not like the fact that Black folks in this community are dying at the rates that we're dying at the hands of police? No one is dealing with it. So, because they left that piece for me, this is still there, I have to attack it as hard and as fast as I can."*[19]

Statistics don't bear up her claim that Blacks are dying at the hands of police in her community. What statistics *do* prove, however, is that St. Louis, the city she represents, is experiencing a spike in violent crime, and has a very high rate of Black-on-Black homicides. As of August 2021, 118 people were murdered in St. Louis since she took office, 108—or 92%—of whom were African American. Sixteen of those victims were juveniles. Of the suspects in these homicides, 58 of them were African American, and 60 of them were of unknown status.[20] In contrast, zero African Americans were killed by police in St. Louis, or the State of Missouri. Zoom out to the entire nation, and four unarmed African Americans were killed by police in the same time frame.[21] Perhaps Bush's crusade, along with many of her contemporaries, should be saving Black men, women, and children, from the violence of their own neighborhoods. The answer to that problem is complex, but it certainly doesn't include defunding the St. Louis Metro Police to the tune of over $4 million and eliminating 100 vacant positions.

Despite St. Louis being ranked the second most dangerous city in the nation in 2020—with a violent crime rate of 1,927 per 100,000 residents—Bush[22] has publicly applauded the defunding of the SLMPD, stating,

> "[The] decision to defund the St. Louis Metropolitan Police Department is historic. It marks a new future for our city."[23]

I agree, it marks a future of continued violence and guarantees that the Gateway to the West will continue to rank high among America's bloodiest cities.

Disarm the Police

In addition to defunding the police, some are suggesting we disarm the police, or replace them altogether with civilian agencies. The logic behind this is terribly flawed—"if we take lethal force capability and authority away from police, then violence will decrease." As I pointed out early in the book, that's about the equivalent of claiming that closing prisons will reduce crime, or taking water hoses away from firefighters will cut back on arsons. Aside from making no sense, it essentially would replace sheepdogs with sheep. It would erase the thin blue line. This is not a parody, this is an actual initiative in some local governments.

Ithaca, New York

Ithaca, New York. Mayor Svante Myrick wants to replace the police department with a new "Department of Community Solutions and Public Safety." He said the Ithaca Police Department does an admirable and professional job but suggested that overpolicing worsens mental illness and drug abuse. The Mayor's new department would be led by a civilian and have two branches: an unarmed branch of community solution workers and an armed public safety branch that responds to and investigates criminal offenses. Oh, and by the way, existing police officers who have served with professionalism will have to reapply if they want one of the new armed public safety positions.[24]

In 2020, then Governor Andrew Cuomo issued a directive to all law enforcement agencies in New York to draft a police reform plan or lose state funding (prompting this proposal), but Ithaca's mayor has proposed the most radical reforms. This is the mayor that announced in 2016 he wanted Ithaca to be the first city with a "supervised injection facility," where people with heroin addictions could be supervised by a nurse when they shoot up.[25]

Notice, also, that the plan calls for armed public safety to respond to and investigate crime. This is commensurate with eliminating proactive policing, which would include traffic enforcement and, therefore, pretextual traffic stops that contribute to so much effective policing. Anti-police government leaders know there is more than one way to skin a cat—they must think we're not smart enough to recognize the bait and switch.

Charlotte, North Carolina

In Charlotte, North Carolina, a city councilman made news in May 2021 when he told a local newspaper police should be disarmed so they are forced to resolve conflicts with words instead of force. He blamed armed police officers for instigating violence and insisted—even when confronting violent and armed criminals—they should use communication skills.[26] Firstly, someone should explain to the councilman that communication skills don't stop bullets. Secondly, perhaps the councilman should go on a ride-along with Charlotte-Mecklenburg's finest and educate himself on the stellar communication skills police officers use and what they *actually* do on a daily basis.

There is a large gap in public perception—albeit a vocal minority—between what is believed police officers do versus what they actually do. At the risk of sounding melodramatic, real police officers don't drive around shooting criminals every shift, like their counterparts who play cops on the screen. Real cops prepare for but dread the day they are confronted by the wolf in a deadly force encounter. We've already discussed the resistance to taking life, and the documented statements made by officers seconds before and after using deadly force—such as "I don't want to shoot you, bro," and the officer collapsing in the street, sobbing—indicating immediate remorse. Therefore, it is a gross misrepresentation to infer that police officers are quick to revert to deadly force.

Officer Safety

A Time Magazine article, entitled, "What the U.S. Can Learn from Countries Where Cops Don't Carry Guns,"[27] published in the summer of 2020, contrasts American policing with nations like Norway, for instance, whose population is about halfway between Los Angeles and New York City—5.3 million to be more specific. Norwegian police are unarmed and deploy special armed units only when dealing with armed and violent subjects. Even then, they must obtain authorization before pulling the trigger. Can you imagine how many more dead American cops we would have on our hands if they had to request permission from a superior officer before they could defend themselves? Paul Hirschfield, a professor of sociology at Rutgers University, was cited in the piece pointing out that the European Convention of Human Rights prohibits officers from shooting unless it is "absolutely necessary." Hirschfield said the following in the way of contrast:

> "[T]he overriding goals of current law, policy, and training on the use of force [in America}... [are] to protect the safety of police."[28]

Insomuch as his assertion points out, American policing doesn't sound far off from that of Norway and countries with similar models, such as Finland and the United Kingdom. The Constitution of the United States and case law—Tennessee v.

Garner, 471 U.S. 1 (1985) and Graham v. Connor, 490 U.S. 386 (1989)—prohibits police use of deadly force unless an officer reasonably believes that his or her life or that of another is in jeopardy, in which case it is *absolutely necessary*. Protecting the safety of a police officer in the performance of his or her duties *should* be the priority. What other goal would make the use of deadly force absolutely necessary, or necessary at all, for that matter?

Another comparison made is that police in Norway work in cooperation with mental health professionals when dealing with mentally ill individuals. This is a popular talking point in the defund the police argument—cut money from police budgets to spend it on mental health professionals, who will then respond to "mental calls" instead of police. This is already taking place in many—if not most—law enforcement agencies in the U.S. This model takes on different shapes, but in my neck of the woods, we call it the "crisis intervention team," or CIT. It is a county-wide cooperative in which officers from each agency are trained by mental health professionals to deal with the unique needs of the mentally ill. Additionally, the county employs licensed clinical counselors who are available for call-outs when police are dealing with a suicidal or mentally ill person. It is not uncommon for these CIT responders—who carry police radios—to be dispatched with officers. In these cases, the counselor evaluates the individual and makes the ultimate determination as to what the next steps should be. We've been doing this for more than a decade; it's not a new idea. The difference is, we send the CIT counselor *with* the police, not *in place of* the police because mentally ill individuals can be irrational and violent during these calls.

This and other arguments for disarming the police, or replacing police officers with unarmed civilian public safety personnel, mediators, violence interrupters, or whatever you want to call them, are based on the false premise that police are the source of violence, as I stated earlier. Deducing that violence will plummet when armed police officers are removed from the equation just doesn't add up. Repeat after me, "The police are not the problem!"

Consent Policing vs. Coercive Policing

The true doctrine behind the *defund* and *disarm the police* movements is a distorted interpretation of "policing by consent," and the elimination of "coercive policing." *Policing by consent*—the model used in the U.K., Norway, and Finland—is based upon "Robert Peel's 9 Principles of Policing," for British police officers. Its definition is best described by principles 2-4.

> *"The power of the police to fulfill their functions and duties is dependent on public approval of their existence, actions, and behavior and on their ability to secure and maintain public respect. To secure and maintain the respect and approval of the public means also the securing of the willing co-operation of the public in the task of securing observance of laws. The extent to which the co-operation of the public can be secured diminishes proportionately the necessity of the use of physical force and compulsion for achieving police objectives."*[29]

To summarize, *policing by consent* means "the power of the police comes from the common consent of the public, rather than the power of the state."[30] The Time article above observes that this is why police in Norway, Finland, and the U.K. are unarmed—because they have the respect and consent of the people—and uses it to make an argument for disarming American police.

Again, this method is already used in American Law Enforcement. If this were not true, the anti-police mob wouldn't be working so hard to void public consent and damage police legitimacy. Where radical anti-police advocates go wrong, however, is in seeking policing by the consent of an individual, rather than the public as a whole. *Policing by consent* doesn't preclude the individual from consenting to the police or the rule of law. The "whole" consents for the police to hold the "one" accountable.

The power and authority of American police are vested in them by the government—by and for the people—however, consent (or moral authority) is granted by public trust (I'll call it public support). Law enforcement can be carried out with the power and authority of government, but it is much easier to do so with the support of the public. When public support decreases, it doesn't decrease the enforcement of law, but it increases the need to use force to do so. This is called, "coercive policing."

Notice above, *Robert Peel's Principles of Policing* draw a connection between public cooperation and use of force and compulsion (or coercion). Increasing the former decreases the latter. But one of the consequences of the latter is the loss of the former. The question before American law enforcement is, Where is the balance? This is the dichotomy of police legitimacy—the balance between consent and coercion.

Those who would defund, disarm, and disband the police argue that the police have no public support because of the use of force (despite legal justification). At the same time, the anti-police mob has pulled no punches in demonizing the whole of police, with the intention of preventing public support. There are multiple cases of police officers being provoked, for the purpose of drawing them into a use of force encounter. If the police respond with force, then the mob points the finger and says, "See! Police officers are violent, racist thugs!" The mobocracy that has been given the louder voice of our nation is crying for *policing by consent*, while sabotaging the efforts of police to increase consent by publicly provoking, abasing, humiliating, accusing, and condemning them. It's a catch-22. We're damned if we do and damned if we don't.

Even nations that operate under a *policing by consent* policy understand that it doesn't always work, and they are prepared to exercise coercive policing when necessary. Robert Peel's 6th Principle of Policing is:

> *"To use physical force only when the exercise of persuasion, advice, and warning is found to be insufficient to obtain public co-operation to an extent necessary to secure observance of law or to restore order, and to use only the minimum degree of physical force which is necessary on any particular occasion for achieving a police objective."*[31]

This closely mirrors the use of force policies of American Law Enforcement agencies. The earlier cited Graham v Connor case establishes the "objective reasonableness" standard in the use of force. Therefore, just about every law enforcement agency in the country includes some version of this language in their policy governing the use of force by police officers. Here are a few examples.

> *Seattle Police Department – An officer will use only force that is objectively reasonable, necessary, and proportional to the threat or resistance of a subject.*

> *Chicago Police Department – Department members may only use force that is objectively reasonable, necessary, and proportional in order to ensure the safety of a member or third person, stop an attack, make an arrest, control a subject, or prevent escape.*

> *Miami Police Department – Officers shall use only the minimum amount of force that is necessary to effect an arrest, apprehension, or physically control a violent or resisting person.*

The American model of policing is not an antithesis of *policing by consent.* But as long as there are wolves living among the sheep, the need for coercive policing—the need for sheepdogs, willing and able to go to battle with wolves— will exist. Defunding the police is a strategy to eliminate coercive policing by overwhelming the law enforcement system. To do this in a political and social climate that has withdrawn their consent (or support) of the police due to deceptive propaganda leaves a vacuum that will be filled with the mobocratic system that has flipped the criminal justice system upside down.

Comparing American policing with other nations that *police by consent* is comparing apples and oranges. Some argue American police agencies should learn from the London Metropolitan Police, for example, the majority of whose officers are unarmed. Only elite squads—comparable to a SWAT team—are trained and authorized to carry guns. England and Wales police officers fatally shot *only* 5 people in the first two months of 2016,[32] compared to 166 fatally shot in the U.S. in the same period.[33] To use these numbers to contrast the styles or success of policing in our separate nations is misleading. For starters, the United States has a population five times greater than England and Wales. However, comparing London and New York City—both with a population of more than 8 million and comparable police manpower—is more representational.

In 2020, The Metropolitan Police in London made 963 gun-related arrests and 2,976 edged weapon-related arrests.[34] NYPD made 4,253 gun-related arrests.[35] An analysis of this comparison may be: "Well, there are more guns in the U.S., therefore, they will make exponentially more gun arrests." This is only partially correct. There *are* more guns in the U.S., but that doesn't necessarily relate to more gun crimes. Guns don't commit crimes. People do.

Shockingly, London's violent crime rate was more than 4 times higher than New York City in the same year, according to the MPD's website and NYPD Compstat reports. New York City's offenses of misdemeanor assault, felonious assault, and homicide total 54,440 incidents.[36] London's offenses of violence without injury (compared to misdemeanor assault), violence with injury (compared to felonious assault), and homicide, total 220,528 incidents.[37] Despite there being fewer guns and gun arrests, the numbers do not necessarily show that the UK's strict *policing by consent* model is more successful in reducing crime than American Policing.

Obviously, demographics and social and political dynamics are much different in the UK, and their crime problem is equally as unique as ours, so the comparison will never be completely parallel. The conclusion that can be drawn, however, is that violent crime is no respecter of persons, or nations, and is not affected by whether or not the police are armed. London may have fewer guns—and therefore, less need to arm their police officers—but they have more reported victims of violent crime than the Big

Apple. And *that* is the most representative comparison.

The bottom line is, the argument to disarm the police is base-less and being used as a distraction from the real issues at hand: The violence being perpetrated by the wolf upon the sheep.

Refund the Police

We've comprehensively established that defunding, disarm-ing, and disbanding the police is a dangerous trend, the dire consequences of which have manifested in soaring violent crime rates nationwide. It has become so bad that some of the bright politicians who took money from the police have been forced by citizen outcry to reverse course and give the money back. In twelve large cities across the country, the cry to defund the police has been replaced by demands of law-abiding citizens to re-fund the police.

Many of the original thirteen cities that defunded their police, including New York City, Oakland, Baltimore, and Los Angeles are now planning to redirect tens of millions of dollars back into their police departments to address the increase in crime that re-sulted from defunding the police the prior year. In the meantime, the price of cowering under the political pressure of the mob was paid for by the blood of victims that didn't have to be victims.[38]

The city of Baltimore—which took $22 million from the po-lice in 2020—is now calling for a $27 million increase, after a group of its business owners threatened to withhold taxes un-til the city starts dealing with its increase in crime.[39] Oakland, California gave back $3.3 million of the $29 million they took, and the mayor has proposed a $24 million increase. Los Angeles' mayor wants to give back $50 million of the $150 million they took. Politicians that are now calling for the refunding of police claim it's a response to pandemic federal stimulus money and the post-pandemic economic revival in their cities, but the demand to defund the police was never about saving money. It was about demonizing and demoralizing America's cops, widening the di-vide between communities of color and law enforcement, and eroding law and order in our nation.

Minneapolis, Minnesota

At the epicenter of the *defund the police* movement was Minneapolis. Much like Seattle, while their police were fighting to protect their city from riotous and violent thugs on the streets in 2020, city hall was passing a measure to dismantle their police department altogether. It took eight residents—who decided to fight back—to force the city to bring to a screeching halt its negligent abandonment of law and order. Eight residents filed a lawsuit against the city, asking the court to grant a Writ of Mandamus to force the city to re-fund the police and hire more cops. In their petition, these residents alleged the City Council and Mayor were violating the city's charter, which prescribes the size of the police force based on population.

> *"The City Council and the Mayor are required by the City Charter to provide for public safety by funding and employing a working police force. The City Charter, in Article VII, section 7.3(c), requires the City Council to fund 0.0017 police per citizen in Minneapolis. Section 7.3(a) gives the Mayor "complete power over the establishment, maintenance, and command of the police department." As a result of these two provisions, the City Council must fund, and the Mayor must employ, 743 officers based on the number of Minneapolis residents in 2020."*[40]

In January 2020, the Minneapolis Police Department had 825 sworn officers,[41] well above the minimum required by the city charter. However, by July approximately 80 officers had either resigned or retired in the wake of several months of protests and rioting over the killing of George Floyd.[42] Additionally, Mayor Jacob Frey said on August 14, 2020, that he expected 100 officers to retire by the end of the year. These numbers, compounded by the cancellation of all 2020 academies, decreased the police department's manpower—and its ability to fill the vacancies—drastically.[43]

To make matters worse, the City Council announced that a veto-proof majority supported dismantling its police department. The lawsuit claimed that this effort, in addition to multiple public remarks made by city leadership disparaging the police department, created a hostile working environment. By the end of July, 111 officers were on medical leave (many for PTSD), leaving the police force at a strength of 634 sworn officers. Additionally, 200 officers had applied for disability retirement.[44]

The residents' petition painted a scathing and convincing portrait of a disintegrating Minneapolis Police Department. In an unprecedented decision, Judge Jamie Anderson of the Fourth Judicial District of Minnesota granted the Writ of Mandamus on July 1, 2021, ordering the City of Minneapolis to hire more cops. The Judge's order states in part:

> *"The City Charter... unambiguously creates a public right of the residents of the City of Minneapolis to a properly funded police force of at least 0.0017 employees per resident."*[45]

A "public right" is something created by a legislature that citizens can expect from their government, and hold them accountable for. The citizens of Minneapolis said, "Our city charter (an enactment of local legislature) established our *right* to have a certain number of police officers per resident. Our local government (the Mayor and City Council) is depriving us of that lawful right." The judge ruled in favor of the petitioners on the basis of that public right.

In August 2021, the city appealed the decision to the Minnesota Supreme Court, which upheld the order.[46] City leaders didn't give up, though. They put an amendment to the city charter on the ballot in November of 2021 which would've removed the police department. The citizens of Minneapolis resoundingly squashed the amendment in a show of support for their police department.[47]

Seattle, Washington

Seattle—another city hit hard by the *"defund the police"* movement—has a similar provision in its charter:

The Police Department shall consist of a Chief of Police and as many subordinate officers and employees as may by ordinance be prescribed. There shall be maintained adequate police protection in each district of the City. (The Charter of the City of Seattle, Article VI, Section 1).[48]

A strong argument could be made in Seattle for their public right to adequate police protection, and the city's failure to provide it. Were the innocent bystanders and business owners in the CHOP zone entitled to adequate police protection? What about the people who were killed there? The months of riots, attacks on police, and lack of police support from the City Council and community leaders demoralized Seattle's cops, leading to the resignation of an embattled chief, and the loss of more than 250 officers by the Summer of 2021. These events are the basis for a strong argument that Seattle city leaders have negligently deprived its citizens of their lawful right to "adequate" police protection.

Although criticized for her handling of the unrest, Mayor Jenny Durkan vetoed the City Council's measure that would've cut the police budget in half in 2020. In July 2021 she called for the rebuilding of the Seattle Police Department, making the following statement:

"It is a false choice between community-led solutions and police officers. We need both."[49]

Those 15 words should have been a sound bite on every news outlet in the country. They illustrate a point of commonality where we all can agree. Those of us who condemn the *defund the police* movement are not condemning social and community services, mental health services, or other programs that prevent crime and improve the lives of citizens. We do not have to choose between police and community programs; we do not have to choose between safety and health. Those two are separate issues that just happen to intersect on the streets of our nation. Conversely, it has been argued that proponents of the *defund the police* movement are not advocating for completely eliminating police, but increasing resources for non-police programs that target the root causes of crime. However, stripping funds from police to finance those programs has already proven to have deadly consequences.

Hidden in the Fine Print

After all the political back and forth, the unfair slighting of America's police officers, and the promises of local, state, and federal politicians to defund the police, the United States Congress passed pro-police language hidden deep within a 2022 budget resolution which *"may include funding the hiring of 100,000 new police officers nationwide."* And which also *"may include limiting or eliminating Federal payments…to local governments that defund the police."*[30] This proves two things. One, no one reads the fine print and, two, there *are* members of Congress who stand behind the brave men and women of American law enforcement.

If only every American could see and understand that police officers are so much more than armed enforcers of law. They are men and women who serve with compassion and empathy who *"become all things to all people so that by all possible means [they] might save some."*[31]

Chapter 10
War on Police

"A society that makes war against its police had better learn to make friends with its criminals." —Unknown

Police officers have become weary, wounded, and demoralized. They didn't enter this profession to fight the daily media battle that has put them in the crosshairs. Many of them have had enough. They are walking away from the profession they so diligently earned, so honorably served, and so thoroughly loved. As one cop put it, "[They're] forming a conga line down at the pension office!"[1] It has become unclear to many cops whether they're fighting the criminal element or their own government, who is supposed to provide the support and overwatch that is needed to successfully do their jobs. Police officers perform their duties under siege every day; they are already the target of organizations like Antifa and BLM. They endure the disdain and jeers of the self-righteous and the complaints of the underbelly of the population on a daily basis, and they do so with dignity and professionalism. But when police command staff, government executives, activist prosecutors, liberal judges, and local and state legislatures begin to target the cops instead of the criminals, that's when cops start planning their exit strategy. Unfortunately, that is *exactly* what is happening.

Senator John Thune of South Dakota echoed the consequences of abusing America's cops on July 15, 2021, during a Senate speech.

> *"It turns out that when you spend months vilifying police officers and demonizing them for doing their jobs, some of them no longer want to stay, and this is perhaps the worst consequence of the defund the police movement."*[2]

Mass Exodus

After the Asheville, North Carolina city council cut their police budget by $770,000 in September 2020,[3] Deputy Chief of Police Mike Yelton announced a laundry list of complaints that officers will no longer respond to. The list includes misdemeanor theft, theft from vehicles, minor property damage, and graffiti unless there is a known suspect for any of these offenses. Additionally, police will not respond to non-life-threatening harassing phone calls (unless it is domestic violence or stalking related), fraud, scams, identity theft, simple assaults that have already occurred, lost or found property, or any other call that doesn't require immediate police action. Citizens will instead have the option to fill out an online report on the department's website for those incidents. The citizens of Asheville are feeling the effects of the mass exodus of more than 80 officers since the beginning of 2020.[4] But the mass exodus of cops is not limited to just Asheville. It is playing out in cities all over the country.

There are many reasons cops leave the business before their time. Some retire for medical reasons. Some leave because of bad leadership and low morale. Some wash out because of poor performance. Some just arrive at the conclusion the job is not for them, and change careers. All those aside, the question is, why do career cops—who love the job and have never wanted to do anything else—walk away? Because the country has unequivocally declared war on its police.

This war is being waged at every level of society by community leaders, city leaders, state and federal legislators, educators, athletes, and influencers. There are few subcultures in the nation that have not directly or indirectly waged war on our police. The weapons are not always guns. Sometimes they come in the form of biased media scrutiny, absence of police leadership, hyper-politicization of law enforcement, the loss of civil rights, violation of due process for cops, elimination of qualified immunity, and risk of wrongful prosecution. Often, these are the weapons that cause the most damage.

The war on police has reached a fever pitch just since 2020 and has crippled the effectiveness of law enforcement in America. We can't expect our officers to continue to expose themselves to these unwarranted abuses and still remain on the job; everyone has their breaking point. Unless something changes, the attrition rates and recruit deficits will continue the negative trend, leading to inadequate police protection, even higher crime rates, and governance by mobocracy—which is exactly what the anti-police mob is hoping for.

War Waged By Community Leaders

By Growing Negative Perception & Biased Media Scrutiny

Community leaders, advocates, and activists form the grassroots of the war on police. The love-hate relationship between the public and the police is nothing new, but the public's perception has become increasingly negative over the last three decades amid the growing availability of videos of police encounters, and the subsequent knee-jerk reactions of those with a voice in society. Whether from dash-cameras, body-worn cameras, or mobile device video, what was once only visible through the windshield of a patrol car or cop's first-hand perspective is now viewable on-demand for anyone who wants to see it, thanks to the Freedom of Information Act.[5] Why has that contributed to the negative perception of police? It's not because the police have intentionally hidden something that is now coming to light, but because the raw reality of what it takes to conduct law enforcement activities—which is not always pretty—is more visible. The 18th Century French writer, Nicholas Chamfort described it perfectly when he wrote,

> *"One would risk being disgusted if one saw politics, justice, and one's dinner in the making."*[6]

When video footage of a violent or fatal encounter with police goes viral, it is a two-dimensional, clipped version of events. It is only one piece in an entire body of evidence that will be examined in the official investigation into that incident. However, Joe and Jane Public—driven by the premature outrage of prominent community leaders—will often make judgments based on what they saw without any context. This combination leads to an uninformed and unfair conclusion that the police officers acted unjustly or, if the suspect is African American, the officers are racist.

Granted, public suspicion is not without cause. After all, one of the first times Americans watched a violent encounter with police in primetime was in 1991, when the beating of Rodney King by LAPD officers was caught on a home video camera. The four officers were acquitted of criminal charges, sparking the infamous 1992 Los Angeles riots during which 90 people were killed, 2,000 were injured, more than 9,000 were arrested, and the city sustained $1 billion in property damages. Ultimately the Department of Justice tried and convicted two of the four former officers for violating King's civil rights. Rodney King became a household name and a national symbol of racial tension and police brutality.[7] It was one of the darkest days for law enforcement in American history. A transgression we have been fighting to overcome ever since.

The difference between the infamous Rodney King video and today's police videos, though, is the distance of the camera. Instead of a stranger discretely filming police from across the street, now those who record police do so up close and often while verbally challenging the officers. This is a more subtle sign of the deterioration of the public's perception of police over the last 30 years. People are so unafraid and contemptuous of police that they will get in a cop's face with a mobile device without hesitation. The justification of an officer's actions seems to be irrelevant. Within minutes, a video is posted to one of many social media platforms, and within hours it goes viral. More often than not, community leaders and biased media—with a responsibility to advocate for truth—stir controversy and incite anger, resulting in a quick public verdict and a rapidly growing negative perception of police.

Kansas City, Missouri

For example, in March 2021 an African American man by the name of Malcolm Johnson was fatally shot by police in a gas station in Kansas City, Missouri. The store's surveillance video captured the incident but does not provide the entire context of the incident. From one angle, two officers are seen entering the store, guns drawn, attempting to arrest Johnson at the front counter. Johnson appears to fight the officers, and the altercation goes out of frame. The second angle then shows officers on top of Johnson trying to get him under control, as more officers are seen coming through the front door. Someone is heard shouting, "He has a gun in his pocket!" While four or five officers are struggling with Johnson, a gunshot is heard. Someone is immediately heard yelling out in pain. Then, two more gunshots are heard, ending the altercation and leaving Johnson dead and an officer shot.[8]

With the knowledge obtained only from the video footage, one could arrive at a variety of conclusions. Conclusion 1: Officers believed Johnson had a gun in his pocket, and fatally shot him to prevent him from obtaining the gun, accidentally hitting an officer in the process. Conclusion 2: White officers fatally shot a black man because they are racists, and claimed he had a gun to justify their actions. Conclusion 3: Johnson shot an officer and the officer returned fire in retribution. If you ask ten people to watch the video and tell you what happened, you'll likely get ten different answers. The point is, the video is just *one piece* of the entire body of evidence. It doesn't tell the whole story. That's why there must be a thorough and impartial investigation.

Joe and Jane Public, watching this viral video on the evening news from their couch, may make judgments about the incident without hearing a word of explanation. Human beings always see things through the filter of their own experiences. Their judgments may be biased based on their upbringing, their race, their belief system, their own interactions with police, etc. If they come to the conclusion that the police acted unjustly—based only on what they saw—their perception of police will be negative. If you multiple this process exponentially across the nation, it amounts to a growing negative perception of police.

The investigation into the shooting was conducted by the Missouri Highway Patrol. Their initial statement at the time of the shooting indicated officers from the Kansas City, MO Police Department had been surveilling Johnson who was wanted for a previous shooting incident. When officers entered the gas station to apprehend Johnson, he fought with them, pulled a gun from his pocket, and shot one of the officers in the leg. Officers returned fire in self-defense, killing Johnson.[9]

By the end of June, the MHP completed its investigation and submitted it to the local prosecutor's office. Ultimately a special prosecutor was appointed to examine the case to avoid a conflict of interest that arises out of Jackson County's previous prosecutions of Johnson. As of the date of this writing, the investigation is still underway.

On June 1, 2021,—while the MHP investigation was still in progress—local faith leaders and activists went on the news calling the incident an execution, claiming video footage they had independently obtained was in conflict with the statement of the Missouri Highway Patrol. A prominent local pastor was quoted as saying, "What I saw was an execution."[10] It is one thing to call for police transparency because of a history of tension between the community and police. It's another thing to make a biased judgment based on video footage of the incident. For a community leader to publicly accuse the police of executing some-one—with nothing more than a limited surveillance video and an initial statement by police—before a formal investigation has even been completed, is one of the reasons why there is a growing negative perception of police. Individuals with a platform have a responsibility to promote truth instead of conspiracy, to seek justice and not what looks right to *just us*.

The French writer Nicholas Chamfort was right. The more the public sees the inner workings and making of justice, the more disgusted they become.

War Waged By City Hall

By the Absence of Police Leadership, Violation of Due Process, and Wrongful Prosecution

Local government leaders—Police Officials, Mayors, City Councils, and Prosecutors—have waged war on police as well, by unjust terminations, violating officers' due process rights, and engaging in wrongful prosecutions.

The faith leaders in Kansas City not only publicly accused police of performing an execution, but also called for the immediate firing and indictment of all officers involved and the resignation of the Chief of Police—before an investigation was even completed.[11] In other words, they want punishment to be exacted without due process. The demand was followed up with a threat to call for a U.S. Department of Justice probe into the shooting.[12] They want the officers involved to be tried on the optics rather than the evidence.

Due process is a constitutional right, held to be so sacred that it is the only one recorded twice: in the Fifth and Fourteenth Amendments. It references the procedures that the government must follow before it deprives an individual of life, liberty, or property. Those procedures include but are not limited to an unbiased tribunal, the right to present evidence (including the right to call witnesses), the right to be represented by counsel, etc.[13] To comply with the demands of these and many other activists—

calling for officers to be immediately charged in fatal encounters—is a violation of officers' constitutional rights.

We, as a nation of law and order, cannot violate a police officer's constitutional rights in the pursuit of truth and justice any more than a police officer can violate a citizen's constitutional rights in pursuit of the same. It doesn't work both ways, yet it is happening in use of force cases around the country. There is not a more befitting example of this injustice against police officers than the story of Officer Garrett Rolfe of the Atlanta Police Department.

Atlanta, Georgia

On June 12, 2020, Atlanta Police Officer Garrett Rolfe fatally shot Rayshard Brooks, an African American male, in the parking lot of a Wendy's restaurant. Officer Rolfe and his partner were attempting to arrest Brooks for drunk driving when Brooks resisted and fought them off. He punched one of the officers in the face and used a Taser (he had managed to obtain during the struggle) on the other officer. Subsequently, Officer Rolfe fatally shot Brooks.[14] Unless you've been living under a rock, you have seen the viral video.

The very next day, Chief Erika Shields tendered her resignation to Mayor Keisha Lance Bottoms, who also announced Officer Rolfe had been terminated. Four days after that, Fulton County District Attorney Paul Howard charged Officer Rolfe with murder. The investigation wasn't even off the ground, there was no disciplinary hearing, and no grand jury had been empaneled. Officer Rolfe had not even given his own statement yet but was summarily fired and charged without even a hint of due process, three months before the Georgia Bureau of Investigation (GBI) had completed their investigation into the shooting.[15]

On August 4, 2020, Officer Rolfe filed a lawsuit against the Mayor and Interim Chief of Police Rodney Bryant, alleging he was denied his constitutional right to due process. The complaint states in part:

"On June 13, 2020, The Petitioner was summarily dismissed from his employment... without an investigation, without proper notice, without a pre-disciplinary hearing, and in direct violation of the municipal code of the City of Atlanta. Contrary to city policy as well as the policies, procedures, customs, and practices of the City of Atlanta Police Department, petitioner was never interviewed by the Office of Professional Standards or any individual regarding this incident to provide his statement"[16]

It's bad enough—if not expected—when a community activist or Joe and Jane Public form an opinion and judge an incident only by its video footage. But when a Chief of Police, Mayor, and County Prosecutor do so and then take official or legal action against the officer, it's a violation of the officer's constitutional rights. Investigators are entrusted to examine all the evidence impartially, paying meticulous attention to detail, before forming an educated, official opinion on a case. That's why police officials will not comment on an ongoing investigation. In this case, however, the Chief of Police fired Officer Rolfe and then resigned within hours of the shooting. Regardless of what opinions *you* may have formed about this incident, surely we can at least agree that this doesn't pass the smell test.

Two months later Officer Rolfe dismissed his lawsuit.[17] But, in May of 2021, he was retroactively reinstated by the Atlanta Civil Service Board, who acknowledged Rolfe had been terminated without due process.[18] During the board's hearing, Officer Rolfe testified that he didn't learn of the "Notice of Proposed Adverse Action" (NPAA) against him until June 13, 2020, at 3:45 PM— less than 24 hours after the shooting. He was given one hour to respond rather than the customary five days. At 5:00 PM that day the Mayor announced his termination at a national press conference.[19]

The man who signed Officer Rolfe's "Notice of Final Adverse Action" (NFAA), Assistant Chief Todd Coyt, also testified at the board hearing. Even he knew the action he was ordered to take was inconsistent with policy and procedure. When speaking of the shooting, he stated Officer Rolfe and his partner *"were trying to show compassion and did everything they could to calm the situation down.*[20]

Mayor Keisha Lance Bottoms' response to the Civil Service Board's ruling was to stand by her decision. She released the following statement.

> *"Given the volatile state of our city and nation last summer, the decision to terminate this officer, after he fatally shot Mr. Brooks in the back, was the right thing to do. Had immediate action not been taken, I firmly believe that the public safety crisis we experienced during that time would have been significantly worse."*[21]

It would appear the wrongful termination of Officer Garrett Rolfe was a political move to appease the violent and riotous mob, who would later that evening burn down the Wendy's restaurant where the shooting occurred, and three weeks later murder little 8-year-old Secoriea Turner, when they fired into her mother's vehicle near one of their barricades. Ironically, two days after Officer Rolfe was reinstated, Mayor Bottoms announced she would not run for re-election.[22]

As of the date of this writing, no trial date has been set for Officer Rolfe. He hasn't even been formally indicted. Yet, he is still required to wear an ankle monitor and abide by a 6 PM to 6 AM curfew, he is prohibited from carrying a gun or having any contact with other members of the APD, and is not allowed to leave the state, all of which are conditions of his bond. It gets worse. It has now been alleged that prosecutors lied in his bond hearing. According to Officer Rolfe's attorneys, the GBI report contradicts the statements made by the former district attorney and his assistants at the hearing.[23]

At his bond hearing, it was alleged that Office Rolfe—after shooting Brooks—said, "I got him." However, there was no witness corroboration of that statement. Additionally, prosecutors alleged that Officer Rolfe had kicked Brooks after he had shot him. Yet the video proves that Rolfe was stepping over Brooks, not kicking him. It was alleged in court that Rolfe waited two and a half minutes to render aid to Brooks after the shooting. Witnesses testified only that they saw Rolfe rendering aid; there was no corroboration of a delay. The district attorney also announced that Officer Rolfe's partner had agreed to testify against him, which was also found to be untrue.[24] Regardless of these alleged falsehoods, his bond conditions still stand.

Former District Attorney Paul Howard was defeated in a runoff election in the summer of 2020 by Fani T. Willis. She was granted a motion to recuse her office from the case, and a subsequent special prosecutor, the third to be tapped, was appointed from St. Louis County to reinvestigate the case to determine its future.[25]

The treatment of Officer Garrett Rolfe in the aftermath of this deadly force encounter is the perfect example of the absence of adequate leadership, the violation of due process, and wrongful prosecution, all mixed together in one large stew of injustice. His chief and his city abandoned him to appease the mobocracy. Even Interim Chief Bryant—who was later appointed permanent Chief—acknowledged the violation of due process and stated he believes Rolfe was charged prematurely.[26]

When something like this happens, it sends a strong message to the nation's police officers: If things go bad, you're on your own. It struck the men and women of the Atlanta PD with fear and anger. The day Officer Rolfe and his partner were charged, several officers walked off the job and approximately 170 officers called in sick. Police leadership realized they had a crisis on their hands and began to request help from surrounding agencies for coverage.[27]

This was reported by local media as a protest, or "Blue Flu," as it has been dubbed. It is illegal for police officers to protest, due to the nature of their job and the interest of public safety. The Blue Flu is said to be a protest tactic used by police officers in which they coordinate the use of sick time. Historically it has been used in collective bargaining contract disputes, such as in 1971 when approximately 20,000 NYPD officers called in sick for six consecutive days.[28] Atlanta police officers, however, were not protesting over a contract dispute. Who is to say they were even protesting? They were afraid to go to work and end up being fired and prosecuted for doing their jobs. And rightfully so.

In response to this supposed Blue Flu, Georgia State Senator Randy Robertson made the following statement to WRBL in Atlanta.

> *"While I have never condoned any action by law enforcement that might impact the safety and welfare of the citizens, it has become obvious during the past few days that those who were elected to lead the City of Atlanta and the Fulton County DA's Office have chosen to surrender law and order, due process, and the safety of citizens to rioters, vandals, and criminals. This failure of leadership has placed every man and woman who wears a badge in the City of Atlanta directly into the cross-hairs of hate."*[29]

Being a retired Georgia police officer himself, Senator Robertson said what a majority of Atlanta Police officers—as well as officers around the country—must have been thinking and feeling.

The Dominoes Are Falling

There has been a recent trend across the nation of activist prosecutors wrongfully prosecuting cops.

A police sergeant in Oklahoma City was charged with manslaughter after fatally shooting a mentally disturbed homeless man who charged him with a knife on December 11, 2020. Officers were called to a business to investigate the man whom business owners didn't want to be camped out there. When officers arrived they confronted the man who was armed with a knife. After multiple attempts were made to de-escalate the situation, and after less-lethal weapons—CEWs and OC Spray—were used to attempt to safely end the situation, the man charged the sergeant, who subsequently shot him in self-defense.[30]

An Austin, Texas police officer was indicted with murder in August of 2021, for the fatal shooting of a mentally disturbed man coming at him with a knife in 2019.[31] The prosecutor's office wouldn't allow their own hand-picked use of force expert to testify before the grand jury after he told them the officer's actions were justified. A month earlier, the same prosecutor dropped aggravated assault charges against another Austin PD officer after it was discovered an assistant in his office withheld exculpatory evidence that would've exonerated the officer.[32]

In June of 2021, Honolulu Police Officers were engaged in a high-speed pursuit with a stolen vehicle that had been involved in an armed robbery. The vehicle was forced to stop at an intersection when it was blocked in by patrol cars. As officers were ordering the occupants out at gunpoint, The driver began to drive away, putting officers at risk. Three officers opened fire, killing the 16-year-old driver. Their actions were deemed justified by the police department. When the grand jury voted not to indict the officers, the prosecutor charged them anyway. Two months later a District Court Judge ruled there was no probable cause to charge the officers.[33]

In Kay County, Oklahoma, police were called when a woman fired a gun at her mother in May of 2019. When the police arrived on the scene, she then opened fire on officers and fled the scene in a vehicle, continuing to fire at police vehicles that pursued her. A police lieutenant returned fire, killing the woman. The lieutenant was cleared by an independent investigation by the Oklahoma Bureau of Investigation. However, seven months later the district attorney presented the case to a grand jury which indicted the Lieutenant for second-degree murder and first-degree manslaughter. Fortunately, In August of 2021, a district court judge dismissed the indictment. Jason Smith, the Oklahoma Fraternal Order of Police president alleged the district attorney withheld exculpatory evidence—bullet holes in the patrol car—from the grand jury. He said,

> "I've yet to see in American history when an active shooter was taken out by a police officer or civilian who was then charged with murder – murder isn't defined by that in America."[34]

If you think the trend of wrongful prosecutions is limited to police officers, think again. In Austin, Texas in July of 2020, a U.S. Army sergeant was driving downtown when he happened upon a road blocked by protesters. When he stopped, a man armed with an AK-47 walked up to his window and pointed the rifle at him. The sergeant, who feared he was about to be shot, pulled his own weapon and fatally shot the protester. Almost a year later he was indicted for murder—by the same prosecutor that wrongfully charged the two Austin Police Officers above.[35]

War Waged By State and Federal Legislatures

By Loss of Civil Rights and Qualified Immunity

The U.S. Supreme Court introduced the qualified immunity doctrine in 1967 to protect law enforcement officers from frivolous lawsuits and financial liability in cases where they acted in good faith in unclear legal situations.[36] This legal protection is one of the ways America stands behind its cops who have sacrificed and risked their lives to stand between the sheep and the wolf. It gives cops the peace of mind that—as long as they are acting in good faith—they cannot be successfully sued and suffer personal financial loss.

Some believe that police reform should include the elimination of qualified immunity. If this were to happen, the anti-police mob would begin collectively funding mass lawsuits against officers all over the country for use of force incidents, no matter how minor. Activist judges who legislate from the bench would begin to rule against officers, who would then be liable out of their own pockets. The only way cops would be able to escape is to go to work and do nothing. The demoralization that would be caused by eliminating qualified immunity and its trickle-down effects would make police stations around the country look like schools out, as cops run from the building.

The reason qualified immunity is on the chopping block is because some believe this will make cops "think twice" before violating someone's civil rights. In other words, it is a method of deterring cops from doing their jobs by removing the shield that protects them from frivolous civil action when they—in good faith and conscience—perform their duties. There are two problems with this idea. Firstly, the war on police is systematically removing the deterrent factor in society that makes criminals think twice but seeks to take measures to deter cops from aggressively fighting crime. That logic should make you scratch your head. Secondly, qualified immunity does not protect cops who willfully violate someone's civil rights. Therefore, eliminating this protection would only expose cops who are doing the right thing, and uncover their personal assets for seizure by an activist judge or jury anytime someone has a beef with the police holding them accountable. Senator Marco Rubio of Florida agrees.[37] This is *exactly* what qualified immunity is supposed to prevent. In *Pearson v Callahan*, U.S. Supreme Court Justice Alito said the following:

> *"Qualified immunity balances two important interests—the need to hold public officials accountable when they exercise power irresponsibly and the need to shield officials from harassment, distraction, and liability when they perform their duties reasonably."*[38]

Proponents of cutting qualified immunity claim they want to hold cops accountable, but all it does is make cops less safe. What cutting qualified immunity will do is make cops "think twice" before they do anything. It will create another level of hesitation in a job where hesitation kills. Regardless, legislation has been introduced in the United States Congress and many State legislatures to strip officers of this important shield.

In March of 2021, The U.S. House of Representatives passed "HR-1280 The George Floyd Justice In Policing Act," which eliminates qualified immunity for law enforcement officers. The language is as follows:

Section 1979 of the Revised Statutes of the United States (42 U.S.C. 1983) is amended by adding at the end the following:

"It shall not be a defense or immunity in any action brought under this section against a local law enforcement officer (as such term is defined in section 2 of the George Floyd Justice in Policing Act of 2021), or in any action under any source of law against a Federal investigative or law enforcement officer (as such term is defined in section 2680(h) of title 28, United States Code), that—

"(1) the defendant was acting in good faith, or that the defendant believed, reasonably or otherwise, that his or her conduct was lawful at the time when the conduct was committed; or

"(2) the rights, privileges, or immunities secured by the Constitution and laws were not clearly established at the time of their deprivation by the defendant, or that at such time, the state of the law was otherwise such that the defendant could not reasonably have been expected to know whether his or her conduct was lawful.".[39]

Colorado, New Mexico, Massachusetts, Connecticut, and New York City have already passed laws abolishing or limiting qualified immunity, and similar legislation has been introduced in several other states.[40] If the U.S. Congress passes its bill, it will decimate police manpower across the country, as cops begin looking for other professions. Cops will risk their lives, but they won't risk the well-being of their families. Period.

War Waged By Educators, Athletes, and Others

Assault on Police Officers

The brave men and women of law enforcement knew they were taking risks when they signed up. They knew they would put on their uniform and go to work everyday with the chance they wouldn't come home. They knew it would be difficult, exhausting, and even damaging mentally and emotionally. They knew they were entering a subculture that would make them a target of hate and violence. And they did it anyway. They did it, and continue to do it to protect the sheep and hold the line of law and order.

Out of every 1,000 police officers, 12 of them will be assaulted. That amounted to 56,034 officers in 2019. While the media and politicians are condemning police use of force, who is condemning the brazen attacks on police officers? What is it going to take to convince a nation that the police are not the problem?

Aurora, Illinois, July 2021 — A police officer was attacked during a traffic stop by the vehicle's occupants who repeatedly struck and kicked him and then choked him unconscious. The attackers were apprehended and indicted for attempted murder.[41]

Birmingham, Alabama, January 2019 — A police detective stopped a vehicle for a possible connection to several burglaries. While he waited for backup, the driver got out of the car and attacked the detective, disarmed him, and pistol-whipped him with his own gun until he was unconscious. After an extensive manhunt involving local agencies and the U.S. Marshall's Office, the attacker was apprehended and charged with attempted murder.[42]

Nashville, Tennessee, May 2021 — A police officer was shot by a man who they believe made a phony 911 call with the intention of ambushing police. Immediately upon officers' arrival, a man started shooting at them, hitting one officer in the arm. Despite taking fire, no officers fired a single shot in the incident. The shooter ultimately took his own life.[43]

New York City, April 2021 — An NYPD officer was dragged by a vehicle after asking the driver he stopped to get out of the vehicle. The suspect fled, broke into a home in Queens, and took an elderly woman hostage, before being apprehended. At the time of the attack, he was out on no bail for an attempted murder charge.[44]

There are 56,030 more stories just like these that occurred in 2019 alone. It has become worse in the last two years, with ambush-style attacks on police officers almost doubling from 2020 to 2021.[45] As the lawless become more brazen, the attacks will continue to increase.

Contempt of Cop

Not every cop-hater is going to physically assault an officer, but many are those who are not shy about their contempt of law enforcement. Cop-haters are very diverse; they include professional athletes, politicians, activist prosecutors, judges, college professors, and even fast-food employees—to say nothing of the lawless. The America that raised my generation—and taught us to respect authority and honor those in uniform—is now the America that is surrendering to the will of a few people who seek to undermine law and order and overwhelm our police.

It's difficult to understand. It's difficult to understand why a bystander would record the assault of a Birmingham police officer instead of coming to his aid, and would then post pictures of him on social media laying unconscious on the sidewalk, commending whomever "pistol-whipped his ass to sleep."[46]

It's difficult to understand why school administrators would dismiss a school resource officer for a statement she made in support of the thin blue line flag that is incorporated into the department's shoulder patch.[47] Or, why the University of Wisconsin Police Chief would ban the flag after someone saw it in the background of a photo and complained,[48] claiming it is a symbol of hate.

It's difficult to understand why the Los Angeles District Attorney would petition the court to drop the gun enhancement in the murder charge of an accused cop-killer to get a reduced sentence.[49]

It's difficult to understand why a group of employees at a Starbucks in St. Paul, Minnesota would refuse to work while police directed the traffic in front of the business, that was caused *by* their business.[50]

It's difficult to understand why the NFL would honor a gunman who was fatally shot while trying to murder cops. 21-year-old Dreasjon Reed was in possession of a stolen gun, which evidence showed he used in two drive-by shootings before attempting to kill an Indianapolis Metro Police Officer in May of 2020. Reed live-streamed the police pursuit and the shooting that led to his demise. Despite the Indiana State Police ruling the shooting justified, the NFL painted Reed as a victim[51] in a video entitled, "Say Their Stories." Officer De'Joure Mercer of the IMPD has now filed a lawsuit against the NFL for defamation. His lawsuit states:

> *"The video gives rise to the inference, implication, and imputation that Mercer committed occupational misconduct and even criminal acts during the May 6 encounter with Reed, similar to that which were inflicted upon George Floyd."*[52]

Cops like Officer Mercer are tired of being attacked and are fighting back.

It's difficult to understand why a convicted cop-killer would be appointed to the Ithaca and Tompkins County, New York police reform advisory group. On January 12, 1981, a 16-year-old Richard Rivera was one of five men who committed armed robbery at a bar and grill establishment in New York City. Off Duty NYPD Officer Robert Walsh was inside the bar, and was shot by Rivera while trying to intervene. Wounded but still alive, Officer Walsh lay on the floor as Rivera stood over him, put a gun to his head, and fatally shot him execution-style. Rivera served 39 years in prison and is now on the Governor-mandated panel tasked with proposing police reform measures. The NYPD Police Benevolent Association called it, "despicable."[53]

It's difficult to understand why San Francisco would defund their police department by $3.75 million,[54] then turn right around and pay criminals $500 per month for not shooting anyone! Not even kidding. Their Human Rights Commission and Economic and Workforce Development program are going to identify those who are considered "high-risk" for gun violence, then pay them $500 every time they go a whole month without shooting someone. The director of the Human Rights Commission said, *"Six thousand dollars per person, when you look at it annually, is nothing if it helps deter criminal activity."*[55]

It's difficult to understand why so many people in America could have such contempt and hatred of the police. These stories just keep piling up, as those who have swallowed the poison pill of propaganda look for their golden opportunity to make a debut on the stage of "I'm offended."

Remember the Victims

"[I]n talking out about crime, we intend to speak for a group that has been frequently overlooked in the past – the innocent victims of crime... The victims of crime have needed a voice for a long, long time, and this administration means to provide it."[56] —*President Ronald Regan*

A violent crime occurs every 24.6 seconds in America. In the time it has taken you to read this book—about three and a half hours—213 people were murdered, 53 people were raped, 123 people were robbed, 323 people were violently assaulted, and 557 homes were burglarized.[57] This doesn't factor in unreported crime. Studies suggest 69% of sexual assaults are unreported, 38% of robberies are unreported, and 37% of assaults are unreported.[58] A study by the DOJ Bureau of Justice Statistics reports approximately 3.4 million violent crimes per year were unreported between 2006-2010.[59] The Pew Research Center published similar findings, claiming 47% of violent crimes in the U.S. were not reported in 2015.[60]

A more recent study from Vanderbilt University says 121 million crimes (against persons and property) were committed in the United States in 2017. However, only an estimated 21.7% of those crimes were reported, which accounts for approximately 26 million offenses and approximately 11.2 million arrests. The Vanderbilt study estimates the annual financial impact of crime at $2.6 trillion. This figure is divided into $620 billion in direct monetary costs—for things like emergency services, legal expenses, victims services, medical and mental healthcare, and stolen and damaged property—and $1.95 trillion for intangible pain, suffering, and lost quality of life costs. The direct monetary costs alone are the equivalent of 3.2% of the U.S. Gross Domestic Product (GDP) and are more than the nation spends on military or social welfare programs.[61] However the anti-police mob may twist the facts, crime is still a serious national problem.

When you compare those statistics to the $193 billion America spent on policing in 2017—roughly $340 per person[62]—it would appear as if we're already trying to fight a forest fire with a garden hose. Defunding the police reduces the garden hose to a trickle and makes it virtually impossible to be effective.

For those who advocate for draining police budgets to fund behavioral health services—as a crime prevention or mediation initiative—consider this: $90 billion is what was spent nationally for crime-related medical and mental healthcare in 2017.[63] Most of that was paid by insurance companies. Theoretically, if we re-source our police to fight and reduce crime (we've already established that defunding the police has caused a spike in crime), wouldn't that reduce the money spent on crime-related medical and mental healthcare? If so, we've found the funds available to pay for social and mental services on the preventative side of crime. For example, wouldn't it make more sense for San Fransisco to take their $500 per month per person and use it to get that high-risk individual needed behavioral health services such as anger management, life-skills education, and other preventative services, instead of paying them cash for not shooting anyone? Of course, it makes more sense! There must be creative ways to redirect money from government's wasteful spending into initiatives that will reduce crime, other than taking it from the police.

American Law Enforcement provides the most comprehensive and effective crime prevention and education programs of any organization in the nation. These programs include D.A.R.E (Drug Abuse Resistance Education), in which police officers reach 1.5 million children in public schools in all 50 states, and C.O.P.S. (Community Oriented Policing Services), a program that is championed by the Department of Justice and has become a major doctrine in a majority of U.S. police agencies. Additionally, citizens' police academies, youth police academies, National Night Out, Shop-With-a-Cop, prescription drug drop-off locations and other programs provide opportunities for the police to interact and work closely with their communities on a personal level. *No one* is doing more than the police to prevent crime. Defund the police, and all that goes away.

On April 1, 1981, President Ronald Reagan signed a declaration creating National Crime Victims' Rights Week. He said,

> *"For too long, the victims of crime have been the forgotten persons of our criminal justice system. Rarely do we give victims the help they need or the attention they deserve. Yet the protection of our citizens — to guard them from becoming victims — is the primary purpose of our penal laws. Thus, each new victim personally represents an instance in which our system has failed to prevent crime. Lack of concern for victims compounds that failure."*

America's war on police ultimately creates more victims. Victims should matter to us. When our society turns the perpetrators of crime into the victims, we are saying to the true victims, "You don't matter." Portraying the lawless as victims is the equivalent of social gaslighting, leaving the true victims to feel invalidated and alone. To call the lawless the victims is to turn the police into the predators. This is the ultimate Blue Lie.

When there exists such an overwhelming body of evidence to debunk the lies that have put police under siege, why are they still believed? Two words: psychological warfare. Hannah Arendt wrote in *The Origins of Totalitarianism*,

> *"If everybody always lies to you, the consequence is not that you believe the lies, but rather that nobody believes anything any longer... And a people that no longer can believe anything cannot make up its mind. It is deprived not only of its capacity to act but also of its capacity to think and to judge. And with such a people you can then do what you please."*[64]

She was speaking of the propaganda warfare used by Adolf Hitler to deceive the Germans. It is based on the philosophy of Nazi Joseph Goebbels: If you repeat a lie long enough, it will eventually become the "truth." Arendt went on to say,

> *"Hitler, who knew the modern chaos of opinions from first-hand experience, discovered that the helpless seesawing between various opinions and 'the conviction that everything is balderdash' could best be avoided by adhering to one of the many current opinions with 'unbendable consistency."*[65]

In our modern society overloaded with information, I've heard Joe and Jane Public say, "I don't know what to believe anymore." That is in fact *exactly* what the mobocracy wants. It will continue to disseminate its Blue Lies with such frequency and consistency that it will eventually become the official doctrine of American society. The uprising of the lawless will continue—dare I say, with the sanction of a weary and beleaguered government unable to resist the force of domestic terrorism. Law enforcement will be reduced to an ever-shrinking force, equivalent to society's hall monitors. "Protect and serve" will become "observe and document." The sheepdogs will no longer have teeth with which to deter the wolves and it will be open season on the sheep *and* sheepdogs. The rule of law will be replaced by the license of the lawless to do as they see fit. This is what anarchy will look like. Only then will the infamous chant of protesters be truly understood, "No justice, no peace."

About the Author

Jeff Wolf had aspirations of becoming a police officer since childhood. After college, however, he entered the ministry and held his first pastorate by the age of twenty-four. During that pastorate, he found a way to serve in both capacities and accepted a position as a chaplain at his local police department. Soon after, this experience prompted him to enroll in the Ohio Peace Officer Training Academy, and begin his bivocational journey as a pastor *and* police officer. During his twenty years of service, he served as a chaplain, patrol officer, field training officer, I.T. officer, and patrol sergeant. He was twice decorated for performing life-saving actions, twice recognized by Mothers Against Drunk Driving for his DUI enforcement, received multiple drug interdiction awards, and numerous other commendations.

In 2020, Jeff took an early retirement to again focus on ministry on a full-time basis. He has distinguished himself as a Christian author with three previous books, and is now making his non-fiction debut with *Blue Lies: The War on Justice and the Conspiracy to Weaken America's Cops*. Jeff lives in the Cincinnati area with his wife, Christal. They have three children and two grandsons.

www.jeffwolf.org

Notes

Chapter 1: Black and Blue

1   Withrow, E. (2021, April 28). Charlotte City Councilman Advocates for gun-free CMPD. FOX 46 Charlotte. Retrieved September 17, 2021, from https://www.fox46.com. Quoted in: Malone, Sandy, Tom Gantert, and Holly Matkin. "Councilman Wants To Disarm Police So Cops Must Use Words Instead Of Force." The Police Tribune, May 3, 2021. https://policetribune.com.

2   McMahon, Julie. "Ithaca Mayor Unveils Proposal to Replace City's Police Department." syracuse, February 23, 2021. https://www.syracuse.com. Quoted in: Matkin, Holly, and Sandy Malone. "Mayor Proposes Ending City's Police Force, Replacing It With New Civilian-Led Agency." The Police Tribune, April 25, 2021. https://policetribune.com.

3   Heffernan, Erin. "Proposed St. Louis Spending Plan Cuts $4m to Police, Removes 98 Vacant Officer Jobs." STLtoday.com, July 14, 2021. https://www.stltoday.com. Quoted in: Matkin, Holly, and Sandy Malone. "St. Louis Mayor Votes To Defund Police, Cut 100 Sworn Positions From Force." The Police Tribune, May 3, 2021. https://policetribune.com.

4   Moore, Tina. "NYPD Cop-Killer Is Now Helping Reform the Police in New York." New York Post. New York Post, March 29, 2021. https://nypost.com. Quoted In: Malone, Sandy. "Cop Killer Given Seat On Governor-Mandated Police Reform Panel." The Police Tribune, March 31, 2021. https://policetribune.com.

5   Matkin, Holly, and Sandy Malone. "NFL Honors Gunman Killed While Trying To Murder Cops." The Police Tribune, December 17, 2020. https://policetribune.com.

6   "Fatal Force: Police Shootings Database." The Washington Post. WP Company, January 22, 2020. https://www.washingtonpost.com.

7   Dean Knox, Jonathan Mummolo. "Perspective | A Widely Touted Study Found No Evidence of Racism in Police Shootings. It's Full of Errors." The

Washington Post. WP Company, July 15, 2020. https://www.washingtonpost.com.

8   Donald, Heather Mac. Opinion "I Cited Their Study, So They Disavowed It." The Wall Street Journal. Dow Jones & Company, July 8, 2020. https://www.wsj.com.

9   "Views from behind the Badge: Rebuilding the Public's Trust in the Police." CBS News. CBS Interactive. Accessed June 15, 2021. https://www.cbsnews.com.

Chapter 2: Courage Under Fire

1   Unless otherwise indicated, the facts and circumstances cited in the case in this chapter are taken from the following:

State of Ohio v James Trimble (Ohio Supreme Court, Case No: 05-2436 June 18, 2007).

State v. Trimble, 122 Ohio St.3d 297, 2009-Ohio-2961.

Multiple Officers. 2005. Ohio Uniform Incident Report. 05-0445. Brimfield Twp Police.

Multiple Officers. 2005. Ohio Uniform Incident Report. 05-0446. Brimfield Twp Police.

2   "Daily Kent Stater, 5 October 2005." Daily Kent Stater 5 October 2005 - Kent State University. Accessed April 15, 2021. https://dks.library.kent.edu.

3   "Daily Kent Stater, 24 January 2005." Daily Kent Stater 24 January 2005 - Kent State University. Accessed April 15, 2021. https://dks.library.kent.edu.

4   Meyer, Ed. "Parents of Slain Kent State Student Break Silence, Maintain Existence of 'Rogue' Sniper as Reason Daughter Died." Akron Beacon Journal. Akron Beacon Journal, January 23, 2015. https://www.beaconjournal.com.

5   Dave O'Brien | staff. "Trimble Death Penalty Re-Imposed by U.S. Court." Record. Record-Courier, October 23, 2015. https://www.record-courier.com.

Chapter 3: The Making of a Sheepdog

1   Smith, Hayley. "Woman Goes on Racist Rant during L.A. County Traffic Stop, Tells Deputy 'You'll Never Be White'." Los Angeles Times. Los Angeles

Times, May 6, 2021. https://www.latimes.com.

2   Grossman, Dave, and Loren W. Christensen. On Combat: the
Psychology and Physiology of Deadly Conflict in War and in Peace. Millstadt, IL:
Warrior Science Pub., 2008.

3   Ibid.

4   Murray, Kenneth R. Training at the Speed of Life the Definitive
Textbook for Military and Law Enforcement Reality Based Training. Gotha,
FL, USA: Armiger Publications, Inc, 2006. Essay in: Asken, Michael J., Loren W.
Christensen, and Dave Grossman. Warrior Mindset: Mental Toughness Skills for
a Nation's Defenders: Performance Psychology Applied to Combat. United States:
BookBaby, 2011.

5   Reaves, Brian A. "State and Local Law Enforcement Training
Academies, 2013." Bureau of Justice Statistics (BJS). U.S. Department of Justice, July
21, 2016. https://www.bjs.gov.

6   Welch, William M. "2 Police Officers Ambushed, Killed at Vegas
Restaurant." USA Today. Gannett Satellite Information Network, June 9, 2014.
https://www.usatoday.com/.

7   "McDonald's Employee Arrested for Allegedly Tampering with
Officer's Food." KERO. KERO, November 17, 2019. https://www.turnto23.com.
Quoted In: Law Officer. "McDonald's Management Catches Employee Tampering
with Officer's Food, Arrest Made." Law Officer, November 17, 2019. https://www.
lawofficer.com.

8   Rector, Kevin. "LAPD after George Floyd: Fewer Officers, Fewer
Arrests But Hardly Defunded." Los Angeles Times. Los Angeles Times, May 30,
2021. https://www.latimes.com. Quoted in: "LAPD after George Floyd: Fewer
Officers, Fewer Arrests ." Police1, May 31, 2021. https://www.police1.com.

9   Berrien, Hank. "NYPD Officers Leaving in Droves, 75% Increase in
Quitting or Retirement in 2020." The Daily Wire. The Daily Wire, April 25, 2021.
https://www.dailywire.com.

10   Berman, Mark, and Jessica Wolfrom. "After 50 Police Officers Resign,
Portland Grapples with Its Message Vs. Rising Violence." Yahoo! Yahoo! Accessed
August 30, 2021. https://www.yahoo.com.

11   Haney, Author: Addie. "Atlanta Police down 220 Officers since Start

of January, Department Says." 11Alive.com, December 9, 2020. https://www.11alive.com.

12   McEvoy, Jemima. "Historic Police Exodus in Cities Most Impacted by Racial Justice Unrest, New Data Shows." Forbes. Forbes Magazine, April 29, 2021. https://www.forbes.com.

13   Ibid.

14   Macfarquhar, Neil. "Departures of Police Officers Accelerated during a Year of Protests." The New York Times. The New York Times, June 11, 2021. https://www.nytimes.com.

15   Ibid.

16   Ahtra Elnashar, "Police Officer Shortage Part OF 8-Year Nationwide Trend." WJLA. WJLA, May 7, 2021. https://wjla.com.

17   Ibid.

18   "The Workforce Crisis, and What Police Agencies Are Doing ..." Accessed August 30, 2021. https://www.policeforum.org.

19   Rago, Gordon. "Chesapeake Will Spend $2.7 Million for Police 'Retention' Bonuses." The Virginian-Pilot, August 13, 2021. https://www.pilotonline.com. Quoted in: "Va. City to Spend $2.7 Million for Police 'Retention' Bonuses." Police1, August 23, 2021. https://www.police1.com.

20   Fernandez, Paige. "Defunding the Police Will Actually Make Us Safer." American Civil Liberties Union, June 11, 2020. https://www.aclu.org.

21   Ibid.

22   Campanile, Carl. "AOC's Answer to Reducing Violent Crime? Stop Building Jails." New York Post. New York Post, June 4, 2021. https://nypost.com.

23   Andrew, Scottie. "There's a Growing Call to Defund the Police. Here's What It Means." CNN. Cable News Network, June 17, 2020. https://www.cnn.com.

24   Calibre Press. "10,000 Officers Respond to Policing Poll: Only 7% Would Recommend Becoming a Cop." Police1, June 30, 2020. https://www.police1.com.

Chapter 4: Ferguson, Missouri

1   Lowry, Rich. "How Did It Become Normal for Every Police Shooting

to Bring Ruinous Rioting?" New York Post. New York Post, April 13, 2021. https://nypost.com.

2   Madhani, Aamer. "'Ferguson Effect': 72% of U.S. COPS Reluctant to Make Stops." USA Today. Gannett Satellite Information Network, January 11, 2017. https://www.usatoday.com.

3   Unless otherwise indicated, the facts and circumstances cited in the case in this chapter are taken from the following:

State of Missouri v Darren Wilson (Transcript of Grand Jury August 24-November 24, 2014).

Official Statement of St. Louis County Prosecutor Robert McCulloch, November 24, 2014

Multiple Officers. 2014. Investigative Report #14-43984. St. Louis County Police Department. St. Louis, MO.

4   Grossman, Dave. On Killing: the Psychological Cost of Learning to Kill in War and Society. New York, NY: Little, Brown and Co., 2009.

5   "Robbery in the Second Degree 570.025." Missouri Revisor of Statutes - Revised Statutes of Missouri, RSMo, Missouri Law, MO Law, Joint Committee on Legislative Research. Accessed May 8, 2021. https://revisor.mo.gov.

6   Fletcher, Bill. "A Black Life Is Worth Less than a $50 Box of Cigars?" The Philadelphia Tribune, August 25, 2014. https://www.phillytrib.com.

7   Cronkleton, Robert. "With New Michael Brown Video Footage, Documentary Asserts He Didn't Rob Ferguson Store." Kansas City Star, March 12, 2017. https://www.kansascity.com.

8   Municode Library. Accessed May 8, 2021. https://library.municode.com/mo/ferguson/codes/code_of_ordinances.

9   "2005 Missouri Revised Statutes - § 565.082. - Assault of a Law Enforcement Officer, Emergency Personnel, or Probation and Parole Officer in the Second Degree, Definition, Penalty." Justia Law. Accessed May 10, 2021. https://law.justia.com/codes/missouri/2005/.

10   "2005 Missouri Revised Statutes - § 565.081. - Assault of a Law Enforcement Officer, Emergency Personnel, or Probation and Parole Officer in the First Degree, Definition, Penalty." Justia Law. Accessed May 10, 2021. https://law.justia.com/codes/missouri/2005/.

11   Miller, Joshua Rhett. "Retired Connecticut Cop Killed in One-Punch Attack on Las Vegas Strip." New York Post. New York Post, March 4, 2021. https://nypost.com.

12   "2014 Missouri Revised Statutes :: Title XXXVIII Crimes And Punishment; Peace Officers And Public Defenders (556-600) :: Chapter 563 Defense of Justification :: Section 563.046 Beginning January 1, 2017–Law Enforcement Officer's use of force in Making an Arrest." Justia Law. Accessed May 12, 2021. https://law.justia.com/codes/missouri/2014.

13   McClam, Erin. "'Beyond Outraged': Michael Brown's Family Accuses Ferguson Police of Smear." NBCNews.com. NBCUniversal News Group, June 11, 2015. https://www.nbcnews.com.

14   Fieldstadt, Elisha. "Michael Brown Rally: 'We Have Had Enough,' Rev. Al Sharpton Says." NBCNews.com. NBCUniversal News Group, June 11, 2015. https://www.nbcnews.com.

15   McClam, Erin. "'Beyond Outraged': Michael Brown's Family Accuses Ferguson Police of Smear." NBCNews.com. NBCUniversal News Group, June 11, 2015. https://www.nbcnews.com.

16   Bacon, John. "Darren Wilson: Ferguson Made Me Unemployable." USA Today. Gannett Satellite Information Network, August 5, 2015. https://www.usatoday.com.

17   Carter, Mike. "Kirkland Man Sentenced for Threats against Ferguson Cop." The Seattle Times. The Seattle Times Company, March 19, 2015. https://www.seattletimes.com.

18   Nelson, Shellie. "Death Threats Drive Former Ferguson Officer Darren Wilson into Hiding." wqad.com. WQAD, December 3, 2014. https://www.wqad.com.

19   United States v Jaleel Tariq Abdul-Jabbaar (United States District Court for the Western District of Washington and Seattle, Case No: 2:14-MJ-00467-BAT December 1, 2014).

20   Ibid, Grossman, On Killing, 168-169.

21   Kmov. "Wesley Bell Announces He Reopened Michael Brown Case, but Will Not File Charges." KMOV.com, July 31, 2020. https://www.kmov.com.

22   Ibid.

23   Staff, POL. "Democratic Presidential Candidates Accuse Former Ferguson Officer of Murdering Michael Brown." Police Magazine. Police Magazine, August 12, 2019. https://www.policemag.com.

24   Ibid.

25   Sharyl Attkisson. "Time to Retire Ferguson Narrative." TheHill. The Hill, August 12, 2019. https://thehill.com.

26   Ibid.

Chapter 5: Baton Rouge, Louisiana

1   Unless otherwise cited, the facts and circumstances cited in the case in this chapter are taken from the following:

Multiple Officers. 07-05-2016. Incident Report #16-00068253. Baton Rouge Police Department. Baton Rouge, LA.

Hill, Kyle, Corporal. 2016. Internal Affairs Investigation #044-16. Baton Rouge Police Department. Baton Rouge, LA.

Official Statement of Louisiana Attorney General Jeff Landry, March 27, 2018

Louisiana Department of Justice Report of the Investigation and the Determination of Criminal Responsibility and use of force by Officers Blane Salamoni and Howard Lake of the Baton Rouge Police Department in the Officer Involved Death of Alton Sterling Occurring July 5, 2016. March 27, 2018

Hillar C. Moore, Iii, 19Th Judicial District Attorney Parish Of East Baton Rouge. The final report of the circumstances, the investigation, and the determination of criminal responsibility for the officer involved death of Gavin Long on July 17, 2016.

United States District Court Middle District Of Louisiana, Officer John Doe Smith Vs. Deray Mckesson; Johnetta Elzie; Black Lives Matter; Black Lives Matter Network, Inc.; #Blacklivesmatter; Alicia Garza;, Patrisse Cullors, And Opal Tometi, Case 3:17-cv-00429-JWD-EWD, July 7, 2017.

2   Louisiana Laws - Louisiana State Legislature. Accessed June 2, 2021. http://www.legis.la.gov.

3   White, Byron Raymond, and Supreme Court Of The United States. U.S. Reports: Terry v. Ohio, 392 U.S. 1. 1967. Periodical. https://www.loc.gov/item/usrep392001/.

4   Sara Burnett, Michael Balsamo. "Despite Growing Chorus, DOJ Is Limited in Police Probes." AP NEWS. Associated Press, April 21, 2021. https://apnews.com.

5   "Federal Officials Close Investigation Into Death of Alton Sterling." The United States Department of Justice, May 3, 2017. https://www.justice.gov.

6   Grossman, On Killing, 45-46

7   Sharrar v. Felsing, 128 F.3d 810, 822 (3d Cir. 1997); Edwards v. Giles, 51 F.3d 155, 156-57 (8th Cir. 1995); Courson v. McMillian, 939 F.2d 1479, 1496 (11th Cir. 1991); Collins v. Nagle, 892 F.2d 489, 495-97 (6th Cir. 1989).

8   Staff, NBC 5. "Sniper Ambush Kills 5 Officers, Injures 7 in Dallas Following Peaceful Protest." NBC 5 Dallas-Fort Worth. NBC 5 Dallas-Fort Worth, June 3, 2020. https://www.nbcdfw.com.

9   Mike Kunzelman And Melinda Deslatte, The Associated Press. "Police: 3 Arrested in 'Credible Threat' to Harm Officers." telegram.com. July 13, 2016. https://www.telegram.com.

10   Carrero, Jacquellena, Elisha Fieldstadt, and Gabe Gutierrez. "Three Baton Rouge Officers Killed, Three Injured in 'Ambush'." NBCNews.com. NBCUniversal News Group, July 18, 2016. https://www.nbcnews.com.

11   Holloway, Philip., America's Newsroom, Fox News, Interview on June 11, 2021.

12   Mettler, Katie. "The Ex-Police Officer Who Killed Alton Sterling Is Allowed to Undo His Firing and Resign Instead." The Washington Post. WP Company, August 2, 2019. https://www.washingtonpost.com.

13   Ibid.

14   Ibid.

15   Starkes, Taleeb. Black Lies Matter. Createspace Independent Publishing Platform, 2016.

Chapter 6: Black Lies Matter

1   Starkes, Taleeb. Black Lies Matter. Createspace Independent Publishing Platform, 2016.

2   Edwards, Frank, Hedwig Lee, and Michael Esposito. "Risk of Being

Killed by Police use of force in the United States by Age, Race–Ethnicity, and Sex." PNAS. National Academy of Sciences, August 20, 2019. https://www.pnas.org/content/116/34/16793.

3 editor, Letters to the. "Letters: Better Chance Being Struck by Lightning than Killed by Police." The Enquirer. Cincinnati Enquirer, April 16, 2021. https://www.cincinnati.com.

4 Private conversation between the author and Judge Roller.

5 "Fatal Force: Police Shootings Database." The Washington Post. WP Company, January 22, 2020. https://www.washingtonpost.com.

6 Donald, Heather Mac. "There Is No Epidemic of Fatal Police Shootings against Unarmed Black Americans." USA Today. Gannett Satellite Information Network, July 6, 2020. https://www.usatoday.com.

7 Johnson, Richard R. "Dispelling the Myths Surrounding Police Use of Lethal Force." Dolan Consulting Group, July 2016. https://www.dolanconsultinggroup.com.

8 Perrin, Andrew. "23% Of Users in U.S. Say Social Media Led Them to Change Views on an Issue; Some Cite Black Lives Matter." Pew Research Center. Pew Research Center, October 16, 2020. https://www.pewresearch.org.

9 https://Blacklivesmatter.com/2020-impact-report/

10 https://Blacklivesmatter.com/about/

11 https://malcontentment.com/wp-content/uploads/2021/01/Understanding-Antifa-and-Urban-Guerilla-Warfare-edited-by-Dan-Dickerson.pdf

12 Henry Redman, Wisconsin Examiner December 14. "Police Group Tied to Wisconsin Spreads Claim That BLM Is 'Terrorist'." Wisconsin Examiner, December 16, 2020. https://wisconsinexaminer.com.

13 Press, The Associated. "Police Guide That Calls BLM a Terrorist Group Draws Outrage." ajc. The Atlanta Journal-Constitution, December 2, 2020. https://www.ajc.com.

14 "Dec 3, 2020: Police Association Spreads Paranoia - AM Quickie." Fans.fm. Accessed June 16, 2021. https://fans.fm/p/qdqrzPV.

15 Kaplan, Talia. "NJ Police Officer Says She Was Fired over Facebook Post Calling Black Lives Matter Protesters 'Terrorists'." Fox News. FOX News Network, May 5, 2021. https://www.foxnews.com.

16   Wallace, Danielle. "Oklahoma DA Slaps Teens with Terrorism Charges, Accuses BLM of Intimidating Officers, Protecting Criminals." Fox News. FOX News Network, July 21, 2020. https://www.foxnews.com.

17   Ibid.

18   Wallace, Danielle. "Oklahoma DA Slaps Teens with Terrorism Charges, Accuses BLM of Intimidating Officers, Protecting Criminals." Fox News. FOX News Network, July 21, 2020. https://www.foxnews.com.

19   Key, Pam. "Biden: Former Military, Police Fueling 'Growth of White Supremacy' Groups." Breitbart, February 17, 2021. https://www.breitbart.com.

20   Prestigiacomo, Amanda. "Model, BLM Activist: 'All Hell Will Break Loose' If Chauvin Not Convicted, Buildings Will Be 'On Fire'." The Daily Wire. The Daily Wire, April 5, 2021. https://www.dailywire.com.

21   Mueller, Benjamin, and Al Baker. "2 N.Y.P.D. Officers Killed in Brooklyn Ambush; Suspect Commits Suicide." The New York Times. The New York Times, December 20, 2014. https://www.nytimes.com.. Quoted in "Starkes, Taleeb, Black Lies Matter, 2016."

22   https://oversight.house.gov/sites/democrats.oversight.house.gov/files/White_Supremacist_Infiltration_of_Law_Enforcement.pdf

23   https://fas.org/irp/eprint/rightwing.pdf

24   Speri, Alice. "The FBI Has Quietly Investigated White Supremacist Infiltration of Law Enforcement." The Intercept, January 31, 2017. https://theintercept.com.

25   German, Michael. "Hidden in Plain Sight: Racism, White Supremacy, and Far-Right Militancy in Law Enforcement." Brennan Center for Justice, June 16, 2021. https://www.brennancenter.org.

26   CBS Sacramento. "Multiple People Stabbed During Rally At State Capitol." CBS Sacramento. CBS Sacramento, June 26, 2016. https://sacramento.cbslocal.com.

27   German, Michael. "Hidden in Plain Sight."

28   "Oath Keepers Bylaws." Oath Keepers, July 25, 2018. https://oathkeepers.org/bylaws/#article-viii.

29   https://www.californiathreepercenters.org

30   "Patriots." Urban Dictionary. Accessed June 23, 2021. https://www.

urbandictionary.com.

31   Gerda, Nick. "OC Sheriff Says Deputy on Leave for Wearing Symbols 'Associated with Extremist Groups'." Voice of OC, December 8, 2020. https://voiceofoc.org.

32   Fowler, Sarah. "Ferguson Unrest: Who Are the Mysterious 'Oath Keepers'?" BBC News. BBC, August 11, 2015. https://www.bbc.com.

33   Klemko, Robert. "Behind the Armor: Men Seek 'Purpose' in Protecting Property despite Charges of Racism." The Washington Post. WP Company, October 6, 2020. https://www.washingtonpost.com.

34   https://www.splcenter.org/hate-map

35   Lussenhop, Jessica. "How Black Lives Matter Was Blamed for Killing of US Police Officers." BBC News. BBC, September 13, 2015. https://www.bbc.com.

36   German, Michael. "Hidden in Plain Sight." https://www.plainviewproject.org/data

37   Will Carless and Michael Corey. "Inside Hate Groups on Facebook, Police Officers Trade Racist Memes, Conspiracy Theories and Islamophobia." Reveal, April 14, 2021. https://revealnews.org.

38   The Breathe Act, February 1, 2021. https://breatheact.org/.

39   "Edward Byrne Memorial Justice Assistance Grant (JAG) Program: Overview." Bureau of Justice Assistance. Accessed June 23, 2021. https://bja.ojp.gov/program/jag/overview.

40   "Police Officer Edward R. Byrne." The Officer Down Memorial Page (ODMP), February 27, 2021. https://www.odmp.org.

41   Biden, Joe. "Biden: We Must Urgently Root out Systemic Racism, from Policing to Housing to Opportunity." USA Today. Gannett Satellite Information Network, June 11, 2020. https://www.usatoday.com.

42   "Staffing and Budget." DEA. Accessed June 23, 2021. https://www.dea.gov/data-and-statistics/staffing-and-budget.

43   Evans, David G. "Marijuana Legalization Will Cause Many Problems for Missouri Law Enforcement and Schools." Missouri medicine vol. 116,3 (2019): 164-167.

44   Goff, Andrew. "Humboldt County Coroner IDs Remains of Garret Rodriguez." Lost Coast Outpost. Lost Coast Outpost, December 17, 2013. https://

lostcoastoutpost.com.

45   NIDA. "Drugged Driving DrugFacts." National Institute on Drug Abuse, 31 Dec. 2019, https://www.drugabuse.gov.

46   "The Legalization of Marijuana in Colorado: The Impact Volume 5 – 2018, UPDATE." Mothers Against Drunk Driving, September 2018.

47   Gonzalez, Mike, and Andrew Olivastro. "The Agenda of Black Lives Matter Is Far Different from the Slogan." New York Post. New York Post, July 2, 2020. https://nypost.com.

48   Gebel, Meira. "The Story behind Thousand Currents, the Charity That Doles out the Millions of Dollars Black Lives Matter Generates in Donations." Insider. Insider, June 25, 2020. https://www.insider.com.

49   "Black Lives Matter PAC - Committee Overview." FEC.gov. Accessed June 28, 2021. https://www.fec.gov.

50   Loiaconi, Stephen. "As Black Lives Matter Donations Surge, Some Want to Know Where the Money Goes." WSYX. WSYX, June 15, 2020. https://abc6onyourside.com.

51   "Fact Sheet: National Strategy for Countering Domestic Terrorism." The White House. The United States Government, June 15, 2021. https://www.whitehouse.gov.

52   "18 U.S.C. § 2331 - U.S. Code Title 18. Crimes and Criminal Procedure § 2331." Findlaw. Accessed June 28, 2021. https://codes.findlaw.com/us/.

53   "Seattle Police Department." SPD Blotter. Accessed June 29, 2021. https://spdblotter.seattle.gov/.

54   "Official Statement on use of force During Friday Night Protests." SPD Blotter, May 30, 2020. https://spdblotter.seattle.gov.

55   Supreme Court Of The United States. U.S. Reports: Brandenburg v. Ohio, 395 U.S. 444. 1968. Periodical. https://www.loc.gov/item/usrep395444/.

56   Black Lives Matter Seattle-King County, et al. vs. City of Seattle (United States District Court, Western District of Washington at Seattle, Case No. 2:20-cv-887 June 9, 2020).

57   Ibid.

58   Daniels, Author: Chris. "Record Number of Seattle Police Officers Leaving the Department, New Report Shows." king5.com, October 16, 2020. https://

www.king5.com.

59	"Seattle Loses Almost 20% of Police Force amid Year of Nationwide Protests: 'We're Not Allowed to Intercede.'" CBS News. CBS Interactive, May 19, 2021. https://www.cbsnews.com.

60	Craighead, Callie. "2020 Crime Report: Seattle Saw Highest Homicide Number in 26 Years; Overall Violent Crimes Lower." seattlepi.com. Seattle Post-Intelligencer, January 12, 2021. https://www.seattlepi.com.

61	French, David. "Black Lives Matter: Radicals Using Moderates to Help Tear America Apart." National Review. National Review, August 5, 2016. https://www.nationalreview.com.

62	Ruiz, Michael. "Black Lives Matter Utah Chapter Calls American Flag 'Symbol of Hatred'." Fox News. FOX News Network, July 8, 2021. https://www.foxnews.com.

Chapter 7: Deadly Force Encounters

1	Grossman, Dave. Essay. In On Killing: the Psychological Cost of Learning to Kill in War and Society, 44. New York, NY: Little, Brown and Co., 2009.

2	"Remarks by the President at Memorial Service for Fallen Dallas Police Officers." National Archives and Records Administration. National Archives and Records Administration. Accessed July 28, 2021. https://obamawhitehouse.archives.gov.

3	"Joe Biden Says He's Spoken to George Floyd Family, Calls on Nation to Confront Racism." C. Accessed July 28, 2021. https://www.c-span.org.

4	MacDonald, Heather. "Opinion | the Myth of Systemic Police Racism." The Wall Street Journal. Dow Jones & Company, June 2, 2020. https://www.wsj.com.

5	"North Olmsted Police Officer Delivering Food and Friendship during Pandemic." WEWS. WEWS, April 20, 2020. https://www.news5cleveland.com. Quoted in: Staff, POL. "Ohio Officer Delivering Meals to Needy Residents During COVID-19 Pandemic." Police Magazine. Police Magazine, April 21, 2020. https://www.policemag.com.

6　　　CBS New York. "Coronavirus Update: Toms River Police Support Local Residents and Businesses with Pizza Giveaway." CBS New York. CBS New York, March 26, 2020. https://newyork.cbslocal.com. Quoted in: Staff. "New Jersey Officers Give Away 300 Pizzas to Needy Families." Police Magazine. Police Magazine, March 26, 2020. https://www.policemag.com.

7　　　Robinson, Carol. "Eufaula Police Offer Helping Hand to Big Rigs Who Can't Access Drive-thru Food." al, March 18, 2020. https://www.al.com. Quoted in: Staff. "Alabama Officers Help Truckers Buy Drive-Through Fast Food." Police Magazine. Police Magazine, March 20, 2020. https://www.policemag.com.

8　　　Staff. "Idaho Officer Gives Man a Bicycle to Help Him Get to Work." Police Magazine. Police Magazine, April 3, 2020. https://www.policemag.com.

9　　　Cosfobserver. "South Fulton Police Officers Honored for Acts of Kindness, Compassion." South Fulton Observer, January 28, 2020. https://cosfobserver.com.

10　　　Houck, Jeanne. "Officers Declare 9-Year-Old Warren County Boy a Hero for Saving His Little Brother's Life." The Enquirer. Cincinnati Enquirer, May 8, 2021. https://www.cincinnati.com.

11　　　Team, FOX TV Digital. "Police Officer Delivers Food after DoorDash Driver Arrested." FOX 5 Atlanta. FOX 5 Atlanta, July 7, 2021. https://www.fox5atlanta.com.

12　　　A., Marshall S L. Men against Fire: the Problem of Battle Command. 76, Norman Okla.: University of Oklahoma Press, 2000. Quoted in Grossman, On Killing, 40.

13　　　Grossman, On Killing, 44

14　　　Office of Justice Programs, Joel H Garner, and Christopher D Maxwell, Measuring the Amount of Force Used By and Against the Police in Six Jurisdictions § (1997). https://www.ojp.gov.

15　　　Harrell, Erika. "Contacts Between Police and the Public, 2018 - Statistical Tables." Bureau of Justice Statistics. Accessed July 3, 2021. https://bjs.ojp.gov.

16　　　Grossman, On Killing, 88

17　　　Ibid, 67.

18　　　Pinizzotto, Anthony, Edward Davis, Shannon Bohrer, and Benjamin

Infanti. "Restraint in the Use of Deadly Force." FBI Law Enforcement Bulletin. FBI, June 1, 2012. https://leb.fbi.gov.

19   This is a survey and not a scientific study.

20   Ibid.

21   Jones, Tom. "Officer and Teen Injured after Being Hit by Stolen Vehicle Driven by Another Teen, Police Say." WSB. WSB-TV Channel 2 - Atlanta, June 6, 2021. https://www.wsbtv.com. Quoted in: Malone, Sandy, and Holly Matkin. "Officer Run over by Teen Car Thief Says He Didn't Want to Use Deadly Force." The Police Tribune, June 10, 2021. https://policetribune.com.

22   Rubin, Neal. "MSP Identifies Woman Killed in Apparent Juneteenth Shootout with Flint Officer." The Detroit News. The Detroit News, June 21, 2021. https://www.detroitnews.com. Quoted In: Matkin, Holly, Sandy Malone, and Tom Gantert. "Video: Woman Ambushes Cop During Parade, He Breaks Down Sobbing After Returning Fire." The Police Tribune, June 23, 2021. https://policetribune.com.

23   Grossman, On Killing, 410

24   "Tactical/Hogan's Alley." FBI. FBI, June 9, 2016. https://www.fbi.gov.

25   Grossman, On Killing, 17

26   Federal Bureau of Investigation, Anthony J. Pinizzotto, Edward F. Davis, and Charles E. Miller, Violent encounters: A study of felonious assaults on our nation's law enforcement officers § (2006).

27   Ibid, 156.

28   Ibid.

29   Ibid.

30   Kellermkeller, Mary Grace. "Sheriff Pillories Frederick County Councilman On Radio, Says Hagen Interfered With Traffic Stop." Post, June 30, 2021. Https://Www.Fredericknewspost.Com. Quoted In: Malone, Sandy, Holly Matkin, And Tom Gantert. "Sheriff Blasts Councilman For Interrupting Traffic Stop To Check On Black Driver." The Police Tribune, July 1, 2021. Https://Policetribune. Com.

31   Kellermkeller, Mary Grace, and Jack Hogan. "Sheriff Pillories Frederick County Councilman on Radio, Says Hagen Interfered with Traffic Stop." Frederick News Post, June 30, 2021. https://www.fredericknewspost.com.

32   Ibid.

33   Ibid, Federal Bureau of Investigation, Anthony J. Pinizzotto, et al. §
(2006).

34   Ricks, Thomas E. Fiasco: The American Military Adventure in Iraq.
New York: Penguin, 2007. Quoted in Thomas, Ricks. "Fiasco.'" Armed Forces Journal,
January 13, 2014. http://armedforcesjournal.com/fiasco/.

35   Ibid, Federal Bureau of Investigation, Anthony J. Pinizzotto, et al. §
(2006).

36   "Law Enforcement Facts." National Law Enforcement Officers
Memorial Fund, July 27, 2021. https://nleomf.org.

37   "Detective Jorge Rene DelRio." The Officer Down Memorial Page
(ODMP), November 7, 2020. https://www.odmp.org.

38   Transcribed   from   public   Facebook   video.   https://
fb.watch/7bGtHLbxDV/

Chapter 8: Traffic Stops

1   "Fugitive Wanted In Colorado, Apprehended After Routine Traffic
Stop In Johnson City." SuperTalk 92.9, July 5, 2021. http://www.supertalk929.com.

2   Haworth, Jon. "Half-Ton of Marijuana Valued at over $8 Million
Found by Dog on Routine Traffic Stop." ABC News. ABC News Network. Accessed
July 21, 2021. https://abcnews.go.com.

3   Martin, Izzy. "Routine Traffic Stop Leads to 50 Kgs of Crystal Meth,
Value Estimated at over $1 Million." WLNS 6 News. WLNS 6 News, June 10, 2021.
https://www.wlns.com/news/michigan/routine-traffic-stop-leads-to-50-kgs-of-
crystal-meth-value-estimated-at-over-1-million/.

4   Sandler, Rachel. "Berkeley Will Become 1st U.S. City To Remove
Police From Traffic Stops." Forbes. Forbes Magazine, July 16, 2020. https://www.
forbes.com.

5   Har, Janie. "Berkeley to Consider Removing Police from Traffic
Stops." AP NEWS. Associated Press, July 14, 2020. https://apnews.com.

6   Semenov, Rose. "City of Minneapolis Looking into Creating
Unarmed Traffic Safety Division." FOX 9 Minneapolis-St. Paul. FOX 9 Minneapolis-
St. Paul, April 16, 2021. https://www.fox9.com. Quoted in: "Minneapolis Takes Step

toward Unarmed Traffic Enforcement." Police1, April 19, 2021. https://www.police1.com.

7   Woods, Jordan Blair, Traffic Without the Police (June 30, 2021). 73 Stanford Law Review 1471 (2021)., Available at SSRN: https://ssrn.com/abstract=3702680

8   Chapman, Steve. "Column: Police Traffic Stops Are a Needless Danger." chicagotribune.com. Chicago Tribune, April 14, 2021. https://www.chicagotribune.com.

9   Scalia, Antonin, and Supreme Court Of The United States. U.S. Reports: Whren v. United States, 517 U.S. 806. 1995. Periodical. https://www.loc.gov.

10   "Drug-Impaired Driving." NHTSA. Accessed July 22, 2021. https://www.nhtsa.gov.

11   Dineen, Hannah. "Legislature Debates Bill about 'Pretextual Traffic Stops'." newscentermaine.com, June 17, 2021. https://www.newscentermaine.com.

12   An Act to Protect Maine's Drivers from Pretextual Traffic Stops. Bill (n.d.). http://www.mainelegislature.org.

13   Schaeffer, Jack. "Commentary: Why Pretext Stops by Police Should Be Allowed." Tribune. San Diego Union-Tribune, June 14, 2019. https://www.sandiegouniontribune.com.

14   Simon, Richard. "Traffic Stops–Tickets to Surprises." Los Angeles Times. Los Angeles Times, May 15, 1995. https://www.latimes.com.

15   "Ted Bundy." Biography.com. A&E Networks Television, July 14, 2021. https://www.biography.com.

16   Staff, WMPI Web. "Ted Bundy Arrested in Pensacola 41 Years Ago." WPMI. WPMI, February 15, 2019. https://mynbc15.com.

17   Ward, Bob. "MSP Most Wanted Fugitive Shot, Killed during Traffic Stop in Tenn." Boston 25 News. Boston 25 News, April 27, 2021. https://www.boston25news.com.

18   reports, Staff. "New Jersey Fugitive Arrested in Martinsburg Traffic Stop." Mail. The Herald-Mail, October 9, 2016. https://www.heraldmailmedia.com.

19   Schmidt, Caitlin. "Louisiana Fugitives Arrested in Casa Grande Traffic Stop." Arizona Daily Star, September 22, 2016. https://tucson.com.

20   "Traffic Stop Leads to Fugitive Arrest." WTOC, December 12, 2012.

https://www.wtoc.com.

21   Simon, Richard. "Traffic Stops–Tickets to Surprises." Los Angeles Times.

22   State of Washington v Thomas Ladson (Washington Supreme Court, Case No: 65801-3, July 1, 1999).

23   Ibid.

24   Scalia, Antonin, and Supreme Court Of The United States. U.S. Reports: Whren v. United States, 517 U.S. 806. 1995. Periodical. https://www.loc.gov.

25   Associate Chief Justice Charles W. Johnsont, and Scott P. Beethamtt. "The Origin of Article I, Section 7 of the Washington State Constitution." Seattle University Law Review Vol. 31:431. Accessed July 27, 2021. https://digitalcommons. law.seattleu.edu.

26   State of Washington v Gilberto Chacon Arreola (Washington Supreme Court, Case No: 86610-4, December 20, 2012).

27   Ibid.

28   State of Iowa v Scottize Danyelle Brown (Iowa Supreme Court, Case No: 17-0367 June 28, 2019).

29   "An Average Drunk Driver Has Driven Drunk over 80 Times before First Arrest." MADD. Accessed July 26, 2021. https://www.madd.org.
"Alcohol-Impaired Driving among Adults - United States, 2012." Centers for Disease Control and Prevention. Centers for Disease Control and Prevention. Accessed July 26, 2021. https://www.cdc.gov.
https://ucr.fbi.gov.

Chapter 9: Defund the Police

1   McEvoy, Jemima. "At Least 13 Cities Are Defunding Their Police Departments." Forbes. Forbes Magazine, September 29, 2020. https://www.forbes. com.

2   Pagones, Stephanie. "Police Defunded: Major Cities Feeling the Loss of Police Funding as Murders, Other Crimes Soar." Fox News. FOX News Network, April 1, 2021. https://www.foxnews.com.

3   Heffernan, Erin. "Proposed St. Louis Spending Plan Cuts $4M to

Police, Removes 98 Vacant Officer Jobs." STLtoday.com, July 14, 2021. https://www.stltoday.com. Quoted in: Matkin, Holly, and Sandy Malone. "St. Louis Mayor Votes to Defund Police, Cut 100 Sworn Positions from Force." The Police Tribune, May 3, 2021. https://policetribune.com.

4   "PERF Daily COVID-19 Report." Police Executive Research Forum, August 3, 2020. https://www.policeforum.org.

5   Colton, Emma. "As Defund the Police Movement Trickles down from Big Cities, Small-Town America Pays the Price." Fox News. FOX News Network, August 3, 2021. https://www.foxnews.com.

6   Nisa Khan, Dustin Dwyer. "A Year After 'Defund' Protests, Most Large Michigan Cities Spending More on Police, Not Less." Michigan Radio. Accessed August 6, 2021. https://www.michiganradio.org.

7   Saad, Lydia. "Black Americans Want Police to Retain Local Presence." Gallup.com. Gallup, June 22, 2021. https://news.gallup.com.

8   "Majority of Public Favors Giving Civilians the Power to Sue Police Officers for Misconduct." Pew Research Center - U.S. Politics & Policy. Pew Research Center, March 2, 2021. https://www.pewresearch.org. Quoted in: "Gallup Poll: Abolishing Police Is Not Popular." Police Magazine. Police Magazine, July 22, 2020. https://www.policemag.com.

9   Harris, Anthony R., Stephen H. Thomas, Gene A. Fisher, and David J. Hirsch. "Murder and Medicine: The Lethality of Criminal Assault 1960-1999." Homicide Studies 6, no. 2 (May 2002): 128–66. https://doi.org/10.1177/108876790200600203. Quoted in Grossman, Dave. Essay. In On Killing: the Psychological Cost of Learning to Kill in War and Society, 391. New York, NY: Little, Brown and Co., 2009.

10   Grossman, Dave. Essay. In On Killing: the Psychological Cost of Learning to Kill in War and Society, 396-397. New York, NY: Little, Brown and Co., 2009.

11   Stats extracted from compstat reports and FBI Uniform Crime Reporting for the first half of 2021.

12   Asher, Jeff. "Murder Rate Remains Elevated as New Crime Reporting System Begins." The New York Times. The New York Times, March 16, 2021. https://www.nytimes.com.

13   Matkin, Holly, and Sandy Malone. "Oakland Police Chief Speaks out after City Council Defunds Police BY $18.4 Million." The Police Tribune, July 1, 2021. https://policetribune.com.

14   Ibid.

15   "Weekly Briefing: Budget Impact, A's Update." Mayor Libby Schaaf. Accessed August 7, 2021. Quoted in Matkin, Holly, and Sandy Malone. "Oakland Police Chief Speaks out after City Council Defunds Police BY $18.4 Million." The Police Tribune, July 1, 2021. https://policetribune.com.

16   Saad, Lydia. "Black Americans Want Police to Retain Local Presence." Gallup.com. Gallup, June 22, 2021. https://news.gallup.com.

17   Zanotti, Emily. "'Defund The Police' Advocate Rep. Cori Bush Spent $70K On Private Security: Report." The Daily Wire. The Daily Wire, July 16, 2021. https://www.dailywire.com.

18   "Cori Bush Explains Her Position On 'Defund the Police' While Paying for Private Security. Her Full Response." CBS News. CBS Interactive. Accessed August 20, 2021. https://www.cbsnews.com.

19   Sotomayor, Marianna. "Cori Bush Tests the Bounds of What an Activist Turned Lawmaker Can Accomplish." The Washington Post. WP Company, August 18, 2021. https://www.washingtonpost.com.

20   St. Louis Metropolitan Police Department, Uniform Crime Reporting Homicide Analysis, August 20, 2021. www.slmpd.org

21   "Fatal Force: Police Shootings Database." The Washington Post. WP Company, January 22, 2020. https://www.washingtonpost.com.

22   Fieldstadt, Elisha. "The Most Dangerous Cities in America, Ranked." CBS News. CBS Interactive, November 9, 2020. https://www.cbsnews.com.

23   Phillips, Morgan. "'Squad' Dem Cori Bush Praises St. Louis' 'Historic' Vote To 'Defund' Police." Fox News. FOX News Network, April 30, 2021. https://www.foxnews.com.

24   jmcmahon@syracuse.com, Julie McMahon |. "Ithaca Mayor Unveils Proposal to Replace City's Police Department." syracuse.com, February 23, 2021. https://www.syracuse.com.

25   jmulder@syracuse.com, James T. Mulder |. "Ithaca Mayor Wants to Let Heroin Users Shoot up under Medical Supervision." syracuse.com, February 22,

2016. https://www.syracuse.com.

26   Withrow, Emma. "Charlotte City Councilman Advocates for Gun-Free CMPD." FOX 46 Charlotte. FOX 46 Charlotte, April 28, 2021. https://www.fox46.com. Quoted in: Malone, Sandy. "Councilman Wants to Disarm Police so Cops Must Use Words Instead of Force." The Police Tribune, May 3, 2021. https://policetribune.com.

27   Godin, Mélissa. "What the U.S Can Learn from Countries Where Cops Are Unarmed." Time. Time, June 19, 2020. https://time.com.

28   Ibid.

29   Office, Home. "Definition of Policing by Consent." GOV.UK. GOV.UK, February 11, 2016. https://www.gov.uk.

30   Ibid.

31   Ibid.

32   Smith, Alexander. "The Vast Majority of U.K. Police Don't Carry Guns. Here's Why." NBCNews.com. NBCUniversal News Group, September 15, 2017. https://www.nbcnews.com.

33   "Fatal Force: Police Shootings Database." The Washington Post. WP Company, January 22, 2020. https://www.washingtonpost.com.

34   https://www.met.police.uk/sd/stats-and-data/

35   "CompStat 2.0." Crime Stats - COMPStat - NYPD. Accessed August 31, 2021. https://www1.nyc.gov.

36   Ibid.

37   https://www.met.police.uk/sd/stats-and-data/

38   Park, Sumner. "Major Cities 'Refund the Police' as Crime Skyrockets and Businesses Backfire." Fox Business. Fox Business, June 19, 2021. https://www.foxbusiness.com.

39   Ibid.

40   Kathy Spann, et al. vs. City of Minneapolis and Mayor Jacob Frey (State of Minnesota Fourth Judicial District, Case No. 27-CV-20-10558 August 17, 2020).

41   Navratil, Liz. "What You Need to Know about the Proposal to End the Minneapolis Police Department." Star Tribune. Star Tribune, July 21, 2020. https://www.startribune.com.

42   Bruch, Michelle. "The Causes of Minneapolis' Summer Crime Spree." Southwest Journal, August 12, 2020. https://www.southwestjournal.com.

43   Kathy Spann, et al. vs. City of Minneapolis and Mayor Jacob Frey

44   Ibid.

45   Ibid.

46   Navratil, Liz. "Minnesota Supreme Court Denies Minneapolis' Appeal on Ruling Requiring It to Hire More Police Officers." Star Tribune. Star Tribune, August 11, 2021. https://www.startribune.com. Quoted in: Navratil, Liz. "Minn. Supreme Court Denies Minneapolis' Appeal on Order to Hire More Cops." Police1, August 11, 2021. https://www.police1.com.

47   Kaste, Martin. "Minneapolis Voters Reject a Measure to Replace the City's Police Department." NPR. NPR, November 3, 2021. https://www.npr.org/.

48   "The Charter of the City of Seattle." Municode library. Accessed August 26, 2021. https://library.municode.com/wa/seattle/codes/.

49   Bernstein, Brittany. "Seattle Mayor Proposes Rebuilding Depleted Police Force after Violent Weekend." Yahoo! Yahoo! Accessed August 27, 2021. https://www.yahoo.com.

50   Congress.gov. "S.Con.Res.14 - 117th Congress (2021-2022): A concurrent resolution setting forth the congressional budget for the United States Government for fiscal year 2022 and setting forth the appropriate budgetary levels for fiscal years 2023 through 2031." August 24, 2021. https://www.congress.gov.

51   1 Corinthians 9:22 (NIV)

Chapter 10: War on Police

1   Balsamini, Dean. "Are NYPD Officers Rushing To Retire Amid City's Anti-Cop Climate?" New York Post. New York Post, April 24, 2021. https://nypost.com.

2   "Thune: Law Enforcement Officers Deserve Much Better Than Far-Left's Anti-Police Rhetoric." U.S. Senator John Thune, July 15, 2021. https://www.thune.senate.gov.

3   Wicker, Mackenzie. "Asheville 'Defund Police' Vote: City Reallocates $770,000 From APD Budget." The Asheville Citizen Times. Asheville Citizen Times,

September 23, 2020. https://www.citizen-times.com.

4   "Police Department Releases List of Calls Officers Will No Longer Respond To." WYFF. WYFF, June 23, 2021. https://www.wyff4.com. Quoted in the Police Tribune

5   "Foia.gov (Freedom of Information Act) Freedom of Information Act Statute." Freedom of Information Act: Freedom of Information Act Statute. Accessed September 3, 2021. https://www.foia.gov/foia-statute.html.

6   Esar, Evan. The Dictionary of Humorous Quotations. New York: Dorset Press, 1989.

7   Biography.com Editors. "Rodney King." Biography.com. A&E Networks Television, October 19, 2020. https://www.biography.com

8   "A Break down of the Malcolm Johnson Shooting Videos." Yahoo! Yahoo!, June 3, 2021. https://www.yahoo.com.

9   Rice, Glenn, and Katie Moore. "Witness Recounts Gas Station Shootout That Left Man Dead, KCPD Officer Injured." The Kansas City Star, March 26, 2021. https://www.kansascity.com.

10   Hartle, Sam. "Kansas City Faith Leaders Raise Concerns in March 25 Police Shooting." KSHB. KSHB, June 1, 2021. https://www.kshb.com.

11   Martin, Luke X. "Once Considered Partners, These Religious Leaders Have Lost Faith In Kansas City Police Leadership." KCUR 89.3 - NPR in Kansas City. Local news, entertainment and podcasts., June 8, 2021. https://www.kcur.org.

12   Ibid.

13   Strauss, Peter. "Due Process." Legal Information Institute. Legal Information Institute. Accessed September 3, 2021. https://www.law.cornell.edu.

14   Corson, Pete. "A Timeline of the Rayshard Brooks Case." ajc. The Atlanta Journal-Constitution, June 11, 2021. https://www.ajc.com.

15   Boone, Christian. "Gbi Investigation Sheds New Light On Rayshard Brooks Shooting." ajc. The Atlanta Journal-Constitution, May 10, 2021. https://www.ajc.com. Quoted in: Malone, Sandy, and Holly Matkin. "GBI Report Indicates DA May Have Lied to Charge Officer Rolfe With Rayshard Brooks' Murder." The Police Tribune, May 12, 2021. https://policetribune.com.

16   Garrett Rolfe vs. Chief Rodney Bryant and Mayor Keisha Lance Bottoms (Superior Court of Fulton County, State of Georgia, Case No. 2020CV338972

August 4, 2020).

17   Ibid.

18   "Read the Civil Service Board Order Reinstating Atlanta Police Officer Garrett Rolfe." ajc. The Atlanta Journal-Constitution, May 5, 2021. https://www.ajc.com.

19   Boone, Christian. "Atlanta Criticized as Police Officer Who Shot Rayshard Brooks Is Reinstated." ajc. The Atlanta Journal-Constitution, May 5, 2021. https://www.ajc.com.

20   Ibid.

21   "Statement on Civil Service Board's Reinstatement of Officer Rolfe." Press Releases | City of Atlanta, GA, May 5, 2021. https://www.atlantaga.gov.

22   Corson, Pete, A Time Line of the Rayshard Brooks Case., Atlanta Journal-Constitution.

23   Malone, Sandy, and Holly Matkin. "GBI Report Indicates DA May Have Lied to Charge Officer Rolfe With Rayshard Brooks' Murder." The Police Tribune, May 12, 2021. https://policetribune.com.

24   Ibid.

25   Pierrotti, Andy. "Third Da Assigned to Prosecute Officers in Rayshard Brooks Case Speaks: 11Alive Exclusive." 11Alive.com, August 18, 2021. https://www.11alive.com.

26   Staff, WSBTV.com News. "Atlanta Interim Police Chief Says DA Was Too Quick to Bring Charges in Rayshard Brooks Shooting." WSB. WSB-TV Channel 2 - Atlanta, July 10, 2020. https://www.wsbtv.com.

27   Wrbl. "Blue Flu: A Number of Atlanta Police Officers Walk out in Apparent Protest." WRBL. WRBL, June 18, 2020. https://www.wrbl.com.

28   Maeder, Jay. "Blue Flu Cops on Strike, December 1970 - January 1971 Chapter 384." nydailynews.com, June 25, 2001. https://www.nydailynews.com.

29   Wrbl. "Blue Flu: A Number of Atlanta Police Officers Walk out in Apparent Protest." WRBL. WRBL, June 18, 2020.

30   Raache, Hicham. "Homeless Man Shot & Killed by Oklahoma City Police While Allegedly Running With Knife; Community Members Gather to Protest His Death." KFOR.com Oklahoma City. KFOR.com Oklahoma City, December 11, 2020. https://kfor.com. Quoted in: Malone, Sandy, and Holly Matkin.

"Video: Sergeant Charged for Shooting Man Armed with Knife Who Charged at Cops." The Police Tribune, March 7, 2021. https://policetribune.com.

31 Gates, Billy, Jaclyn Ramkissoon, and Tahera Rahman. "'He Didn't Have a Chance': Attorneys Say Murder Indictment of Two Officers 'a Step toward Ju Stice'." KXAN Austin. KXAN Austin, August 28, 2021. https://www.kxan.com. Quoted in: Matkin, Holly, and Sandy Malone. "Austin PD Officers Indicted for Shooting Man Coming at Them with Knife." The Police Tribune, August 30, 2021. https://policetribune.com.

32 Plohetski, Tony. "Case against Austin Officer Dismissed after DA Says Prosecutor Withheld Evidence." Statesman. Austin American-Statesman, July 19, 2021. https://www.statesman.com. Quote in: Malone, Sandy, and Holly Matkin. "Anti-Cop Da Forced to Drop Charges On Austin Cop He Was Making Example Of." The Police Tribune, July 24, 2021. https://policetribune.com.

33 "Judge Rejects Charges for Hawaii Officers in Fatal Shooting." Police1, August 20, 2021. https://www.police1.com.

34 Malone, Sandy, and Holly Matkin. "Judge Dismisses DA'S Murder Indictment Against Cop Who Killed Active Shooter." The Police Tribune, August 12, 2021. https://policetribune.com.

Horn, Chase, and Kaylee Douglas. "Blackwell Officer Indicted in May Officer-Involved Shooting." KFOR.com Oklahoma City. KFOR.com Oklahoma City, November 27, 2019. https://kfor.com.

35 Malone, Sandy, and Holly Matkin. "Army Sergeant Indicted for Shooting Protester Who Pointed AK-47 at Him." The Police Tribune, July 2, 2021. https://policetribune.com.

Peiser, Jaclyn. "An Armed Black Lives Matter Protester Confronted a Car That Drove toward a March. the Driver Fatally Shot Him." The Washington Post. WP Company, July 27, 2020. https://www.washingtonpost.com.

Staff. "Fort Hood Sergeant Indicted for Murder in 2020 Death of Austin Protester." https://www.kwtx.com. Accessed September 19, 2021. https://www.kwtx.com.

36 "Qualified Immunity." Wikipedia. Wikimedia Foundation, July 5, 2021. https://en.wikipedia.org.

37 DeBonis, Mike. "Policing Deal Remains out of Reach on Capitol Hill as the Anniversary of George Floyd's Death Approaches." The Washington Post. WP

Company, May 20, 2021. https://www.washingtonpost.com.

38   Alito, Samuel A, and Supreme Court Of The United States. U.S. Reports: Pearson v. Callahan, 555 U.S. 223. 2008. Periodical. https://www.loc.gov.

39   Congress.gov. "H.R.1280 - 117th Congress (2021-2022): George Floyd Justice in Policing Act of 2021." March 9, 2021. https://www.congress.gov.

40   Wise, Justin. "State Lawmakers Tackle Qualified Immunity Defense." Law360, May 2, 2021. https://www.law360.com.

41   Jones, Megan. "Dashcam Video Shows Officer Strangled, Beaten at Traffic Stop." Police1, July 22, 2021. https://www.police1.com.

42   Robinson, Carol |. "Man with Violent Past Charged in Bpd Detective Attack." al, August 8, 2015. https://www.al.com.

43   Shapiro, Emily. "Nashville Officer Shot While Responding to 'Setup' 911 Call; Suspect Dead: Police." ABC news. ABC News Network, May 5, 2021. https://abcnews.go.com.

44   Casiano, Louis. "Driver Drags NYPD Officer with Car, Was out with No Bail at Time despite Attempted Murder Charge, Police Say." Fox News. FOX News Network, April 24, 2021. https://www.foxnews.com.

45   Pagones, Stephanie. "Ambush Attacks on Police Officers up 91% in 2021 Compared to Last Year, Group Says." Fox News. FOX News Network, July 1, 2021. https://www.foxnews.com.

46   Robinson, Carol |. "Man with Violent Past Charged in Bpd Detective Attack." al, August 8, 2015.

47   Kaplan, Talia. "Illinois Officer Says She Lost Job Protecting Local High School over Defense of Thin Blue Line Patch." Fox News. FOX News Network, June 24, 2021. https://www.foxnews.com. Quoted in: Malone, Sandy, and Holly Matkin. "SRO Dismissed by School Administrators for Supporting Thin Blue Line." The Police Tribune, June 28, 2021. https://policetribune.com.

48   Jim Piwowarczyk & Jessica McBride. "UW-Madison Police Chief bans Thin Blue Line." Wisconsin Right Now, February 13, 2021. https://www.wisconsinrightnow.com.

49   Matkin, Holly, and Sandy Malone. "New Da Wants to Drop Enhancements against Alleged Cop-Killer to Reduce Sentence." The Police Tribune, December 16, 2020. https://policetribune.com.

50   Malone, Sandy, and Holly Matkin. "Starbucks Employees Refuse to Work While Police Direct Traffic Outside." The Police Tribune, April 28, 2021. https://policetribune.com.

51   Matkin, Holly, and Sandy Malone. "NFL Honors Gunman Killed While Trying to Murder Cops." The Police Tribune, December 17, 2020. https://policetribune.com.

DePompei, Elizabeth. "Grand Jury: No Charges FOR Impd Officer Who Fatally Shot Dreasjon Reed." The Indianapolis Star. Indianapolis Star, November 11, 2020. https://www.indystar.com/.

52   Matkin, Holly, and Sandy Malone. "Cop Sues NFL for Defamation Over Portrayal of Justified Shooting OF Dreasjon Reed." The Police Tribune, June 15, 2021. https://policetribune.com.

staff, WTHR.com. "IMPD Officer Who Shot Dreasjon Reed Sues NFL for Defamation over Social Justice Campaign." IMPD officer files suit over NFL's 'Inspire Change' campaign. wthr.com, June 15, 2021. https://www.wthr.com

53   Moore, Tina. "NYPD Cop-Killer Is Now Helping Reform the Police in New York." New York Post. New York Post, March 29, 2021. https://nypost.com. Quoted In: Malone, Sandy. "Cop Killer Given Seat On Governor-Mandated Police Reform Panel." The Police Tribune, March 31, 2021. https://policetribune.com.

54   Monroe, Nick. "San Francisco Mayor Takes $3.75 Million from Police, Giving to Black Businesses Instead." The Post Millennial. The Post Millennial, May 8, 2021. https://thepostmillennial.com.

55   Colton, Emma. "San Francisco Will Pay People to Not Shoot Others: 'Cash for Criminals'." Fox News. FOX News Network, September 2, 2021. https://www.foxnews.com. Quoted in: Matkin, Holly, and Sandy Malone. "San Francisco Program Pays Criminals up to $500 per Month to Not Shoot People." The Police Tribune, September 2, 2021. https://policetribune.com.

56   Reagan, Ronald. "Remarks at the Annual Meeting of the International Association of Chiefs of Police in New Orleans, Louisiana." Ronald Reagan. Accessed September 10, 2021. https://www.reaganlibrary.gov.

57   "Crime Clock." FBI. FBI, September 11, 2018. https://ucr.fbi.gov.

58   "The Criminal Justice System: Statistics." Rainn. Accessed September 13, 2021. https://www.rainn.org/statistics/criminal-justice-system.

59   "Victimizations Not Reported to the police, 2006-2010." Bureau of Justice Statistics, August 9, 2012. https://bjs.ojp.gov.

60   Gramlich, John. "Most Violent and Property Crimes in the U.S. Go Unsolved." Pew Research Center. Pew Research Center, May 30, 2020. https://www.pewresearch.org.

61   Miller, Ted R., Mark A. Cohen, David Swedler, Bina Ali, and Delia V. Hendrie. "Incidence and Costs of Personal and Property Crimes in the United States, 2017." SSRN Electronic Journal, 2020. https://doi.org/10.2139/ssrn.3514296.

62   USAFacts. "Police Departments, Funding, Stats & Data." USAFacts. USAFacts, April 28, 2021. https://usafacts.org.

63   Miller, et al., Incidence and Costs of Personal and Property Crimes in the United States, 2017.

64   Arendt, Hannah. The Origins of Totalitarianism. San Diego, NY, London : Harcourt Brace, 1985. Quoted in: Pierre, Joe. "Illusory Truth, Lies, and Political Propaganda: Part 1." Psychology Today. Sussex Publishers. Accessed September 15, 2021. https://www.psychologytoday.com.

65   Ibid.